English 2600

FOURTH EDITION WITH INDEX

A Programed Course
in Grammar and Usage

JOSEPH C. BLUMENTHAL

HARCOURT BRACE JOVANOVICH, INC.

New York   Chicago   San Francisco   Atlanta   Dallas

THE SERIES

ENGLISH 2200

ENGLISH 2600

ENGLISH 3200

Tests for English 2200

Tests for English 2600

Tests for English 3200

TEACHER'S MANUAL for Each Textbook

ABOUT THE AUTHOR

Joseph C. Blumenthal received his A.B. and A.M. degrees from the University of Michigan. He also did graduate work at the University of Chicago and at Columbia University. From 1938 to 1959 he was Head of the English Department at Mackenzie High School in Detroit. He is now devoting his full time to textbook writing. Among his writings are the *Common Sense English* series, the *English Workshop* series (with John F. Warriner and others), and *The English Language* series (with Louis Zahner and others).

ABOUT THE FOURTH EDITION

The inclusion of an index in this edition is intended to make ENGLISH 2600 more useful to students and teachers by giving them ready access to the entire body of material treated in the text. Each entry is indexed by frame and page numbers to facilitate reference.

THE TEST BOOKLET

The 64-page Test Booklet designed for use with ENGLISH 2600 consists of a Pre-Test, two Mastery Tests for each of the twelve units, two Halfway Tests, and a Final Test.

ISBN School Printing: 0-15-314337-1
       College Printing: 0-15-522690-8

TO THE STUDENT

ENGLISH 2600 is a programed course in grammar, sentence-building, correct usage, and punctuation. A new feature of this edition is an index which can help you locate a particular topic quickly when you need it for reference or review.

If this is your first experience with a programed textbook, you may be puzzled by its appearance. As you leaf through its pages, you may wonder why it looks so different from other books you have studied.

Why the zebra-like pages with alternating bands of gray and white?

Why is the material divided into small bits or *frames*?

Why don't you read the pages from top to bottom as you do other books?

Why are the answers printed in the marginal strips where they can be so easily seen?

ENGLISH 2600 looks so different because it is built upon some modern learning principles. For many years, the problems of learning have been studied scientifically in colleges and universities all over our country. As a result, new discoveries have been made which can make learning faster, surer, more thorough (and, we hope, more fun). **ENGLISH 2600** is based on some of the most important of these discoveries.

1. In a programed course, often called simply a *program*, the material is broken down into very small and carefully arranged steps—approximately 2600 in this book—through which you reason your way, one step at a time. There is no separation between explanation and exercise, as in other language textbooks; the two are tightly interwoven. Every step, or *frame*, calls for a written response, which requires both *thinking* and *concentration*. The advantages of "reasoning your own way" instead of "being told" have been known to good teachers ever since the days of Socrates. By thinking your way through the program, you are likely to understand better and to remember longer.

2. Programs are constructed to prevent mistakes before they happen. The psychologists call this "errorless learning" and have proved its importance by scientific experiment. The steps are so small and their arrangement is so orderly that you are not likely to make many errors. When an error occurs, you catch it immediately by turning the page for the answer. You are corrected before a wrong habit can become established. You spend your time *learning*—not *unlearning*. Using a programed textbook is like having a private teacher who watches you as you work and who sets you back on the track the moment you wander off.

3. A very important factor in this method is what the psychologists call *reinforcement*. Its importance in learning cannot be stated too strongly.

With the usual textbook, you first study the lesson (which you may or may not understand completely). Then you apply what you have studied to an exercise. Unfortunately, you do not find out until some time later (often the next day) whether you did the exercise correctly. With **ENGLISH 2600** you discover immediately whether your answer is right or wrong. At this point something very interesting and mysterious happens. The instant you find out you are right, the idea "takes root," so to speak, in your brain. This does not happen as successfully when time (even a moment or two) is allowed to elapse before you discover that you are right.

Finding out immediately that you are right is called *reinforcement,* and the quicker and more often this happens, the better you learn and remember. A reinforcement is something like a reward; and if you have ever taught a dog tricks, you know from experience how the biscuits speed up learning.

4. With programed instruction you can advance at your own speed. Since you work by yourself, no one needs to wait for you, and you don't need to wait for anyone else. Many students complete an entire course of study in a fraction of the time usually required by the traditional textbook method. The time you save by this method can be used profitably in other language activities.

How to Use **ENGLISH 2600**

Each step (or frame) requires that you perform some operation. For example, in many of the frames you will do one of two things:

1. If there is a blank line, write in the missing word or letter.
   Example: Jones is the name of a *person* .
2. If there are two or more words or letters in parentheses, underline the correct answer.
   Example: Jones is the name of a (*person,* place).

(*Note:* Your teacher will tell you whether to write your answers in this book, in a notebook, or on sheets of paper.)

The first work frame is Frame 2 (on page 3). After you complete Frame 2, turn to Frame 3 *in the same position* on the next *right-hand* page (page 5). In the column to the left of Frame 3, you will find the correct answer to Frame 2. If your answer is not correct, turn back and correct it before doing Frame 3. You will always find the answer to a frame in the column to the left of the frame that you are to do next. Thus you find the answer to Frame 3 to the left of Frame 4, the answer to Frame 4 to the left of Frame 5, and so on.

Go completely through the book, taking only the top gray frame on each *right-hand* page (3, 5, 7, 9, 11, etc.) until you reach the end. When you reach the end of the book, turn back to page 1 and follow the second band—a white one—through the book, still working only on the *right-hand* pages. Then proceed to the third horizontal band, which is gray, going through all the *right-hand* pages. Continue in this way through the fourth, fifth, and sixth bands. When you come to the last white band on the *right-hand* page (Frame 1320), turn back to page 2 and start reading the gray bands at the top of the *left-hand* pages. Continue through the book, following each horizontal band through the *left-hand* pages. The last frame is 2633 on page 436.

The alternating bands of white and gray will make it easy for you to stay on the same horizontal band as you advance through the book. Since both frame and answer are numbered (each in the lower right corner), you will always know where you are and where to go next.

Getting the Most from ENGLISH 2600

1. Whenever you are unsure about the correct answer to a frame, read the frame again very carefully, looking for clues. You will generally find a clue that guides you to the right answer. As the lesson advances, fewer and fewer clues will be given; so if you make a mistake, you will need to go back a few frames to try to correct your thinking. If you still don't understand where your mistake lies, ask your teacher for help.

2. Take as much time as you need in figuring out your answer. But once you write your answer, turn immediately to the next frame to check its correctness. Scientific experiment has proved that the more quickly you check your answer, the better you learn. *Even the delay of a few seconds makes a big difference!*

3. Don't cheat yourself out of the valuable experience of thinking! Don't look at the answer in the next frame until *after* you have figured it out for yourself. Thinking things through takes effort, but it is this kind of effort that results in the most effective kind of learning. You are not working for grades on these lessons because the lessons will not be scored. In fact, you will always end with a perfect score because you are expected to correct each error immediately (and you will probably make very few). However, your teacher may want to evaluate your work by administering and scoring the tests that accompany **ENGLISH 2600**. "Peeking ahead" for the answer will not give you the reasoning ability you will need to pass the tests.

If you will use **ENGLISH 2600** in the mature way in which it is designed to be used, you may discover that, working at your own pace, you have achieved a better command of the fundamentals of your language—and in a much shorter time. You may also find that you have developed your ability to think and concentrate in ways that will help you in your other studies. You will have profited from letting science help you with its most recent and exciting discoveries about how people learn.

JOSEPH C. BLUMENTHAL

CONTENTS

bath 220	**Carl invited** . . . (Whom?) **Carl invited his best friend.** The word that completes the meaning of the verb **invited** is _____ . 221
feels, looks 440	A linking verb must always be completed by a subject complement. A subject complement is so called because it completes the meaning of the verb and describes or identifies the _____ . 441
b 660	If you can move a modifier to another position in the sentence, it is likely to be an (*adverb, adjective*). 661
map 880	Here, again, are the **pronouns** that can be used as clause signals to start **adjective clauses:** ADJECTIVE CLAUSE SIGNALS: **who (whom, whose),** **which, that** Are these the same signal words that start adverb clauses? (*Yes, No*) 881
S F 1100	**Slipping through a hole in the fence. The rabbit disappeared.** ____ ____ 1101

sits 1320	**To set** means "to put or to place something." Never use this word unless you name the "something" that is put or placed somewhere (or use a pronoun in its place). **You can set (put) the bag on the floor.** What is the "something" that you can **set** (put) on the floor? It is the _____. 1321
are 1539	**The trees on the hillside** (*prevent, prevents*) **soil erosion.** 1540
most 1758	With some words, we have the choice of forming the second degree by adding either **-er** or **more** and of forming the third degree by adding either **-est** or **most**. **Let's play a livelier game.** or: **Let's play a** _____ **lively game.** 1759
Karen's 1977	<u>Yours</u> **writes better than** <u>Gails</u>. Which underlined word does *not* require an apostrophe because it is a pronoun? _____ 1978
Ȼaptain, Ɱajor 2196	Cross out each capital letter that is not correct: **Andy's Mother asked my Father to drive Betty to school.** 2197
March, 2415	**We shall be at the Webers' house in Houston from June 18 to the end of the month.** 2416

Here is a *complete sentence* of only two words:

Birds fly.

We know what this sentence is about. It is not about *dogs* or *horses*. It is about _____.

2

---

friend

221

Some verbs can be either complete or incomplete, depending on the sense in which they are used.

    a. **The weather changed.**

    b. **Bob changed the tire.**

In which sentence does the verb **changed** require a noun to complete the intended meaning? ____

222

---

subject

441

    a. **Gloria's favorite candy is** *fudge*.
    b. **Gloria made some** *fudge* **for the party.**

In which sentence is *fudge* a subject complement? ____

442

---

adverb

661

A preposition is a word that shows the _____ between the noun or pronoun that follows it and some other word in the sentence.

662

No

881

Use **who (whom, whose)** to refer to **persons.**

Underline the correct pronoun for the clause signal:

The witness (*which, who*) *had seen the accident* **could not be found.**

882

F S

1101

A passer-by, seeing our difficulty. Came over to our car.

____   ____

1102

bag
 	
1321
	Once again, **to sit** means "to take a sitting position" or "to be in place."
	
	In which of the following sentences does this definition fit —*a* or *b*?
	
	    a. **I prefer to . . . in the balcony.**
	    b. **Don't . . . the hot pan on the table.**
	
	                                              1322

prevent 1540	**One of the ladies** (*remind, reminds*) **me of my mother.** 1541
more 1759	**This is the pleasantest spot in the park.** or: **This is the _____ pleasant spot in the park.** 1760
Yours 1978	**My <u>friends</u> car was behind <u>ours</u>.** Which underlined word does *not* require an apostrophe because it is a pronoun?_____ 1979
M̸other, F̸ather 2197	In this and the following frames, copy only the words that require capitalization, adding the needed capitals: **Poe's story "The pit and the pendulum" has a gruesome plot.** _____ 2198
None 2416	**We will be staying at Columbine Lodge Denver from Monday July 1 through Saturday July 6.** (Add five commas.) 2417

birds	**Birds . . .** **Birds fly** is a sentence, but the word **birds** by itself is not a _____ .
2	3

b	**Fred laughed.** **Fred tore . . .** Both verbs—**laughed** and **tore**—show actions. Which of these action verbs fails to make a *complete* statement about the subject **Fred?** _____
222	223

a	1————————→ 2 a. **Howard polished his** _____ . 1 ←———————— 1 b. **Howard was our best** _____ . Which sentence would be completed by a subject complement? ____
442	443

relationship	The noun or pronoun that follows a preposition is called its (*object, subject*).
662	663

who	Use **which** to refer to **things** or **animals.** Underline the correct pronoun for the clause signal: **A dog** (*which, who*) *has been properly trained* **will not chase cars.**
882	883

F F	**Will James wrote "Smoky." A story about a horse.** ____ ____
1102	1103

a 1322	**I prefer to . . . in the balcony.** The meaning we want is "to take a sitting position." Therefore, the correct word is _____. 1323
reminds 1541	**The car with many extras** (*cost, costs*) **$2,700.** 1542

most
 	
 1760
	Never use both **-er** and **more** or both **-est** and **most** with the same word. This is needless duplication.
	
	   a. **Let's play a more livelier game.**
	   b. **Let's play a more lively game.**
	
	 Which sentence is wrong because both **-er** and **more** are used with the same word? ____
	 1761

ours 1979	Which words can show ownership without the use of apostrophes—*nouns* or *pronouns?* _____ 1980
Pit, Pendulum 2198	Copy the words that require capitals: **His father is a close friend of superintendent Andrews and mayor Sanders.** _____ 2199
Lodge, Denver, Monday, July 1, Saturday, 2417	**Jack Karr of Baltimore will wrestle Sam Lutz of Chicago at Soldiers' Field Chicago.** 2418

sentence 3	The word **birds** by itself merely *names* a topic that we might talk about. To make a sentence of it, we must *tell* something about _____. 4
tore 223	**Fred tore . . .** (What?) What did Fred tear—his hair, his sock, or his shirt? The sentence fails to tell *what* received the action of the verb **tore.** Therefore, the meaning of the sentence is (*complete, incomplete*). 224
b 443	a. **The Milners were frequent** *visitors* **in our home.** b. **My parents invited many** *visitors* **to our home.** In which sentence is the italicized word a subject complement? ____ 444
object 663	A group of words that begins with a preposition and ends with its object is called a _____ *phrase.* 664
which 883	Use **that** to refer to anything—**persons, things,** or **animals.** Underline the correct pronoun: **The clerk** (*which, that*) *waited on me* **was very helpful.** 884
S F 1103	**Mr. Corey, the owner of the boat. Gave us permission to use it.** _____ _____ 1104

sit 1323	Here are the forms of the verb **sit**: PRESENT SIMPLE PAST PAST WITH HELPER **sit** (on chair) **sat** **have sat** The two past forms of **sit** are (*different, alike*). 1324
costs 1542	**The printing on these sheets** (*come, comes*) **out in the wash.** 1543
a 1761	a. **The de luxe model is fancier than the standard.** b. **The de luxe model is more fancy than the standard.** c. **The de luxe model is more fancier than the standard.** The above sentences are correct except for sentence _____. 1762
pronouns 1980	a. <u>**Our's**</u> **was parked in front of our** <u>**neighbors**</u> **house.** b. <u>**Ours**</u> **was parked in front of our** <u>**neighbor's**</u> **house.** Which sentence is correct? _____ 1981
Superintendent, Mayor 2199	**This morning father Corrigan and sister Magdalene visited our class.** _____ 2200
Field, 2418	**Eleanor Grayson of 310 Fulton Street was chosen Queen of the Cherry Festival.** 2419

birds 4	**Birds fly.** In this sentence, the word that *tells* something about **birds** is _____. 5
incomplete 224	**Fred <u>tore</u> his shirt.** Now the meaning of the sentence is complete. We know *what* Fred tore. He tore his **shirt.** Which word *receives the action* of the verb **tore?** _____ 225
a 444	a. **Liszt won great** *fame* **all over Europe.** b. **Liszt became** *famous* **all over Europe.** In which sentence is the italicized word a direct object? ____ 445
prepositional 664	A prepositional phrase can be used either as an adjective or an adverb. (*True, False*) 665
that 884	The main point to remember is never to use **which** to refer to **persons.** Underline the correct pronoun: **the teacher** (*who, which*) 885
F F 1104	**Mr. Corey is the owner of the boat. He gave us permission to use it.** ____ ____ 1105

alike 1324	PRESENT SIMPLE PAST PAST WITH HELPER **sit** (on a chair) **sat** **have sat** **Ernie _____ in the same seat all semester.** 1325
comes 1543	Lesson **50** Words That Mean One [Frames 1545–1573]
c 1762	a. **This was the most happiest day in my life.** b. **This was the happiest day in my life.** Which sentence is right because it avoids duplication? _____ 1763
b 1981	Make a special effort to hold back your apostrophes whenever you write these words: POSSESSIVE PRONOUNS **his** **its** (**its** name) **yours** **hers** **ours** **theirs** Which of the above pronouns means "belonging to it"? _____ 1982
Father, Sister 2200	**I received gifts from my uncle George, aunt Helen, and my two cousins.** _____ 2201
None 2419	Every address in the United States has a ZIP Code number. Write this number after the state with no comma between them. The state and ZIP Code number form a single unit. Supply the necessary commas: **You can write Pete at 5225 Cornelius Avenue Indianapolis Indiana 46208 until July 15.** 2420

fly 5	**Birds fly.** This sentence doesn't tell us that birds *eat, sleep,* or *sing.* It tells us that birds _____. 6
shirt 225	**The <u>class</u> <u>elected</u> Henry.** Which word *receives the action* of the verb **elected?** _____ 226
a 445	a. **The President gave a medal to the** *astronaut.* b. **The President gave the** *astronaut* **a medal.** In which sentence is the italicized word an indirect object? ____ 446
True 665	A prepositional phrase that modifies a noun or pronoun is called an _____ *phrase.* A prepositional phrase that modifies a verb is called an _____ *phrase.* 666
who 885	Underline the correct pronoun: **the elephant** (*who, which*) 886
S S 1105	**Being interested in music. I made my report on Caruso.** **A great Italian opera singer of the early 20th century.** ____ ____ ____ 1106

sat 1325	**Ernie sat in the same seat all semester.** If we added the helper **has** to the verb, would we need to change the word **sat?** (*Yes, No*) <div align="right">1326</div>
  1543	The words **each, every, either,** and **neither** can be used as adjectives and (except for **every**) also as pronouns. <center>*Each* **one** *Either* **boy** *Every* **house** *Neither* **road**</center> When these words modify nouns or pronouns, they are used as _____. <div align="right">1545</div>
b 1763	In this and the following frames, underline the correct form of the adjective or adverb: **Personality is** (*importanter, more important*) **than good looks.** <div align="right">1764</div>
its 1982	Do not confuse the possessive (ownership) pronoun **its** with the contraction **it's** (= it is). <center>a. **What is <u>its</u> name?** b. **<u>It's</u> time to eat.**</center> In which sentence does the underlined word show ownership? _____ <div align="right">1983</div>
Uncle, Aunt 2201	**Lesson 71 Capitals—Not Too Many, Not Too Few** <div align="right">[Frames 2203–2226]</div>
Avenue, Indianapolis, 46208, 2420	Supply the necessary commas: **I wrote to the British Information Service 30 Rockefeller Plaza New York N.Y. 10020** for their latest film catalogue. (Remember that the state and ZIP Code number which follows it are a single unit.) <div align="right">2421</div>

fly	To tell about something means to make a statement about it.
	Birds fly.
	The word **fly** makes a statement about _____.
6	7
Henry	Sometimes the word that completes the verb *receives the action*. At other times, it *shows the result of the action*.
	Mother bakes her own bread.
	Which word *shows the result of the action* of the verb **bakes?** _____
226	227
b	Words that are used to connect words or groups of words are called _____.
446	447
adjective adverb	A phrase that is separated by other words from the word it modifies is likely to be an (*adjective, adverb*) *phrase*.
666	667
which	Underline the correct pronoun:
	any store (*that, who*)
886	887
F S F	Lesson **36** **Run-on Sentences: Three Guilty Words**
	[Frames 1108–1137]
1106	

No 1326	**To set** means "to put or to place something." You can't just put—you have to put *something.* Unless the sentence names this "something," this is not the word you want. **Don't set the hot pan on the table.** The "something" in this sentence is _____. 1327
adjectives 1545	*Each* **comes in a box.** *Either* **fits you well.** *Neither* **plans to go.** When these words are used in place of nouns, they are _____. 1546
more important 1764	**Is Myra** (*older, more older*) **than Floyd?** 1765
a 1983	a. **What is** <u>its</u> **name?** b. <u>It's</u> **time to eat.** In which sentence is the underlined word a contraction for the two words **It is?** ____ 1984
	Too many capitals are as bad as too few. Let's look at some groups of **common nouns** that should *not* be capitalized. ANIMALS: **collie, spaniel, tiger, panther** BIRDS: **robin, pheasant, woodpecker, crow** Supply the missing letters: **At the zoo we saw ____lephants and ____iraffes.** 2203
Service, Plaza, New York, N.Y. 10020, 2421	Lesson **78** Unit Review [Frames 2423–2441] *page 14*

birds 7	A group of words that both names something and makes a _____ about it is a **complete sentence.** 8
bread 227	A word in the predicate that *receives the action* or *shows the result* of this action is called a **direct object.** **Dad <u>repaired</u> the motor.** The noun **motor** *receives the action* of the verb **repaired** and is therefore a _____ _____. 228
conjunctions 447	Three common conjunctions are _____, _____, and _____. 448
adverb 667	a. **I learned about boats <u>from my uncle.</u>** b. **The letter <u>from my uncle</u> contained a check.** In which sentence is the underlined prepositional phrase an adverb phrase? _____ 668
that 887	Underline the correct pronoun: **the nurse** (*which, who*) 888
	<div align="center">**The <u>curtain</u> <u>went</u> up.** **The <u>audience</u> <u>quieted</u> down.**</div> These are two separate and complete sentences. A period shows where the first sentence ends, and a _____ letter shows where the second sentence begins. <div align="center">*page 15*</div> 1108

pan 1327	PRESENT SIMPLE PAST PAST WITH HELPER **set** (put) **set** **have set** Does the word **set** change in any of the verb's three forms? (*Yes, No*) 1328

pronouns
 	
1546
	The following words are singular. We know this because we can use the word *one* with each of them.
	    each (each *one***)** **either (either** *one***)**
	    every (every *one***)** **neither (neither** *one***)**
	In the sentence below, which verb agrees with the singular subject **one?** _____
	            Each one (*is, are*) **in its place.** 1547

older 1765	**Our new house is** (*more comfortable, comfortabler*) **than our old one.** 1766
b 1984	**It's** (= **It is) time to eat.** The apostrophe in the contraction **It's** takes the place of the missing letter ____. 1985

e, g
 	
2203
	The name **collie** would apply to *any* dog of this breed.
	The name of a *particular* dog might be **Lassie** or **Prince.**
	       The name of our collie was blondie.
	In this sentence, capitalize (*collie, blondie*).
	                                          2204

	In this and the following frames, supply the necessary commas. Not every sentence requires a comma. Some sentences require commas according to more than one rule. **Can you come to my graduation Shirley on Friday June 21?** 2423

statement 8	**Birds fly.** This little sentence is like most sentences because it has _____ parts: a *naming part* and a *telling part.* 9
direct object 228	**The cashier made a mistake.** Because it *shows the result of the action* of the verb **made,** the direct object is the noun _____. 229
and, but, or 448	a. **One of my sisters washed and wiped all the dishes.** b. **Andrea and my sister washed all the dishes.** Which sentence has compound verbs? ____ 449
a 668	Underline *two* prepositional phrases: **The future of our country depends on its schools.** 669
who 888	Now we shall continue to combine sentences by changing one of them to an adjective clause. **Jenny had an *uncle. He* was very kind to her.** First, we find a word in the second sentence (*He*) that means the same as a word in the first sentence (_____). 889
capital 1108	**The curtain went up. The audience quieted down.** **The curtain went up,** *and* **the audience quieted down.** We have now combined these two sentences into a single (*complex, compound*) sentence. 1109

No 1328	**Mother . . . the pie on the window sill to cool.** This sentence names the "something" that was put somewhere. It was a **pie.** Therefore, our verb should be a form of (*sit, set*). 1329
is 1547	a. **Each <u>one</u> <u>is</u> in its place.** b. **<u>Each</u> <u>is</u> in its place.** The subject of sentence *a* is the pronoun **one.** The subject of sentence *b* is the pronoun _____. 1548
more comfortable 1766	**The weather gets** (*more cold, colder*) **at night.** 1767
i 1985	Write the contraction of the words **It is.** _____ 1986
Blondie 2204	**There never was a cocker more affectionate than cindy.** In this sentence, capitalize (*cocker, cindy*). 2205
graduation, Shirley, Friday, 2423	Add any necessary commas: **Joe Louis a worker in a Detroit automobile plant became the world's heavyweight champion in 1937.** 2424

two 9	**Flowers fade.** In this sentence, _____ is the *naming part,* and _____ is the *telling part.* 10
mistake 229	A direct object receives the _____ of the verb or shows the _____ of this action. 230
a 449	a. **Mrs. Forbes showed** *Mother* **and** *Rayna* **her beautiful garden.** b. **Mrs. Forbes showed them her** *house* **and** *garden.* In which sentence are the italicized words compound in- direct objects? ____ 450
of our country, on its schools 669	**UNIT 4: BUILDING BETTER SENTENCES** Lesson **23** **Recognizing Compound Sentences** [Frames 671–707]
uncle 889	*———who* **Jenny had an** *uncle.* ~~**He**~~ **was very kind to her.** Next, we change the second sentence into an adjective clause by putting the clause signal *who* in place of the word _____. 890
compound 1109	**The** <u>curtain</u> <u>went</u> **up,** *and* **the** <u>audience</u> <u>quieted</u> **down.** The two statements of this compound sentence are held to- gether by the conjunction _____, with a comma before it. 1110

set 1329	**Mother set the pie on the window sill to cool.** If we added the helper **had** to the verb, would we need to change the word **set**? (*Yes, No*) 1330
Each 1548	a. **Either <u>one</u> <u>is</u> a bargain.** b. **<u>Either</u> <u>is</u> a bargain.** The subject of sentence *a* is the pronoun **one.** The subject of sentence *b* is the pronoun _____. 1549
colder 1767	**It is the** (*beautifullest, most beautiful*) **car I have ever seen.** 1768
It's 1986	a. **See if <u>its</u> ready.** b. **Where <u>is</u> <u>its</u> mother?** In which sentence should **its** be written *without* an apostrophe because it is a possessive pronoun? ____ 1987
Cindy 2205	**After peewee escaped, Mother never wanted another parakeet.** In this sentence, capitalize (*peewee, parakeet*). 2206
Joe Louis, plant, 2424	Add any necessary commas: **An aluminum screen will not rust or warp or swell under any weather conditions.** 2425

Flowers (naming part)	**Glass breaks.**
fade (telling part)	In this sentence, _____ is the *naming part,* and _____ is the *telling part.*
10	11
action, result	PATTERN 2: *Subject—Action Verb → Direct Object* This, our second sentence pattern, consists of three parts. **The hot weather in July drove many people to the beaches.** The third part of the framework of this sentence is the direct object _____.
230	231
a	a. **The heavy rain flooded** *streets* **and** *basements.* b. **Two certainties of life are** *death* **and** *taxes.* In which sentence are the italicized words compound subject complements? ____
450	451
	Glen | buys old cars. This sentence can be divided into two major parts: the **complete subject** and the **complete pred**_____.
	671
He	a. **He was very kind to her.** b. *who was very kind to her* We changed *a,* which is a sentence, to *b,* which is a _____.
890	891
and	a. **The curtain went up, and the audience quieted down.** b. **The curtain went up, the audience quieted down.** Which sentence is wrong because there is no conjunction to hold the two statements together? ____
1110	1111

No 1330	Here are the two verbs to compare: PRESENT SIMPLE PAST PAST WITH HELPER **sit** (on a chair) **sat** **have sat** **set** (put) **set** **have set** The simple past form of **sit** is _____, but the simple past form of **set** is _____. 1331
Either 1549	**Neither** (*is, are*) **a bargain.** Which verb agrees with the subject **Neither?** _____ 1550
most beautiful 1768	**Rhode Island is the** (*smallest, most small*) **state in the Union.** 1769
b 1987	a. **It's not in its cage.** b. **Its not in it's cage.** Which sentence is correct? ____ 1988
Peewee 2206	Here are some more common nouns that should *not* be capitalized: TREES: pine, maple, oak, birch FLOWERS: rose, orchid, aster, dandelion Supply the missing letters: **There was a bed of ____oses around the ____ine tree.** 2207
None 2425	**In the early days of the industry each automobile was practically made by hand and the price of cars was very high.** 2426

Glass (naming part) breaks (telling part) 11	**Water freezes.** In this sentence, **Water** is the ＿＿＿＿＿＿ *part,* and **freezes** is the ＿＿＿＿＿＿ *part.* 12

people
 	
231
	When a sentence includes a direct object, as well as a sub-
	ject and an action verb, it has three parts.
	    a. **The driver of the other car accepted the blame.**
	    b. **The driver of the other car apologized.**
	Which sentence is built around a *three-part* framework—
	a or *b?* ＿＿＿
	                          232

b 451	A verb that is used before the main verb to express our meaning more exactly is called a ＿＿＿＿＿＿ verb. 452
(pred)icate 671	**Glen and Chris | buy old cars.** Although the complete subject now contains two simple subjects, the sentence can still be divided into ＿＿＿＿ major parts. (How many?) 672
clause 891	**Jenny had an uncle** *who was very kind to her.* The clause *who was very kind to her* is an adjective clause because it modifies the noun ＿＿＿＿. 892
b 1111	WRONG: **The curtain went up, the audience quieted down.** This sentence is wrong because a comma by itself can't hold the two statements of a compound sentence together. A ＿＿＿＿＿＿ is needed after the comma. 1112

(sit) sat (set) set 1331	**to sit to set** Which of these verbs means "to take a sitting position" or "to be in place"? _____ 1332
is 1550	The singular words **each, every, either,** and **neither** are often followed by an **of** phrase with a plural noun. Do not let this plural noun trick you into using a plural verb. A verb does not agree with the object of a preposition. It agrees with its _____. 1551
smallest 1769	**Lucille ordered the** (*most expensive, expensivest*) **sandwich on the menu.** 1770
a 1988	Underline the correct word in each pair: **Amy put** (*her's, hers*) **in with** (*their's, theirs*). 1989
r, p 2207	Capitalize a proper adjective that modifies a common noun. **French poodle African violet Scotch pine** **One sees very few russian wolfhounds.** In the above sentence, capitalize (*russian, wolfhounds*). 2208
industry, hand, 2426	**I wrote to the Sterling Stamp Co. 1600 Jefferson Ave. Buffalo N.Y. 14208 for their latest price list.** 2427

naming, telling 12	A complete sentence usually has _____ parts. (How many?) 13
a 232	**The <u>driver</u> of the other car <u>accepted</u> the blame.** The noun **blame** is the _____ _____ of the verb **accepted.** 233
helping 452	a. **surely, soon, always, really, not** b. **must, will, should, may, could, might** Which group consists of helping verbs? _____ 453
two 672	**<u>Glen</u> and <u>Chris</u> | <u>buy old cars</u> and <u>rebuild them</u>.** Now the complete subject has two parts connected by the word **and,** and the complete predicate also has two parts connected by the word _____. 673
uncle 892	**The paper printed a** *notice*. **Few people saw** *it*. The pronoun *it*, in the second sentence, means the same as the noun _____ in the first sentence. 893
conjunction 1112	WRONG: **The curtain went up, the audience quieted down.** A sentence like this is called a **run-on sentence.** In a run-on sentence, one sentence "runs on" into another without a conjunction to connect them or a period and a capital to *sep*_____ them. 1113

to sit 1332	In this and the following frames, underline the correct verb in each pair: **There was no place to** (*sit, set*) **down and wait.** 1333
subject 1551	**One is a bargain.** **Every one is a bargain.** Both sentences have the same subject—the pronoun ____. 1552
most expensive 1770	**Ralph ordered the** (*most cheap, cheapest*) **sandwich on the menu.** 1771
hers, theirs 1989	(*It's, Its*) **too late for** (*it's, its*) **nap.** 1990
Russian 2208	**The oaks were draped with spanish moss.** In this sentence, capitalize (*oaks, spanish, moss*). 2209
Co., Ave., Buffalo, N.Y. 14208, 2427	**When we first met Rosemary had dark brown hair and wore glasses.** 2428

two	We often use the word **subject** to mean *topic;* for example, "What subjects (topics) did you discuss?" In grammar, we call the *naming part* of a sentence the **subject** because it names the topic that the sentence is about. **Water freezes.** **Water** is the sub_____ of this sentence.
13	14
direct object	a. **The <u>argument</u> finally <u>ended</u>.** b. **<u>Dad</u> finally <u>ended</u> the argument.** Which sentence is built around a two-part framework—*a* or *b*? ____
233	234
b	A helping verb can be separated from the main verb by another word. (*True, False*)
453	454
and	**<u>Glen</u> and <u>Chris</u>	<u>buy</u> old cars and <u>rebuild</u> them.** Because the complete subject has more than one part, we say the subject is **compound.** Because the complete predicate also has more than one part, we say that the predicate is _____.
673	674
notice	_____*which* **The paper printed a** *notice.* **Few people saw *it*.** *which* **few people saw.** First, we change *it* to *which.* Then we move *which* to the (*beginning, end*) of the clause, where the clause signal belongs.
893	894
(sep)arate	**The curtain went up the audience quieted down.** **The curtain went up, the audience quieted down.** Both sentences—the one with the comma and the one without the comma—are (*correct, run-on*) sentences.
1113	1114

sit 1333	Don't (*sit*, *set*) the dish so near the edge of the table. 1334
one 1552	**Every <u>one</u> <u>is</u> a bargain.** **One** is the subject of this sentence. Can any prepositional phrase that we put after it change the fact that **one** is the subject? (*Yes*, *No*) 1553
cheapest 1771	In this and the following frames, underline the word that will avoid duplication. If you use **more,** don't also use **–er;** if you use **most,** don't also use **–est,** and vice versa. **Aluminum is (***lighter*, *more lighter***) than steel.** 1772
It's, its 1990	**Does he want to borrow (***yours*, *your's***) or (***ours*, *our's***)?** 1991
Spanish 2209	Do not capitalize— DISEASES: **flu, mumps, pneumonia, diabetes** **After recovering from tonsilitis, Judy caught the asiatic flu.** In this sentence, capitalize (*tonsilitis*, *asiatic*, *flu*). 2210
met, 2428	**Yes I have complete faith ladies and gentlemen in our democratic form of government.** 2429

(sub)ject 14	In grammar, we call the *telling part* of a sentence the **predicate.** **Water freezes.** The **predicate** of this sentence is _____. 15
a 234	a. **The <u>tree</u> behind our garage <u>died</u>.** b. **Our <u>dog</u> <u>chases</u> cars.** Which sentence is built around a three-part framework— *a* or *b*? ____ 235
True 454	In one of the following sentences, the complete verb is interrupted by a word that is not a verb. Underline each word of the verb in this sentence only. **The ship will soon be crossing the equator.** **The author of this article must have lived in Japan.** 455
compound 674	**<u>Glen</u> and <u>Chris</u> │ <u>buy old cars</u> and <u>rebuild them</u>.** Although both the subject and the predicate are compound, we can still divide the sentence into two parts: the **complete subject** and the **complete** _____. 675
beginning 894	**The paper printed a notice** *which few people saw.* The clause *which few people saw* modifies the noun **notice.** It is therefore an _____ *clause.* 895
run-on 1114	*As the curtain went up,* **the audience quieted down.** This sentence is right. It is not a run-on sentence. The word group (*before, after*) the comma could not stand by itself as a complete sentence. 1115

set 1334	You can (*sit, set*) next to us. 1335
No 1553	Every <u>one</u> (of these suits) <u>is</u> a bargain. Now a plural noun—**suits**—has appeared between the subject and the verb. The plural noun **suits** is not the subject. It is the object of the preposition _____. 1554
lighter 1772	I was more (*hungrier, hungry*) than the other boys. 1773
yours, ours 1991	(*It's, Its*) mother knows that (*it's, its*) crying. 1992
Asiatic 2210	The Weather Bureau gives each hurricane a girl's name to identify it—like **Carol** or **Mamie.** However, we do not give each particular case of **measles** or **mumps** a special name like **Betty** or **Winifred.** Since **measles** or **mumps** means any case of measles or mumps, it (*is, is not*) capitalized. 2211
Yes, faith, gentlemen, 2429	Dale of course apologized to Miss Bromley and she accepted his apology very graciously. 2430

freezes 15	**Predicate** is a long word. Let's break it up into three syllables and learn to spell it: **pred-i-cate** The third syllable of **predicate** is _____. 16
b 235	Don't mistake other words that may follow the verb for a *direct object*. To be a *direct object*, a word must either receive the _____ of the verb or show the _____ of this action. 236
will be crossing 455	UNIT 3: **THE WORK OF MODIFIERS** Lesson **16** **Meet the Adjective** [Frames 457–481]
predicate 675	A sentence that can be divided into two parts—a subject and a predicate—is a **simple sentence.** A **simple sentence** may have a *compound subject* and/or a *compound* _____. 676
adjective 895	After changing a sentence to an adjective clause, be sure to put it next to the word it modifies in the other sentence. <div align="center">———————————*who*</div>**Jack forgot to mention the turn.** ~~He~~ *gave us our directions.* Does the clause *who gave us our directions* modify **Jack** or **turn?** _____ 896
before 1115	*As the curtain went up,* **the audience quieted down.** The word group before the comma is an *adverb* _____. 1116

sit 1335	Why does Pete (*sit, set*) around waiting for opportunities to come to him? 1336
of 1554	**Every <u>one</u> of ...** No matter how we complete this **of** phrase, the pronoun **one** will remain the subject of this sentence. For this reason, the verb in this sentence will need to be (*singular, plural*). 1555
hungry 1773	**Mr. Hart is more (*friendly, friendlier*) than Miss Sibley.** 1774
Its, it's 1992	Lesson **65** "We Boys" and the "–*self*" Pronouns [Frames 1994–2015]
is not 2211	**The measles was spreading throughout the Wicker school.** In this sentence, capitalize (*measles, school*). 2212
Dale, course, Miss Bromley, 2430	**Well you should have heard Coach Frankoski talk to the boys between halves.** 2431

cate 16	**Iron bends.** In this sentence, the subject is _____, and the predicate is _____. 17
action, result 236	**Larry drove** *recklessly.* **Larry drove the** *car.* What did Larry drive—a golf ball, a tractor, or a car? Is *recklessly* or *car* a direct object? _____ 237
	a. **dog** b. **large dog** Does *a* or *b* give us a clearer picture of a dog? _____ 457
predicate 676	**My mother is English.** **My father is French.** Each of the above sentences can be divided into a subject and a predicate. Therefore, each of the above sentences is a _____ sentence. 677
Jack 896	a. **Jack forgot to mention the turn,** *who gave us our directions.* b. **Jack,** *who gave us our directions,* **forgot to mention the turn.** Which sentence makes better sense because the clause comes correctly after the noun it modifies? _____ 897
clause 1116	*As the curtain went up,* **the audience quieted down.** This sentence cannot be separated into two sentences. This sentence, therefore, (*is, is not*) a run-on sentence. 1117

sit 1336	**sat set** Which one of these past forms means "took a sitting position" or "was in place"? _____ 1337
singular 1555	Underline the correct verb: **Every one (of these 10,000 stamps)** (*is, are*) **for sale.** 1556
friendly 1774	**This melon is** (*riper, more riper*) **than the other.** 1775
	How can you tell which form of the pronoun to use in expressions like "*We* boys" and "*Us* girls"? By omitting the noun that follows the pronoun **we** or **us**, you will see instantly which pronoun is correct. <div align="center">(*Us, We*) ~~boys~~ **need a rest.**</div>In the above sentence, choose the pronoun _____. 1994
School 2212	Do not capitalize— FOODS: **spaghetti, chop suey, pizza, brownies** GAMES: **football, hockey, bingo, bowling** **After the hockey game, we went to an italian restaurant for pizza.** Capitalize (*hockey, italian, pizza*). 2213
Well, 2431	**Dr. Weiss excused himself and left the party after he received the telephone call.** 2432

(subject) Iron (predicate) bends 17	**Milk sours.** In this sentence, **Milk** is the _____, and **sours** is the _____. 18
car 237	**Peggy cooks the** *dinner.* **Peggy cooks** *well.* Is *dinner* or *well* a direct object? _____ 238
b 457	a. **dog** b. **large dog** **Large dog** gives us a clearer picture than just the noun **dog** because the word _____ describes the dog. 458
simple 677	a. **My mother is English.** **My father is French.** b. **My mother is English, and my father is French.** In b, the two simple sentences are joined into a single sentence by the **conjunction,** or connecting word, _____. 678
b 897	*which* **Our yearbook comes out next week.** ~~It~~ *sells for a dollar.* After we change the second sentence to an adjective clause, we should place the clause after the word it modifies. What is the article *which sells for a dollar?* It is the (*yearbook, week*). 898
is not 1117	a. **The curtain went up, and the audience quieted down.** b. **As the curtain went up, the audience quieted down.** c. **The curtain went up, the audience quieted down.** Which sentence is wrong because it is a run-on sentence— *a, b,* or *c?* ____ 1118

sat 1337	**Mrs. Winkler** (*sat, set*) **on the porch and knitted.** 1338
is 1556	(Remember that a verb agrees with its subject, not with a noun or pronoun that may follow the subject.) a. **Each** <u>was</u> **in its place.** b. **Each (of the tools)** <u>was</u> **in its place.** The subject of both sentence *a* and *b* is the singular pronoun _____. 1557
riper 1775	**We saw the** (*most fiercest, fiercest*) **gorilla in captivity.** 1776
We 1994	<u>We</u> **need a rest.** <u>We</u> **boys need a rest.** The subject form **We** is correct because it is the subject of the verb _____ in both sentences. 1995
Italian 2213	**Later in the evening, Wilma made brownies while we played chinese checkers.** Capitalize (*brownies, chinese, checkers*). 2214
None 2432	From this point on, draw circles around any commas that should be omitted. In several sentences, all the commas need to be removed. **Expressways, buses, and airlines, take passenger business away from the railroads.** 2433

(Milk) subject (sours) predicate 18	A sentence usually has two parts. The grammar names for these two parts are **subject** and _____. 19
dinner 238	**Steve brought . . .** The meaning of this subject and verb is incomplete. We are waiting to hear *whom* or *what* **Steve** _____. 239
large 458	a. **large dog** b. **large brown dog** Does *a* or *b* give us a clearer and more detailed picture of a dog? ____ 459
and 678	**My mother is English, | and my father is French.** Can we divide this sentence into two parts—a subject and a predicate? No, each of its two parts now has *its own* subject and predicate. Is this a **simple sentence?** *(Yes, No)* 679
yearbook 898	a. **Our yearbook comes out next week** *which sells for a dollar.* b. **Our yearbook,** *which sells for a dollar,* **comes out next week.** Which sentence makes better sense because the adjective clause is properly placed? ____ 899
c 1118	Run-on sentences are most likely to occur when two sentences are closely related in thought. WRONG: **The referee blew his whistle, the game ended.** No matter how closely related in thought two sentences may be, they are still two separate sentences unless they are connected by the _____ **and, but,** or **or.** 1119

sat	**You** (*sat, set*) **the trap where someone might step on it.**
1338	1339
Each	<u>Each</u> **(of the tools)** <u>was</u> **in its place.** The noun **tools** is not the subject of the verb. It is the object of the preposition _____.
1557	1558
fiercest	**Julie was the most** (*selfish, selfishest*) **child I have ever seen.**
1776	1777
need	**Will you drive** (*we, us*) **girls to the corner?** To decide which pronoun to use, omit the noun **girls.** In the above sentence, choose the pronoun _____.
1995	1996
Chinese	Do not capitalize— OCCUPATIONS: **engineer, lawyer, minister, plumber** MUSICAL INSTRUMENTS: **piano, violin, accordion, trumpet** **Our doctor plays the french horn as a hobby.** Capitalize (*doctor, french, horn*).
2214	2215
airlines ⊙	Draw a circle around each comma that should be omitted: **It is doubtful, by the way, whether John can graduate, and go to college.**
2433	2434

predicate 19	The predicate makes a statement about the _____. 20
brought 239	**Steve brought** home a friend from college. *Whom* or *what* did **Steve** bring—a **home**, a **friend**, or a **college?** _____ 240
b 459	a. **large dog** b. **large brown dog** In *a*, there is only one word that describes the **dog**. In *b*, there are _____ words that describe the **dog**. 460
No 679	**Our school is small, but we have good teams.** This sentence was made by joining two simple sentences with the conjunction _____. 680
b 899	**Dad goes to Dr. Foster.** *His office is near our house.* Underline the clause signal you would put in place of *His* in changing the second sentence to an adjective clause. **which whose who that** 900
conjunction 1119	a. **When the referee blew his whistle, the game ended.** b. **The referee blew his whistle, the game ended.** c. **The referee blew his whistle, and the game ended.** Which sentence is wrong because it is a run-on sentence— *a, b,* or *c?* ____ 1120

set 1339	The scouts (*sat, set*) around the campfire and told tall stories. 1340
of 1558	Each of the tools was in its place. The subject of this sentence is the singular pronoun _____. 1559
selfish 1777	I discovered the (*most easiest, easiest*) way of making fudge. 1778
us 1996	Will you drive <u>us</u> to the corner? Will you drive <u>us</u> girls to the corner? The object form **us** is correct because it is the object of the verb _____. 1997
French 2215	This stradivarius violin is owned by a chicago banker. Capitalize (*stradivarius, violin*) and (*chicago, banker*). 2216
graduate⊙ 2434	Draw a circle around each comma that should be omitted: **Their fruits, and vegetables are always fresh, and reasonably priced.** 2435

subject 20	wrote talked melted Each of these words could be the _____ of a sentence. 21
friend 240	**Steve brought home a friend from college.** The noun **friend** receives the action of the verb **brought**. The noun **friend** is the _____ _____ of the verb **brought**. 241
two 460	The more words that we have describing a noun, the more (*clear, vague*) our mental picture of it becomes. 461
but 680	**You must shut the gate, or the dog will get out.** This sentence was made by joining two simple sentences with the conjunction _____. 681
whose 900	*whose* **Dad goes to Dr. Foster.** ~~His~~ *office is near our house.* The clause *whose office is near our house* belongs after the noun (*Dad, Dr. Foster*), which it modifies. 901
b 1120	**Floyd washed the car. The car was very dusty.** These are two complete sentences, each with a subject and a verb. They should be written (*apart, together*). 1121

sat 1340	(An object can *sit* on a table, desk, or stove just as a person can *sit* on a chair.) **This dictionary always (*sat, set*) on Mr. Ford's desk.** 1341
Each 1559	Remember the **"Rule of S":** When we add an *s* to the subject, we do not add an *s* to the verb. When we add an *s* to the verb, we do not add an *s* to the _____ . 1560
easiest 1778	**This is the most (*handy, handiest*) tool I have ever used.** 1779
drive 1997	**He offered the use of the gym to (*we, us*) fellows.** To decide which pronoun to use, omit the noun **fellows.** In the above sentence, choose the pronoun _____ . 1998
Stradivarius, Chicago 2216	**The minister of Bethel church plays the cello very well.** Capitalize (*minister, church, cello*). 2217
fruits⊕ fresh⊕ 2435	**I was still holding the king of spades, the queen of spades, and two aces, in my hand at the end of the game.** 2436

predicate 21	**bread pencil engine** Each of these words could be the _____ of a sentence. 22
direct object 241	In analyzing sentences, we shall use *S* for *subject*, *V* for *verb*, and *DO* for *direct object*. **Most Americans eat three meals a day.** Label the three-part framework of this sentence: S _____ _____ **Americans eat meals.** 242
clear 461	Each of the following two-word phrases gives you a different picture of a dog, doesn't it? <u>large</u> dog <u>old</u> dog <u>small</u> dog <u>brown</u> dog The word that changes your picture of the dog is the (*first, second*) word in each phrase. 462
or 681	A sentence made by joining two (or more) simple sentences with the conjunction **and, but,** or **or** is called a **compound sentence.** The most common conjunctions that connect the two parts of a compound sentence are **and, but,** and _____. 682
Dr. Foster 901	In this and the following frames, combine each pair of sentences by changing the italicized sentence to an adjective clause. Write the full sentence in the blank space. **Ernie had a lame shoulder.** *It prevented him from pitching.* _____ _____ 902
apart 1121	*It* **Floyd washed the car.** ~~The car~~ **was very dusty.** Since **car** is mentioned in the first sentence, we do not need to repeat the noun **car** in the second sentence. Therefore we can put the _____ *It* in place of the noun **car** as the subject of the second sentence. 1122

sat 1341	**have sat have set** Which of these helper forms is a form of the verb **sit,** which means "to take a sitting position" or "to be in place"? _____ 1342
subject 1560	**Every one of these suits** (_fit, fits_) **you well.** Since **one,** the subject of this sentence, does not end in _s,_ which verb would you choose? _____ 1561
handy 1779	Lesson **58** One _No_ Is Enough! [Frames 1781–1806]
us 1998	**He offered the use of the gym to us.** **He offered the use of the gym to us fellows.** The object form **us** is correct because **us** is the object of the preposition _____. 1999
Church 2217	Underline the words that require capitals: **Last sunday, my dad played golf with coach Harris at Brookside park.** 2218
aces ⊙ 2436	**You can read,** _Huckleberry Finn,_ **in one, or two evenings.** 2437

subject 22	arrives Henry Which word could be used as the subject of a sentence? _____ 23

V   DO
eat   meals
 	
242
	The old man always wears his hat in the house.
	The framework of this sentence is:
	
	     S V DO
	
	   man _____ _____
	
	243

first 462	In grammar, we frequently use the word **modify.** *To modify* means *to change.* To modify the body style of a car means to change its style. After your mother *modifies* a recipe, the recipe is (*the same, different*). 463

or
 	
682
	_____ ========== { , **and**
	                   { , **but** _____ ==========.
	                   { , **or**
	Notice that in a compound sentence there is a subject and a predicate both *before* and *after* the _____,
	or connecting word.
	
	683

Ernie had a lame shoulder that (which) prevented him from pitching. 902	**He gave facts about crime.** *They startled everyone.* _____ _____ 903
pronoun 1122	a. **The <u>car</u> <u>was</u> very dusty.** b. **<u>It</u> <u>was</u> very dusty.** Both *a* and *b* are complete sentences. If we were writing only one sentence, without any others, we would write sentence (*a, b*). ____ 1123

have sat 1342	You should have (*sat, set*) the bottles right on ice. 1343
fits 1561	Every one of these stones (*come, comes*) from a different state. Which word is the subject of this sentence—**one** or **stones**? _____ 1562
	Yes is a positive word. **No** is a negative word. **Something** is a positive word. **Nothing** is a _____ word. 1781
to 1999	a. (*We, Us*) boys decorated the gym. b. The gym was decorated by (*we, us*) boys. Is the object form **us** correct in sentence *a* or *b*? ____ 2000
Sunday, Coach, Park 2218	His brother has been in the Clippert hospital with pneumonia since labor day. 2219
read⊙ Huckleberry Finn⊙ one⊙ 2437	Call for your dry cleaning at, 1075 Prentis Avenue, after Tuesday, May 10. 2438

Henry 23	**elephants returned** Which word could be used as the predicate of a sentence? _____ 24
V DO wears hat 243	**My very best pen recently disappeared.** The framework of this sentence is: S V _____ _____ 244
different 463	_To modify_ means _to change._ <u>brown</u> dog <u>black</u> dog When we say that **brown** and **black** modify the noun **dog,** we really mean that they _____ our picture or idea of the dog. 464
conjunction 683	A **simple sentence** _cannot_ be divided into two separate sentences. A _____ **sentence** _can_ be divided into two separate sentences. 684
He gave facts about crime that (which) startled everyone. 903	**Mr. Dell would not take any money.** _He owns the boat._ _____ _____ (Be sure to put the clause next to the noun it modifies.) 904
a 1123	a. **The car was very dusty.** b. **It was very dusty.** If the sentence were to follow another sentence that already mentioned the **car,** we would write sentence (_a, b_). ____ 1124

set 1343	His hat looked as if someone had (*sat, set*) on it. 1344
one 1562	Every one of these stones (*come, comes*) from a different state. Since **one,** the subject of this sentence, does not end in *s,* which verb would you choose? _____ 1563
negative 1781	a. **some** ever **something** anybody someone either b. **none** never **nothing** nobody no one neither Which group of words is negative? ____ 1782
b 2000	The gym was decorated by <u>us</u>. The gym was decorated by <u>us</u> boys. The object form **us** is correct because **us** is the object of the preposition _____. 2001
Hospital, Labor Day 2219	In this and the following frames, cross out each capital letter that is not correct: I saw my first Robin this Spring in my Grandmother's back yard. 2220
at⊙ Avenue⊙ 2438	I wrote, and revised, and copied my composition twice before I turned it in. 2439

returned 24	**answered vegetables stumbled** Which word could be used as a subject? _____ 25
S V pen disappeared 244	**His good manners won many friends for him.** S V DO _____ **won** _____ 245
change 464	Words that modify nouns and pronouns are called **adjectives. Adjectives** are another *class* of words. The word **adjective** has three syllables: **ad-jec-tive.** An adjective can modify a _____ or pronoun. 465
compound 684	a. <u>Our class</u> <u>made birdhouses and sold them.</u> b. <u>Our class</u> <u>made birdhouses</u>, and <u>the church</u> <u>sold them.</u> Which sentence has both a subject and a predicate after the conjunction **and?** ____ 685
Mr. Dell, who owns the boat, would not take any money. 904	**He made an announcement.** *None of us heard it.* _____ _____ 905
b 1124	**Floyd washed the car.** *It* **was very dusty.** *It* **was very dusty** is a complete sentence because we know from the previous sentence that *It* means _____. 1125

sat 1344	**The painter had** (*sat, set*) **the ladders against a tree.** 1345
comes 1563	In this and the following frames, underline the verb that agrees with its subject. Remember that **each, every, either,** and **neither** are either singular themselves or modify singular nouns or pronouns. **Each** (*was, were*) **with an escort.** 1564
b 1782	not none never nothing nobody no one neither nowhere Each of these negative words, just like the word **no,** begins with the letter ____. 1783
by 2001	The *"–self"* Pronouns When using pronouns that end with **–self** or **–selves,** be careful not to use words that do not exist. WRONG: **theirselves, themself** RIGHT: **themselves** **The campers washed** _____ **in the lake.** 2002
R̸obin, S̸pring, G̸randmother's 2220	Cross out each capital letter that is not correct: **Because of his Appendicitis operation, Pete fell behind in his English and Math courses.** 2221
wrote ⓘ revised ⓘ 2439	**If you know what's good for you, you won't cut across Mr. Kronk's lawn, when you deliver his paper.** 2440

vegetables

25

---

kitchen   money   boiled

Which word could be used as a predicate? _____

26

S   DO
manners friends

245

The price of oranges suddenly jumped.

S   V

_____   _____

246

---

noun

465

---

brown dog   **gentle** dog
smart dog   **obedient** dog

The adjectives **brown, smart, gentle,** and **obedient** tell us *what kind* of dog and change our picture or idea of it.

In grammar, we say that these adjectives _____ the noun **dog**.

466

---

b

685

---

a. **Our class** **made** **birdhouses** and **sold them.**
b. **Our class** **made** **birdhouses,** and **the church** **sold them.**

Which sentence can be divided into two separate sentences—*a* or *b*? ____

686

He made an
announcement
that (which)
none of us heard.

905

We picked some plums. *They were growing along the road.*

_____

_____

906

---

car

1125

Not only *it* but other pronouns, too, can start a new sentence.

        Wendy is musical. *She* **plays several instruments.**

She **plays several instruments** is a complete sentence because we know from the previous sentence that *She* means

_____.

1126

set 1345	You must have (*sat, set*) on some wet paint. 1346
was 1564	Each of the girls (*was, were*) with an escort. 1565
n 1783	doesn't haven't can't won't shouldn't The n't at the end of each of these verbs is a contraction of the negative word _____. 1784
themselves 2002	WRONG: hisself RIGHT: himself Albert looked at _____ in the mirror. 2003
~~A~~ppendicitis, ~~M~~ath 2221	Cross out each capital letter that is not correct: The boys bought their Mother a corsage of red Carnations for Mother's Day. 2222
lawn⊙ 2440	Very soon, however, I lost my feeling of strangeness, and began to feel at home. 2441

boiled 26	**Birds fly. Water freezes. Iron bends. Milk sours.** In the above sentences, the subject comes (*before, after*) the predicate. (Underline the correct answer.) 27
S V price jumped 246	**His funny story about the dog amused everybody.** S V DO **story** _____ _____ 247
modify 466	**A sharp stone cut the tire.** *What kind* of stone cut the tire? The _____ **sharp** modifies the noun **stone.** 467
b 686	a. **Our class made birdhouses and sold them.** b. **Our class made birdhouses, and the church sold them.** Which sentence is a compound sentence? ____ 687
We picked some plums that (which) were growing along the road. 906	**Pam saw the lightning strike.** *She was standing at the window.* _____ _____ 907
Wendy 1126	**Elephants are intelligent.** *They* **learn tricks quickly.** *They* **learn tricks quickly** is a complete sentence because we know from the previous sentence that the pronoun *They* stands for _____. 1127

sat 1346	They found the baby (*sitting, setting*) in a mud puddle. 1347
was 1565	Every one (*is, are*) on sale. 1566

not
 	
1784
	One negative word is all we need to make a negative statement. A second negative word is useless duplication and a sign of poor speech.
	
	     a. **I couldn't see nothing.**
	     b. **I couldn't see anything.**
	
	Which sentence contains two negative words? ____
	
	1785

himself 2003	WRONG: **yourselfs** RIGHT: **yourselves** **Why don't you girls make _____ some lunch?** 2004
Mother, Carnations 2222	My Uncle plays the Organ every Sunday at the Highland Community Church. 2223
strangeness_(r) 2441	UNIT 12: APOSTROPHES AND QUOTATION MARKS Lesson **79** Spotting the Apostrophe [Frames 2443–2484] *page 54*

before 27	In most English sentences, we usually first name what we are talking about; then we make a statement about what we have named. Most English sentences begin with the _____. 28
V amused DO everybody 247	**The waiter finally removed the dirty dishes from the table.** S V DO _____ _____ _____ 248
adjective 467	**A tame brown bear approached us.** *What kind* of bear approached us? In this sentence, the two adjectives that modify the noun **bear** are _____ and _____. 468
b 687	**Our class made birdhouses, and the church sold them.** This is a **compound sentence**. In a compound sentence, place a comma after the first statement. This comma comes before the _____ **and, but,** or **or**. 688
Pam, who was standing at the window, saw the lightning strike. 907	**We have a watchdog.** *It would lick the face of a burglar.* _____ _____ 908
Elephants 1127	**Elephants are intelligent,** *they* **learn tricks quickly.** This is an incorrect run-on sentence. One way to correct it is to separate the two sentences with a period and a capital. Another way is to connect the two separate sentences with the _____ **and.** 1128

Lesson 43 Straightening Out
Rise and Raise

[Frames 1349–1380]

---

is

Every one of these ties (*is, are*) **on sale.**

(Did you see the word **one** in this sentence? Watch for it, too, in the sentences ahead!)

1566   1567

---

a

The error of using two negative words instead of one is called a **double negative.**

     a. **Jim doesn't want any more.**
     b. **Jim doesn't want no more.**

Which sentence is wrong because it contains a **double negative?** ____

1785   1786

---

yourselves

WRONG: **ourself, ourselfs**   RIGHT: **ourselves**

My dad and I built _____ **a workshop.**

2004   2005

Ⱥncle, Ører̸gan

Next Summer, my Cousin will graduate as an electrical Engineer from Cornell University.

2223   2224

Here we have two nouns in a row:

       boy's bicycle

Which one of these two nouns indicates the owner?

_____

           2443

subject 28	In analyzing a sentence, we often underline the subject with one line and the predicate with two lines. EXAMPLES: <u>Grass</u> <u><u>grows</u></u>. <u>Dogs</u> <u><u>bark</u></u>. Underline this sentence to show the subject (one line) and predicate (two lines): **Ice melts.** 29
S V waiter removed DO dishes 248	# 9 The Indirect Object Pattern Lesson [Frames 250–279]
tame, brown 468	So far, our adjectives have told *what kind* about the nouns they modify. Adjectives are also used to point out *which one*(s) we mean. EXAMPLES: <u>**this** dog</u> <u>**that** dish</u> <u>**these** houses</u> <u>**those** cars</u> The words **this, that, these,** and **those** are _____. 469
conjunction 688	<u>Our class</u> <u><u>made</u></u> <u>birdhouses</u> and <u><u>sold</u></u> <u>them</u>. This is not a compound sentence because there is not a subject and predicate, but only a part of the _____, after the conjunction **and.** 689
We have a watch-dog that (which) would lick the face of a burglar. 908	a. **who (whom, whose), which, that** b. **if, as, when, because, after, although** The words that can be used as adjective clause signals are those in group (*a, b*). ____ 909
conjunction 1128	a. **Elephants are intelligent. They learn tricks quickly.** b. **Elephants are intelligent, they learn tricks quickly.** c. **Elephants are intelligent, and they learn tricks quickly.** Which sentence is wrong because it is a run-on sentence—*a, b,* or *c*? ____ 1129

To rise means "to go up" or "to get up."

> **Farmers rise early.**
> **The curtain rises on time.**

The bubbles of air _____ **to the surface.**

1349

---

is

1567

Don't forget that a final *s* makes a verb *singular* when it expresses present time.

> **Either one** (*look, looks*) **good on you.**

1568

---

b

1786

WRONG: **Jim doesn't want no more.**

This sentence contains a **double negative.**

The first negative word is **doesn't;** the second negative

word is _____.

1787

---

ourselves

2005

All the **–self** pronouns are solid words. Don't split them.

> **I made** (*my self, myself*) **a sandwich.**

2006

~~S~~ummer,
~~C~~ousin,
~~E~~ngineer

2224

Our Principal let the members of the Richmond Science Club sell Popcorn at the Football game on Thanksgiving Day.

2225

---

boy's

2443

boy's bicycle

Which noun names what is owned? _____

2444

<u>Ice</u> <u>melts</u>. 29	Underline this sentence to show the subject and predicate: **Mosquitoes bite.** 30
  	In the previous lesson, we studied two sentence patterns: PATTERN 1: *Subject—Action Verb* PATTERN 2: *Subject—Action Verb → Direct Object* Do both patterns include a direct object? (*Yes, No*) 250
adjectives 469	a. <u>tall</u> glass <u>empty</u> glass <u>green</u> glass <u>broken</u> glass b. <u>this</u> glass <u>that</u> glass <u>these</u> glasses <u>those</u> glasses Do the adjectives point out *which glass* or *which glasses* we mean in group *a* or *b*? _____ 470
predicate 689	**Our class <u>made</u> birdhouses and <u>sold</u> them.** The conjunction **and** does not connect two sentences. It connects two parts of the (*subject, predicate*). 690
a 909	Never use the pronoun **which** as a clause signal to refer to (*things, persons*). 910
b 1129	The word *then* causes many run-on sentence errors. WRONG: **Ed looked at the clock,** *then* **he went back to sleep.** RIGHT: **Ed looked at the clock.** *Then* **he went back to sleep.** *Then* is not a conjunction like *and, but,* and *or,* which can join two sentences into a (*compound, complex*) sentence. 1130

rise 1349	A person **rises,** a wind **rises,** the sun **rises,** and a price _____ . 1350
looks 1568	**Every one of these pieces** (*fit, fits*) **somewhere.** 1569
no 1787	**Mr. Platt could <u>not</u> find work** (*nowhere, anywhere*). To avoid using a double negative, we choose the positive word _____ . 1788
myself 2006	**We were ashamed of** (*ourselves, our selves*). 2007
Principal, Popcorn, Football 2225	**My Aunt Harriet's Collie and her Persian Cat are the best of friends.** 2226
bicycle 2444	**boy's bicycle** The apostrophe appears in the word that shows (*the owner, what is owned*). 2445

Mosquitoes bite. (underlined: Mosquitoes = subject, bite = double underline) 30	Although all are printed as sentences, only *one* of the following pairs of words really is a sentence. Underline this sentence to show the subject and predicate, as you have been doing. **Cold water.**　　**Before noon.**　　**Snow falls.**　　**Broken wheel.** 31
No 250	Often an action verb requires another word to show *who* or *what* receives its action or to show the result of this action. This word often needed to complete the meaning of an action verb is called a *direct* _____. 251
b 470	Some words can be used as either pronouns or adjectives. 　　　a. **This is the correct address.** 　　　b. **This address is not correct.** In which sentence is **This** used as an adjective? _____ 471
predicate 690	**Our class <u>made birdhouses</u> and <u>sold them</u>.** A comma (*is, is not*) used before a conjunction that connects the two parts of a compound predicate. 691
persons 910	Ordinarily, an adjective clause should be put right (*after, before*) the noun or pronoun it modifies. 911
compound 1130	**Ed looked at the clock.** *Then* **he went back to sleep.** *Then* is not a conjunction. It is an adverb that tells (*how, when, where*)—just like the other adverbs in the following sentences: *Then* **he went to sleep.**　　*Soon* **he went to sleep.** *Later* **he went to sleep.**　　*Afterward* **he went to sleep.** 1131

rises 1350	To raise means "to lift something." Don't use this word unless you name the "something" that is lifted (or use a pronoun in its place). This rope raises (lifts) the curtain. What is the "something" that the rope raises? It is the _____. 1351
fits 1569	Neither one of the doors (was, were) unlocked. 1570
anywhere 1788	The baby can hardly walk. Does "hardly walk" mean "walk poorly" or "walk well"? _____ 1789
ourselves 2007	(We, Us) boys rented the cottage for a week. 2008
¢ollie, ¢at 2226	Lesson **72** Unit Review [Frames 2228–2249]
the owner 2445	The apostrophe is a mark we use to show *ownership*. To own something means to possess it. We say, therefore, that a word showing ownership is a *possessive* word. George's book was in my friend's locker. The possessive nouns in this sentence are _____ and _____. 2446

Snow falls. 31	Only *one* of the following pairs of words is a sentence. Underline this sentence to show the subject and predicate. **Barking dog. Almost ready. Falling rain. Gas explodes.** 32
object 251	S V **Dad gave an orchid.** The meaning of the action verb **gave** is completed by the direct object _____. 252
b 471	Adjectives also tell **how many** and **how much** about the nouns they modify. HOW MANY? <u>two</u> cars <u>most</u> boys <u>several</u> trees HOW MUCH? <u>no</u> eggs <u>some</u> sugar <u>enough</u> bread All the underlined words above are _____. 472
is not 691	a. <u>**Shorty reached for the ball**</u> but <u>missed it.</u> b. <u>**Shorty reached for the ball**</u> but <u>he missed it.</u> Which sentence requires a comma because it is a compound sentence? ___ 692
after 911	Lesson **30** **Using Adjective Clauses to Improve Sentences** [Frames 913–937]
when 1131	a. **We ordered our lunch.** *Then* **we discovered that we had no money.** b. **We ordered our lunch,** *then* **we discovered that we had no money.** Which is correct—*a* or *b*? ___ 1132

curtain
 	
1351
	Once again, **to rise** means "to go up" or "to get up."
	In which of the following sentences does this definition fit?
	—*a* or *b*? ____
	
	    a. **The men . . . early to go fishing.**
	    b. **Gentlemen always . . . their hats to ladies.**
	
	                                                            1352

was 1570	**Which one of us (*is, are*) to blame?** 1571

walk poorly
 	
1789
	a. **The baby can hardly walk.**
	    b. **The baby can't hardly walk.**
	If **"hardly walk"** means "walk poorly," which sentence says
	that the baby *can* walk, but poorly? ____
	
	                                                              1790

We 2008	**They rented the cottage to (*we, us*) boys for a week.** 2009

	Each of these frames will present a problem based on one of the rules of capitalization presented in this unit.
	
	Try to recall the specific rule which applies before you make your decision.
	
	    a. **at Niagara falls** b. **at Niagara Falls**
	Which item is correctly capitalized? ____
	
	                                                          2228

George's,
friend's
 	
2446
	my dad's office **the girls' gym**
	    a boy's locker **our soldiers' lives**
	Examine carefully the four examples above.
	
	Does the apostrophe always come *before* the final *s*?
	(*Yes, No*)
	
	                                                              2447

Lesson 2 The Complete Subject and Predicate

---

orchid

252

| S   V   DO |
| **Dad gave** *Mother* **an orchid.** |

Here we find a noun standing between the action verb and its direct object. This noun is _____.

253

---

adjectives

472

Dick bought new tires.

The adjective **new** modifies the noun _____.

473

---

b

692

↓
Shorty reached for the ball, but <u>he</u> missed it.

Would the comma before the conjunction be needed if we dropped the word **he** from this sentence? (*Yes, No*)

693

We can form a **compound sentence** by connecting two simple sentences with the conjunction *and, but,* or *or*.

The coat was too loose, and the sleeves were too long.

The two parts of this compound sentence are connected by the conjunction _____.

913

---

a

1132

Another trouble-maker is the adverb *therefore*.
  WRONG: **Our tires were old,** *therefore* **we drove slowly.**
  RIGHT: **Our tires were old.** *Therefore* **we drove slowly.**
Therefore is not a conjunction. It can't be used like *and* to connect sentences.
Can the adverb *therefore* begin a new sentence? (*Yes, No*)

1133

a 1352	**The men . . . early to go fishing.** The meaning we want is "to get up." Therefore, the correct word is _____. <div align="right">1353</div>
is 1571	**Several of the rooms** (*has, have*) **running water.** <div align="right">1572</div>
a 1790	a. **I couldn't scarcely stand up.** b. **I could scarcely stand up.** Which sentence says that you *could* stand up, but poorly? ____ <div align="right">1791</div>
us 2009	(*We, Us*) **fellows always get the blame.** <div align="right">2010</div>
b 2228	a. **a Negro magazine** b. **a negro magazine** Which item is correctly capitalized? ____ <div align="right">2229</div>
No 2447	How do you decide whether to put an apostrophe *before* or *after* the final *s*? The method is very simple. <div align="center">**A boys locker was left open.**</div>Ask yourself, "Who owns the locker?" The answer is a _____. <div align="right">2448</div>

Until now we have been working with sentences having a one-word subject and a one-word predicate. Usually, however, subjects and predicates have more than one word.

The lock on the front door stuck.

The part of this sentence that has more than one word is the (*subject, predicate*).

34

Mother

253

S   V   DO
Dad gave *Mother* **an orchid.**

The noun *Mother* is not another direct object like **orchid.**

The thing that Dad **gave** was not *Mother* but an _____.

254

---

tires

473

Dick bought _____ **new tires.**

Underline one of the following adjectives which would tell **how many** tires Dick bought:

expensive   good   several   these

474

No

693

We talked to the jockey and learned a lot about horses.

A compound sentence can be divided into two simple sentences, each with its own subject and predicate.

Is this a compound sentence? (*Yes, No*)

694

---

and

913

A sentence that contains a clause is called a **complex sentence.**

     a. **You received a letter which looks important.**
     b. **You received a letter, and it looks important.**

Which sentence is **complex** because it contains an adjective clause? ____

914

Yes

1133

     a. **Our tires were old,** *therefore* **we drove slowly.**
     b. **Our tires were old, and** *therefore* **we drove slowly.**

Which sentence is correct? ____

1134

rise 1353	Here are the forms of the verb **rise:** PRESENT SIMPLE PAST PAST WITH HELPER **rise** (go up) **rose** **have risen** Supply the correct past form of the verb **rise:** **The storm _____ soon after dark.** <div align="right">1354</div>
have 1572	**Neither of these snapshots** (*look, looks*) **a bit like you.** <div align="right">1573</div>
b 1791	**The car** (*would, wouldn't*) **hardly start.** **The car** (*would, wouldn't*) **scarcely start.** Although the car started with difficulty, the fact is that it *did* start. Therefore, we choose the word (*would, wouldn't*). <div align="right">1792</div>
We 2010	**What did she say about** (*us, we*) **girls?** <div align="right">2011</div>
a 2229	a. **St. Mary's Catholic Church** b. **a new Catholic Church** Which item is correctly capitalized? _____ <div align="right">2230</div>
boy 2448	Since the answer to your question is **boy,** put the apostrophe after the word **boy.** **A boy's locker was left open.** The apostrophe goes after the letter _____. <div align="right">2449</div>

subject 34	**John** <u>graduated.</u> <u>My best friend</u> <u>graduated.</u> <u>One of the boys in our club</u> <u>graduated.</u> In how many of the above sentences does the subject have more than one word? ____ 35
orchid 254	S V DO **Dad gave** *Mother* **an orchid.** The noun *Mother* shows *to whom* Dad gave the orchid. We call such a word an **indirect object**. The noun **orchid** is the *direct object,* and the noun *Mother* is the _____ *object.* 255
several 474	**Dick bought several new tires.** The noun **tires** is modified by (*one, two*) adjectives. 475
No 694	**We talked to the jockey and learned a lot about horses.** Should a comma be inserted after **jockey?** (*Yes, No*) 695

a
 	
914
	We can often tighten up a weak **compound sentence** by changing one of the statements to an **adjective clause**.
	    a. **We finally found a restaurant,** *and* **it was still open.**
	    b. **We finally found a restaurant** *which was still open.*
	Which sentence is a complex sentence because it contains a clause? ____
	
	                                                           915

b
 	
1134
	a. **Our tires were old.** *Therefore* **we drove slowly.**
	    b. **Our tires were old,** *therefore* **we drove slowly.**
	Which is correct? ____
	
	                                                           1135

rose 1354	**PRESENT** **SIMPLE PAST** **PAST WITH HELPER** **rise** (go up) **rose** **have risen** **The storm rose soon after dark.** If we added the helper **had** to the verb, we would need to change the word **rose** to _____. 1355
looks 1573	Lesson **51** The *And, Or,* and *Nor* **Problem** [Frames 1575–1596]

would
 	
 1792
	When using the words **hardly** and **scarcely**, do not use a negative word that reverses the meaning.
	
	     a. **Little Sandy could hardly reach the shelf.**
	     b. **Little Sandy couldn't hardly reach the shelf.**
	
	 Which sentence is correct? ____
	
	 1793

us 2011	**We wouldn't let** (*ourselves, ourselfs*) **believe this rumor.** 2012
a 2230	a. **a drifast bathing suit** b. **a Drifast bathing suit** Which item is correctly capitalized? ____ 2231
y 2449	Now suppose that we want to write— **Several boys lockers were left open.** Ask again, "Who owns the lockers?" This time the answer is not **boy,** but _____. 2450

Two 35	John graduated. My best friend graduated. One of the boys in our club graduated. In how many of the above sentences does the predicate have more than one word? _____ 36
indirect 255	S V IO DO **Dad gave Mother an orchid.** The indirect object **Mother** comes (*before, after*) the direct object **orchid.** 256
two 475	**Joe spilled red paint on himself.** The adjective _____ modifies the noun **paint.** 476
No 695	↓ **We talked to the jockey and learned a lot about horses.** Suppose that we added the name **Bob** at the point marked by the arrow. Would it then be correct to insert a comma after **jockey?** (*Yes, No*) 696
b 915	a. **We finally found a restaurant,** *and* **it was still open.** b. **We finally found a restaurant** *which was still open.* The relationship between the two ideas is brought out more clearly by the (*compound, complex*) sentence. 916
a 1135	A pronoun such as *it, she,* or *they* can begin a new sentence even though its meaning depends on a previous sentence. (*True, False*) 1136

risen 1355	Supply the correct form of the verb **rise:** **The price of gasoline has _____ again.** 1356
	"Rudy *and* Vic are coming over tonight." If someone made this remark to you, how many boys would you expect—*one* or *two?* _____ 1575
a 1793	In this and the following frames, underline the word which will not produce a **double negative.** (Some of the sentences require a negative word.) **The price doesn't make (*any, no*) difference to him.** 1794
ourselves 2012	**Why not let the guests serve (*themselves, theirselves*)?** 2013
b 2231	a. **after Memorial day** b. **after Memorial Day** Which item is correctly capitalized? ____ 2232
boys 2450	Since the answer to your question is **boys,** put the apostrophe after the word **boys.** **Several boys' lockers were left open.** Here the apostrophe goes after the letter ____. 2451

None 36	**One of the boys in our club graduated.** In this sentence, the last word of the subject is _____. 37
before 256	Besides showing *to whom* something is done, an **indirect object** can also show *for whom* something is done. **Uncle Frank cooked himself a big breakfast.** The indirect object that shows *for whom* Uncle Frank cooked the breakfast is the pronoun _____. 257
red 476	**Joe spilled _____ red paint on himself.** Underline one of the following adjectives which could tell **how much** paint Joe spilled: **bright some sticky that** 477
Yes 696	**We talked to the jockey, and Bob learned a lot about horses.** Adding the name **Bob** makes this a **compound sentence,** and the comma after **jockey** is therefore (*right, wrong*). 697
complex 916	**Grandfather has as much pep as a boy, and he is 75 years old.** To change the second statement to an adjective clause, drop the conjunction **and,** and put the clause signal **who** in place of the word _____. 917
True 1136	The adverb *then* or *therefore* (*can, cannot*) be the beginning of a new sentence. 1137

risen 1356	**To raise** means "to lift something." **PRESENT** **raise** (lift)　　**SIMPLE PAST** 　　　　　　　**raised**　　　**PAST WITH HELPER** 　　　　　　　　　　　　　　**have raised** The two past forms of **raise** are (*alike, different*). 1357
Two 1575	**Rudy** *and* **Vic** (*is, are*) **coming over tonight.** **Two boys** (*is, are*) **coming over tonight.** The subjects of both these sentences are plural because both mean *two* boys. Therefore, we choose the plural verb _____. 1576
any 1794	**Don't say** (*anything, nothing*) **about the party to Pat.** 1795
themselves 2013	**I blamed** (*my self, myself*) **for this quarrel.** 2014
b 2232	a. **our English test** b. **our Biology test** Which item is correctly capitalized? ____ 2233
s 2451	If the answer to the question "Who is the owner?" is a word *without* an *s*, like **boy, dog,** or **children,** put the apostrophe after this word and before the *s*—**boy's, dog's, children's.** Insert an apostrophe in the following sentence: **Where is your dads office?** *page 74* 2452

club 37	**The back wheels of our car skidded.** The last word of the subject is _____. 38
himself 257	**Uncle Frank cooked himself a big breakfast.** The indirect object _____ comes before the direct object _____. 258
some 477	**<u>Few</u> people enjoyed <u>this</u> movie.** The adjective that tells *which one* is _____. The adjective that tells *how many* is _____. 478
right 697	**Mr. Rice excused himself <u>and</u> he <u>and</u> his wife left the meeting.** This sentence contains two **and**'s. The **and** that connects the two parts of this compound sentence is the (*first, second*) **and**. 698
he 917	*who* **Grandfather has as much pep as a boy,** ~~and he~~ *is 75 years old.* Is the clause *who is 75 years old* where it should be—right after the word it is meant to modify? (*Yes, No*) 918
can 1137	Lesson **37** When Does a Sentence End? [Frames 1139–1159] *page 75*

alike
 	
1357
	The curtain . . . a half hour late.
	
	In this sentence, do we want a verb that means *a* or *b*? _____
	
	    a. **to go up**
	    b. **to lift something**
	
	1358

are 1576	Now suppose that the same person had said— **"Rudy *or* Vic is coming over tonight."** How many boys would you expect—*one* or *two*? _____ 1577
anything 1795	**We fished for several hours, but we caught** (*anything, nothing*). 1796
myself 2014	**Our cat spends most of the day washing** (*its self, itself*). 2015
a 2233	a. **by umpire Todd** b. **by Umpire Todd** Which item is correctly capitalized? _____ 2234
dad's 2452	If the answer to the question "Who is the owner?" is a word *with* an *s*, like **friends, students,** or **neighbors,** put the apostrophe after the entire word, including the *s*—**friends', students', neighbors'.** Insert an apostrophe in this sentence: **Several neighbors trees were uprooted.** 2453

car 38	**The letter from Uncle Bert disappeared.** The last word of the subject is _____. 39
himself (indirect object) breakfast (direct object) 258	PATTERN 3: *Subject—Action Verb→Indirect Object—Direct Object* Always look for an indirect object (*before, after*) the direct object. 259
this (which one) Few (how many) 478	We have seen how **adjectives** give us a clearer picture or idea of **nouns** by telling *what kind, which one*(s), *how many,* or *how much.* **dark** cloud **green** hat **ripe** peach **strong** coffee Do the underlined adjectives answer the question "How many?" or "What kind?" _____ _____ 479
first 698	**Mr. Rice excused himself <u>and</u> he <u>and</u> his wife left the meeting.** A comma should be inserted before the (*first, second*) **and.** 699
No 918	**Grandfather has as much pep as a boy,** *who is 75 years old.* To make this sentence sensible, the clause *who is 75 years old* should be put right after the noun _____, which it modifies. 919
	We have seen that *it* (and other pronouns), *then,* and *therefore* may start a new sentence. However, they may also come in the middle of a sentence. **As I approached the bird,** *it* **flew away.** Can this sentence be divided into two separate and complete sentences? (*Yes, No*) 1139

a 1358	**The speaker raised and lowered his voice.** We use **raised** rather than **rose** because the speaker **lifted** something—his _____. 1359
One 1577	**Rudy _or_ Vic (_is, are_) coming over tonight.** Only _one_ boy is coming. Rudy _is_ coming, or Vic _is_ coming—not both. Since the subject of this sentence is singular, we choose the singular verb _____. 1578
nothing 1796	**I couldn't reach (_either, neither_) of the two doctors.** 1797
itself 2015	Lesson **66** Unit Review [Frames 2017–2050]
b 2234	a. **with my Uncle Harry** b. **with my uncle Harry** Which item is correctly capitalized? ____ 2235
neighbors' 2453	**One students clothes were damaged.** Who is the owner of the clothes? The owner is one (_student, students_). 2454

Bert 39	John graduated. John graduated from our school. John will graduate from our school in June. The parts of these sentences which in some cases have more than one word are the (*subjects, predicates*). 40

before
 	
259
	An indirect object tells *to whom* or *for whom* by its position alone—by coming *before* the direct object. A noun or pronoun used with *to* or *for* is never an indirect object.
	
	  a. **Pam told** *Helen* **a secret.**
	  b. **Pam told a secret** *to Helen.*
	
	In which sentence is *Helen* an indirect object? ____ 260

What kind? 479	a. **clean dish** **sharp pencil** **fresh eggs** **juicy oranges** b. **this dish** **that pencil** **these eggs** **those oranges** Do the adjectives answer the question "Which one?" or "Which ones?" in group *a* or *b*? ____ 480
first 699	**Several boys <u>and</u> girls wrote <u>and</u> produced this program.** This sentence contains two **and**'s. Is either **and** used to connect the two parts of a compound sentence? (*Yes, No*) 700
Grandfather 919	**Grandfather,** *who is 75 years old,* **has as much pep as a boy.** The adjective clause is now correctly placed in this (*complex, compound*) sentence. 920
No 1139	**As I approached the bird,** *it* **flew away.** **As I approached the bird** cannot stand by itself as a separate sentence. Because it tells **when** about the verb **flew**, it is an *adverb* _____. 1140

voice 1359	PRESENT SIMPLE PAST PAST WITH HELPER **raise** (lift) **raised** **have raised** **The roots raised the sidewalk several inches.** If we added the helper **have** to the verb, would we need to change the word **raised**? (*Yes, No*) 1360

is
 	
1578
	Neither means "not the one nor the other."
	
	    Neither **Rudy** *nor* **Vic . . . coming over tonight.**
	
	Rudy *is* not coming—Vic *is* not coming. We are talking about two boys but only *one at a time.*
	With **neither . . . nor,** we use a _____ verb.
	    1579

either 1797	**My dad hasn't** (*never, ever*) **flown in a plane.** 1798
	a. **I** he she we they b. **me** him her us them Which pronouns can be used as the subjects of verbs— those in group *a* or *b*? ____ 2017
a 2235	In this and the following frames, underline only the words that now lack necessary capitals: **The bean crop in Loomis county was seriously damaged by mexican beetles.** 2236
student 2454	**One students clothes were damaged.** Since one **student** is the owner of the clothes, the apostrophe should go after the letter (*t, s*). ____ 2455

predicates	**John** <u>**graduated.**</u>
	John <u>**graduated from our school.**</u>
	John <u>**will graduate from our school.**</u>
	About whom do all the predicates make statements?
	_____
40	41

a	S V IO DO
	Pam told *Helen* **a secret.**
	S V DO
	Pam told a secret *to Helen.*
	When we change *Helen* to a position after the direct object **secret,** we are forced to say _____ *Helen.*
260	261

b	a. <u>**five**</u> **days** <u>**most**</u> **cars** <u>**some**</u> **schools** <u>**no**</u> **trees**
	b. <u>**warm**</u> **days** <u>**fast**</u> **cars** <u>**large**</u> **schools** <u>**tall**</u> **trees**
	Do the adjectives answer the question "How many?" in group *a* or *b*? _____
480	481

No	**Several boys and girls wrote and produced this program.**
	This is not a compound sentence. Therefore a comma (*is, is not*) necessary.
700	701

complex	**I know a child,** *and* **his parents pay him to eat.**
	Underline the pronoun you would use as a clause signal in changing this compound sentence to a complex sentence.
	whose **which** **whom** **that**
920	921

clause	a. **I approached the bird,** *it* **flew away.**
	b. **As I approached the bird,** *it* **flew away.**
	Which sentence is wrong because it is a run-on sentence—*a* or *b*? _____
1140	1141

No 1360	The roots raised the sidewalk several inches. The roots have raised the sidewalk several inches. Both sentences are correct. (*True, False*) 1361
singular 1579	a. **Rudy** *and* **Vic . . . coming over tonight.** b. *Neither* **Rudy** *nor* **Vic . . . coming over tonight.** Which sentence requires the singular verb **is** because the subject is singular? ____ 1580
ever 1798	**I never trust** (*nobody, anybody*) **with secrets.** 1799
a 2017	a. **I** **he** **she** **we** **they** b. **me** **him** **her** **us** **them** Which pronouns can be used as the objects of verbs and prepositions—those in group *a* or *b*? ____ 2018
County, Mexican 2236	Underline the words that require capitals: **In her painting "Christmas at Home," grandma Moses recalls her girlhood memories of a country christmas.** 2237
t 2455	a. **One students' clothes were damaged.** b. **One student's clothes were damaged.** In which sentence is the apostrophe correctly placed—*a* or *b*? ____ 2456

John 41	John **graduated.** John **graduated from our school.** John **will graduate from our school in June.** In how many of the above sentences does the predicate have more than one word? _____ 42
to 261	a. **The trailer saved much money** *for the family.* b. **The trailer saved** *the family* **much money.** In which sentence is *family* an indirect object? ____ 262
a 481	## Lesson 17 More About Adjectives [Frames 483–508]
is not 701	a. **Mr. Potter talks about democracy but he doesn't practice it.** b. **Mr. Potter talks about democracy but doesn't practice it.** Which sentence requires a comma because it is a compound sentence? ____ 702
whose 921	a. **I know a child,** *and* **his parents pay him to eat.** b. **I know a child** *whose parents pay him to eat.* The relationship between the two ideas is brought out more clearly in sentence *b*, which is a (*compound, complex*) sentence. 922
a 1141	a. **Because the price was reasonable,** *he* **bought the car.** b. **The price was reasonable,** *he* **bought the car.** In one of these sentences, the pronoun *he* should start a new sentence. The run-on sentence is ____. 1142

True
 	
 1361
	Be sure not to use **raise** unless the "something" that is lifted up is mentioned.
	
	     We raise the window, but the window rises.
	
	     You raise the price, but the price _____.
	
	 1362

b 1580	Two singular subjects that are connected by **and** are plural since one and one make two. Two singular subjects that are connected by **or** or **nor** are _____ since they mean one or the other— not both. 1581
anybody 1799	**Mr. Armstrong would take** (*no, any*) **money for his help.** 1800
b 2018	Write the object form of each of these subject pronouns: she _____ we _____ they _____ 2019
Grandma, Christmas 2237	Underline the words that require capitals: **The source of the Mississippi river is lake Ataska in minnesota.** 2238
b 2456	**Both students clothes were damaged.** To whom do the clothes belong? They belong to the (*student, students*). 2457

Shirley answered the phone.

Two

The first word of the predicate is _____ .

42

43

---

b

         S   V   IO   DO

The trailer saved *the family* **much money.**

Now we shall put *the family* after the direct object:

         S   V   DO

The trailer saved much money *for the family.*

When *the family* comes after the direct object, we are

262

forced to say _____ *the family.*

263

We generally find adjectives right before the nouns they modify.

    The new <u>owner</u> gave free <u>samples</u> to every <u>customer</u>.

The three underlined words in this sentence are all nouns.

Is each one of these three nouns modified by an adjective? (*Yes, No*)

483

---

a

a. **We can carry our lunch, or eat in the cafeteria.**
b. **The cap must be screwed on tight, or the perfume will evaporate.**

From which sentence should the comma be removed because it is not a compound sentence? ____

702

703

---

complex

Later in this lesson, you will find weak compound sentences in which two ideas are loosely connected by **and.**

You will improve each sentence by changing the italicized part to an adjective clause.

In other words, you are asked to change each weak compound sentence to a stronger _____ sentence.

922

923

---

b

a. **You should try your best,** *then* **no one can blame you.**
b. **If you try your best,** *then* **no one can blame you.**

Which sentence can be divided into two separate and complete sentences? ____

1142

1143

rises 1362	The campers raised their tent, and the tent (*raised, rose*). 1363
singular 1581	a. **Rain** *and* **snow . . . predicted for tonight.** b. **Rain** *or* **snow . . . predicted for tonight.** In which sentence is only one thing expected? ____ 1582
no 1800	**Mother didn't order** (*any, no*) **milk today.** 1801
her, us, them 2019	Write the subject form of each of these object pronouns: **me** _____ **him** _____ **us** _____ 2020
River, Lake, Minnesota 2238	**The Hudson river runs along the Catskill mountains for many miles.** 2239
students 2457	**Both students clothes were damaged.** Since the answer to our question is **students,** the apostrophe should go after the letter (*t, s*). ____ 2458

answered 43	**Firemen discovered the cause of the fire.** The first word of the predicate is _____. 44
for 263	To be an indirect object, a noun or pronoun must stand between the verb and its direct object. This is the position that means *to* or *for* without our using these words. DO DO a. **I wrote** *Dave* **a letter.** b. **I wrote a letter** *to Dave.* In which sentence is the noun *Dave* an indirect object? ____ 264
Yes 483	The normal position of an adjective is just before the noun it modifies. The main exception is adjectives that are used as subject complements. **The sky looks cloudy.** The adjective **cloudy** modifies the subject _____. 484
a 703	**The crowded bus stopped and took on still more people.** Should a comma be inserted before the conjunction **and?** (*Yes, No*) 704
complex 923	In changing a compound sentence to a complex sentence, you first need to (*drop, add*) the conjunction **and.** 924
a 1143	**You should try your best.** *Then* **no one can blame you.** These are two separate and complete sentences, each with a subject and predicate. We must either keep them apart or connect them with the _____ **and.** 1144

rose 1363	The men have raised an argument, and an argument has (*rose, risen*). 1364
b 1582	a. **Rain** *and* **snow . . . predicted for tonight.** b. **Rain** *or* **snow . . . predicted for tonight.** In which sentence would the singular verb **is** be correct because the subject is singular? ____ 1583
any 1801	**We had plenty of sandwiches, but Ray didn't want** (*none, any*). 1802
I, he, we 2020	Pronoun errors occur mainly when pronouns are used in pairs or when a pronoun is paired with a noun. A good way to avoid such errors is to try each pronoun by itself. Then use the same pronouns when they are combined. *He* **was waiting for a bus.** *I* **was waiting for a bus.** Therefore: (*He, Him*) **and** (*I, me*) **were waiting for a bus.** 2021
River, Mountains 2239	**Dr. Meyers shares an office with another doctor over the Pickwick restaurant on Main street.** 2240
s 2458	a. **Both students' clothes were damaged.** b. **Both student's clothes were damaged.** In which sentence is the apostrophe correctly placed? ____ 2459

discovered 44	In many sentences, both the subject and the predicate consist of more than one word. **My best friend graduated from our school.** The subject of the above sentence consists of _____ words, and the predicate consists of _____ words. 45
a 264	To make sure that a word is an indirect object, see if the word *to* or *for* would make sense before it. **Mark sold ( )** *me* **his stamps.** Which word would make sense in the parentheses—*to* or *for*? _____ 265
sky 484	**The sky looks cloudy.** The adjective **cloudy** is used as a _____ *complement.* 485
No 704	**The train whistle woke me up and I couldn't fall asleep again.** Should a comma be inserted before the conjunction **and?** (*Yes, No*) 705

drop
 	
924
	After you drop the conjunction **and,** you will add an adjective clause signal to start your clause.
	
	      a. **who (whom, whose), which, that**
	      b. **if, as, when, because, after, although**
	
	The words that can be used as adjective clause signals are those in group (*a, b*). _____
	
	925

conjunction 1144	a. **You should try your best,** *then* **no one can blame you.** b. **You should try your best, and** *then* **no one can blame you.** Which is the run-on sentence? _____ 1145

risen 1364	Let's compare the two verbs: PRESENT SIMPLE PAST PAST WITH HELPER **rise** (go up) **rose** **have risen** **raise** (lift up) **raised** **have raised** Which verb has two different past forms—**rise** or **raise**? _____ 1365
b 1583	**The teacher** *and* **a student take the attendance.** Since the job is done by *two* persons, we choose the plural verb _____. 1584
any 1802	**The air was so stuffy that we** (*couldn't, could*) **hardly breathe.** 1803
He, I 2021	**Sandra can ride with the** *Hills.* **Sandra can ride with** *us.* Therefore: **Sandra can ride with the** *Hills* **and** (*we, us*). 2022
Restaurant, Street 2240	**George Gershwin's composition "an american in Paris" includes a realistic imitation of french taxicab horns.** 2241

a
 	
2459
	The word that comes before the apostrophe should indicate who the owner is.
	
	    a. **the boy's father**
	    b. **the boys' father**
	
	Which means the father of *one* boy? ____
	
	2460

three four 45	**The early bird catches the first worm.** The subject ends with the word _____, and the predicate begins with the word _____. 46
to 265	**Mark sold** (*to*) *me* **his stamps.** Because the pronoun *me,* in this position, means *to me,* it is an _____ _____. 266
subject 485	a. **Mother makes delicious custard.** b. **Mother's custard is delicious.** Does the adjective **delicious** come after the noun it modifies in sentence *a* or *b?* ____ 486
Yes 705	a. **We started on time but were delayed by a train.** b. **We started on time but a train delayed us.** Only one of these sentences could be split into two separate sentences. Which sentence requires a comma because it is compound? ____ 706
a 925	In making your adjective clause, never use the pronoun **which** as a clause signal to refer to persons. Underline the correct adjective clause signal: **The driver** (*which, who*) *rammed Dad's car* **was not insured.** 926
a 1145	a. **The meeting was very important,** *therefore* **most of the parents attended.** b. **Most of the parents,** *therefore,* **attended this important meeting.** Which can be divided into two separate and complete sentences? ____ 1146

rise 1365	In this and the following frames, underline the correct verb in each pair. Remember to choose **raise** only when the sentence mentions the "something" that is lifted. **Holidays always** (*rise, raise*) **the accident rate.** 1366
take 1584	**The teacher** *and* **a student** (*takes, take*) **the attendance.** If we changed the conjunction *and* to *or*, would we need to change the verb? (*Yes, No*) 1585
could 1803	**There** (*were, weren't*) **scarcely any people at the meeting.** 1804
us 2022	In this and the following frames, underline the correct pronouns. Always choose the same pronoun that you would choose if the pronoun were used alone. **Virginia and** (*she, her*) **prepared the entire dinner.** 2023
An, American, French 2241	**We don't study the French revolution until history (2).** 2242
a 2460	**the boy's father** This means the father of *one* boy because the apostrophe does not come after the plural noun **boys,** but after the singular noun _____. 2461

bird, catches 46	**The fragrant pink blossoms attract the bees.** The subject ends with the word _____, and the predicate begins with the word _____. 47
indirect object 266	**Karen made ( )** _the boys_ **some fudge.** Which word would make sense in the parentheses—_to_ or _for?_ _____ 267
b 486	**Mother's custard is delicious.** The adjective **delicious** is used as a _subject complement_ and modifies the noun _____. 487
b 706	A sentence that can be divided into two separate sentences, each having its own subject and predicate, is a (_simple, compound_) sentence. 707
who 926	In this and the following frames, change the italicized part of each sentence to an adjective clause. Write the full sentence in the blank space. **Fred dreams up stories,** _and they make him feel important._ _____ _____ 927
a 1146	**The meeting was very important.** _Therefore_ **most of the parents attended.** These are two separate and complete sentences. Can we connect them just with a comma without using the conjunction **and?** (_Yes, No_) 1147

raise 1366	On holidays, the accident rate always (*rises, raises*). 1367
Yes 1585	The teacher *or* a student (*takes, take*) the attendance. Since only *one* person does the job, we use the singular verb _____. 1586
were 1804	The water was so shallow that we (*couldn't, could*) hardly swim. 1805
she 2023	The Owens and (*we, us*) share the same telephone line. 2024
Revolution, History 2242	My aunt Jane just won a new ford by writing a jingle telling why she likes krispie cornflakes. 2243
boy 2461	a. the boy's father b. the boys' father Which means the father of *more than one* boy? ____ 2462

blossoms, attract 47	a. **the early train** b. **left his books on the bus** Which group of words could be the *subject* of a sentence— *a* or *b*? ____ 48
for 267	**Karen made** (*for*) *the boys* **some fudge.** Because *the boys*, in this position, means *for the boys*, it is an _____ _____. 268
custard 487	**The soup was too salty for me.** The adjective **salty** comes (*before, after*) the noun it modifies. 488
compound 707	Lesson **24** **Building Good Compound Sentences** [Frames 709–743]
Fred dreams up stories that (which) make him feel important. 927	**We passed a car,** *and its door was partly open.* (Try *whose.*) _____ _____ 928
No 1147	a. **The meeting was very important, and** *therefore* **most of the parents attended.** b. **The meeting was very important,** *therefore* **most of the parents attended.** Which sentence is wrong because it is a run-on sentence? ____ 1148

rises 1367	The passing cars (*rise, raise*) a lot of dust. 1368
takes 1586	As you complete this lesson, don't trust your ear. What sounds right to you may be wrong. Reason out each problem, applying these rules: Two singular subjects that are connected by **and** are plural. Two singular subjects that are connected by **or** or **nor** are _____. 1587
could 1805	There (*wasn't, was*) scarcely any chicken in my salad. 1806
we 2024	What seems to be the trouble between Beverly and (*she, her*)? 2025
Aunt, Ford, Krispie 2243	I don't think that referee Grimes was fair to our pitcher in the game with Westover high. 2244
b 2462	**the boys' father** This means the father of *more than one* boy because the apostrophe comes after the plural noun _____. 2463

a 48	a. **looked at his watch** b. **the driver of the truck** Which group of words could be the *predicate* of a sentence —*a* or *b*? _____ 49
indirect object 268	If a noun or pronoun is an indirect object, we can insert the word _____ or _____ before it. 269
after 488	**The soup was too salty for me.** The adjective **salty** is used as a *subject* _____. 489
	A compound sentence can be made by joining two simple sentences with the conjunction **and, but,** or **or.** In a compound sentence, are there a subject and a predi- cate both before and after the conjunction? (*Yes, No*) 709
We passed a car whose door was partly open. 928	**A stranger helped me,** *and he happened to be a mechanic.* _____ _____ (Be sure to put the clause next to the noun it modifies.) 929
b 1148	In doing the remaining frames, remember that two separate sentences cannot be connected by a comma alone—with- out a conjunction to hold them together. a. **I checked all the tubes, then I put them back in the set.** b. **I checked all the tubes. Then I put them back in the set.** Which sentence is correct? _____ 1149

raise 1368	Used car prices generally (*rise, raise*) in the spring. 1369
singular 1587	In this and the following frames, underline the verb that agrees with its subject. Remember that if a verb showing present time ends in *s*, it is singular, not plural. The doctor or his assistant (*plan, plans*) to see you tonight. 1588
was 1806	Lesson **59** An *A–An* Checkup [Frames 1808–1829]
her 2025	You can leave the key with the Wesbrooks or (*they, them*). 2026
Referee, High 2244	In his poem "to a Waterfowl," Bryant had the feeling that god was guiding his footsteps. 2245
boys 2463	woman women Which one of the above nouns is plural? _____ 2464

a 49	a. **voted for Frank** b. **bought a small farm** c. **a piece of broken glass** Which group of words could be the *subject* of a sentence? _____ 50
to, for 269	S V DO **Mr. Hill offered a ride** *to us.* As this sentence is printed, it contains no indirect object. Rewrite this sentence, changing the italicized words to an indirect object. _____ 270
complement 489	**The small and crowded room became very stuffy.** The adjective **stuffy** is used as a subject complement and modifies the subject _____. 490
Yes 709	**He went his way, and I went mine.** In a compound sentence, the comma should be placed (*before, after*) the conjunction **and, but,** or **or**. 710
A stranger who (that) happened to be a mechanic helped me. 929	**His room was full of books,** *and they showed his interest in science.* _____ _____ 930
b 1149	a. **Explorers do not look for danger. They try their best to avoid it.** b. **Explorers do not look for danger, they try their best to avoid it.** Which sentence is correct? ____ 1150

rise 1369	a. **rose** b. **raised** One of these past forms means "went up" or "got up." The other means "lifted up something." Which word means "went up" or "got up"? ____ 1370
plans 1588	**The doctor and his assistant** (*plan, plans*) **to see you to-night.** 1589
	Whether we use **a** or **an** before a word depends on whether the word begins with a vowel or consonant *sound.* The vowels are **a, e, i, o, u.** **apple brick egg joke infant oven tree uncle** How many of the above words begin with vowels? _____ 1808
them 2026	**Either Dennis or** (*he, him*) **will play first base.** 2027
To, God 2245	Cross out each capital letter that is not correct: **My Dad brought my little Sister several guest-sized bars of Ivory Soap from the Madison Hotel.** 2246
women 2464	a. **the woman's advice** b. **the women's advice** Which means the advice of *more than one* woman? ____ 2465

c 50	a. **three airplanes** b. **improved the flavor of the cake** c. **the price of admission** Which group of words could be the *predicate* of a sentence? ____ 51
Mr. Hill offered us a ride. 270	S V DO **Vic found a good job** *for himself.* Rewrite this sentence, changing the italicized words to an indirect object. _____ 271
room 490	**The new model looks quite different from the old one.** The adjective _____ is a subject complement and modifies the subject _____. 491

before
 	
 710
	Only *similar* ideas of *equal importance* should be combined into a compound sentence.
	
	   a. **The lightning flashed, and the thunder rumbled.**
	   b. **The lightning flashed, and I was walking with Carl.**
	
	 In which sentence do the ideas fit together better? ____
	
	 711

His room was full of books that (which) showed his interest in science. 930	**My uncle plays a violin,** *and he made it himself.* _____ _____ 931
a 1150	a. **Sunburn feels warm at first, then it begins to burn.** b. **Sunburn feels warm at first, and then it begins to burn.** Which sentence is correct? ____ 1151

a	**Our canoe drifted away when the tide** (*rose, raised*).
1370	1371

plan	(Are you checking each sentence for **and, or,** and **nor** before choosing the verb?) **Neither the name nor the address** (*was, were*) **legible.**
1589	1590

five	The vowels are **a, e, i, o, u.**
	All the other letters of the alphabet are consonants.
	
	  a. **dollar pencil ball flower stamp**
	  b. **article effect inch omelet uncle**
	
	In which group do the words begin with consonants? ____

1808	1809

he	**The Fishers invited Verna and** (*I, me*) **to visit them.**
2027	2028

Ⴕad, Ⴕister, Ⴕoap	Cross out each capital letter that is not correct: **The Keynote Glee Club will sing some Spanish Songs at our September meeting in the Church.**
2246	2247

b	When writing a possessive noun, don't forget to ask yourself, "Who is the owner?" Then put the apostrophe right after your answer. In the following sentence, place the apostrophe to show that *one girl* is the owner of the room: **Dad painted the girls room.**
2465	2466

a. **we won**
b. **won the opening game of the season**

Which group of words is a complete sentence? _____

(The capital letter and the period are omitted to avoid revealing the answer.)

b

51

52

Vic found himself
a good job.

271

An indirect object is a noun or pronoun placed (*after, before*) the direct object to show *to whom* or *for whom*, or *to what* or *for what* something is done.

272

---

different,
model

491

The words **a, an,** and **the** are special adjectives. They are usually called **articles.** We generally omit **articles** when identifying modifiers in sentences.

The special adjectives known as **articles** are **a, an,** and

_____.

492

---

a

711

The lightning flashed, and the thunder rumbled.

Because both parts of this sentence are about weather conditions, this compound sentence is (*good, poor*).

712

My uncle plays a
violin that (which)
he made himself.

931

These shirts are a good buy, *and they are on sale today.*

_____

_____

932

---

b

1151

a. **While the young people danced, the older people visited.**
b. **The young people danced, the older people visited.**

Which sentence is correct? _____

1152

rose 1371	At last our guests (*rose, raised*) to go home. 1372
was 1590	Mother or Dad (*do, does*) the shopping. 1591
a 1809	Use the word **a** before any word that begins with a consonant sound. a. **dollar** **pencil** **ball** **flower** **stamp** b. **article** **effect** **inch** **omelet** **uncle** Would you use the word **a** before the words in group *a* or *b*? ____ 1810
me 2028	Neither (*he, him*) nor (*I, me*) could start the car. 2029
₴ongs, ₵hurch 2247	Who took the part of Captain Bligh in *Mutiny On The Bounty?* 2248
girl's 2466	Now place the apostrophe to show that the room belongs to *two or more* girls. **Dad painted the girls room.** 2467

a 52	a. **a heavy rain** b. **a heavy rain spoiled our plans** Which group of words is a complete sentence? ____ 53
before 272	In this and the following frames, write in the missing words of the sentence framework. (S = Subject, V = Verb, IO = Indirect Object, DO = Direct Object) **The accident gave everyone a good scare.** S V IO DO _____ gave _____ scare 273
the 492	**A customer had dropped an egg on the floor.** The *articles* in this sentence are ____, _____, and _____. 493
good 712	**I got an A in Spanish, and Steve is in my English class.** This is a poor compound sentence because the ideas are too (*alike, unlike*) to be combined. 713
These shirts that (which) are on sale today are a good buy. 932	**The witness made statements,** *and he couldn't prove them* _____ _____ 933
a 1152	a. **There was a convention in the city. Therefore all the hotels were full.** b. **There was a convention in the city, therefore all the hotels were full.** Which is correct—*a* or *b*? ____ 1153

rose 1372	**The new manager** (*rose, raised*) **everyone's salary.** 1373
does 1591	**Neither mud nor snow** (*stop, stops*) **a tractor.** 1592
a 1810	Use **a** before every word that begins with a consonant *sound*, not necessarily with a consonant. Some words that begin with the vowel **u** sound as though they begin with the consonant **y**—like the word **unit** (pronounced *you-nit*). Does the word **uniform** begin with a **y** sound? (*Yes, No*) 1811
he, I 2029	**Miss Turner was sitting behind** (*she, her*) **and** (*me, I*). 2030
∅n, ⧸he 2248	**Every pupil who enters High School must take an Arithmetic test before he may enroll in Algebra (1).** 2249

girls'
 	
2467
	lady ladies
	When you write a possessive noun, be sure to have the correct spelling of the owner before the apostrophe.
	    a. **a ladie's husband**
	    b. **a lady's husband**
	Does the husband belong to a **ladie** or a **lady?** _____
	
	2468

b 53	a. **the bottle of red ink** b. **squirrels bury nuts** Which group of words is a complete sentence? ____ 54
S accident IO everyone 273	**My brother made himself a good workbench.** S V IO DO brother _____ _____ _____ 274
a, an, the 493	**Young corn is tender.** The two adjectives in this sentence are _____ and _____. 494
unlike 713	a. **My mother was born in Ohio. She likes music.** b. **My mother was born in Ohio. She grew up in Kentucky.** Which sentences would make a better compound sentence —those labeled *a* or *b*? ____ 714
The witness made statements that (which) he couldn't prove. 933	**I have a friend,** *and he helped me fix the motor.* _____ _____ 934
a 1153	a. **I searched through every pocket, my ticket was gone.** b. **I searched through every pocket, but my ticket was gone.** Which sentence is correct? ____ 1154

raised 1373	The temperature usually (*rose, raised*) in the afternoon. 1374
stops 1592	A sandwich and a glass of milk (*is, are*) all I want. 1593
Yes 1811	Although the word **uniform** begins with the vowel **u**, it is pronounced as though it begins with the consonant **y** (*you-ni-form*). We therefore use the word (*a, an*) before **uniform**. 1812
her, me 2030	In making comparisons, you may be puzzled as to which pronoun to use after **than** or **as.** By supplying the omitted words, you will see which pronoun is needed. **I didn't walk as far as . . . (walked).** Underline two pronouns that would fit in the above sentence. **him he she her** 2031
High School, Arithmetic 2249	UNIT 11: **LEARNING TO USE COMMAS** Lesson **73** Commas in Series [Frames 2251–2285]
lady 2468	a. **a ladie's husband** b. **a lady's husband** Which is correct—*a* or *b*? ____ 2469

b 54	a. **added a room to their house** b. **the owner of the gas station** Which group of words would be a sentence if a *subject* were added? ____ 55
V IO made himself DO workbench 274	**Sandy drew me a map of the camp.** S V IO DO Sandy _____ _____ map 275
Young, tender 494	Do both adjectives—**Young** and **tender**—modify the same noun? (*Yes, No*) 495
b 714	**The food in our cafeteria is good. The prices are very reasonable.** Although each sentence has a different subject, both sentences are about the cafeteria's food—the first about its quality and the second about its _____. 715
I have a friend who (that) helped me fix the motor. 934	**who (whom, whose) which that** These words that are used as adjective clause signals are (*pronouns, adjectives*). 935
b 1154	a. **Gasoline is dangerous, it should never be used indoors.** b. **Because gasoline is dangerous, it should never be used indoors.** Which sentence is correct? ____ 1155

rose 1374	a. **have risen** b. **have raised** Which of these helper forms means "have gone up" or "have got up"? _____ 1375
are 1593	**Oil or wax** (*protect, protects*) **the surface from rust.** 1594
a 1812	**umpire** **union** Both the above words begin with the vowel **u.** Before which of these words do we use **a** because the word sounds as though it begins with the consonant **y?** _____ 1813
he, she 2031	**The coach used Dave more often than (he used) . . . .** Underline two pronouns that would fit in the above sentence. **me I him he** 2032
	A **series** is a number of similar things in a row, like a series of games, a series of treatments, a series of explosions—one coming after another. *Men, women,* **and** *children* **will enjoy this film.** How many kinds of people does this sentence list? _____ 2251
b 2469	Now suppose you want to write about the husbands of *several* ladies. a. **several ladies' husbands** b. **several ladys' husbands** Which is correct—*a* or *b?* _____ 2470

a 55	a. **the heaviest boy on the team** b. **needs a good pitcher** Which group of words would be a sentence if a *predicate* were added? ____ 56
V IO drew me 275	**The new lamp gives the room a cheerful look.** S V IO DO lamp gives _____ _____ 276
Yes 495	**Young corn is tender.** Because the adjective **tender** comes after the noun it modifies, it is a _____ _____. 496
prices 715	**The food in our cafeteria is good. The prices are very reasonable.** Both these sentences are about food, and the ideas are of (*equal, unequal*) importance. 716
pronouns 935	Ordinarily, an adjective clause should be placed right (*after, before*) the noun or pronoun it modifies. 936
b 1155	a. **When the football season ended, the students turned to basketball.** b. **The football season ended, the students turned to basketball.** Which sentence is correct? ____ 1156

a 1375	Underline the correct verb: Taxes have (*rose, risen*) again. 1376
protects 1594	**Neither Stratton nor Central High** (*has, have*) **a pool.** 1595
union 1813	<p align="center">**empty useless awful**</p>All the above words begin with vowels. Before which word would we use **a** because it begins with a consonant *sound?* _____ 1814
me, him 2032	**I can't remember names as well as** (*him, he*). 2033
Three 2251	In grammar, a series is a succession of three or more words, phrases, or clauses in a sentence—all used in the same way. To form a series, there must be _____ or more similar items in a row. (How many?) 2252
a 2470	<p align="center">a. **several ladies' husbands** b. **several ladys' husbands**</p>The correct answer is *a* because the husbands belong not to **ladys** but to _____. 2471

Lois sings.

a

If you added the word **beautifully** to this sentence, it would be a part of the (*subject, predicate*).

56 · 57

IO   DO
room look

The graduates bought their school some new equipment.

S	V	IO	DO
graduates	_____	_____	_____

276 · 277

---

subject complement

Adjectives modify nouns and pronouns. However, we seldom use adjectives before pronouns, as we do before nouns. We are not likely to say *pretty she* or *delicious them*.

a. _____ **cities have** _____ **problems.** (nouns)

b. _____ **she bought** _____ **them.** (pronouns)

It would be difficult to insert adjectives in sentence _____.

496 · 497

---

equal

The food in our cafeteria is good, and the prices are very reasonable.

This is a (*good, poor*) compound sentence.

716 · 717

---

after

A sentence that consists of a main statement and an adjective clause is a (*compound, complex*) sentence.

936 · 937

---

a

a. **Highways will be jammed, resorts will be overflowing.**

b. **Highways will be jammed, and resorts will be overflowing.**

Which sentence is correct? _____

1156 · 1157

risen 1376	The accident rate has (*risen, rose, raised*) **nearly every year.** 1377
has 1595	The heat, the noise, and the crowd (*was, were*) **too much for Mother's nerves.** 1596
useless 1814	It is difficult to pronounce two vowels in a row. Notice how difficult it is to say **a apple, a egg, a Indian, a omelet, a uncle.** To make pronunciation easier, we use **an** before a word beginning with a vowel sound—**an egg, an Indian,** etc. We must use **an** before (*apple, banana*). 1815
he 2033	**Myra's report card upset her mother more than** (*her, she*). 2034
three 2252	*Men, women,* **and** *children* **will enjoy this film.** All three italicized nouns in this sentence are used as subjects of the verb **will enjoy.** These three nouns, taken together, are called a _____. 2253
ladies 2471	**baby babies** The plural of **baby** is **babies.** How would you write that the doctor kept a record of the birthdays of *all* the babies under his care? **The doctor kept a record of all the _____ birthdays.** 2472

predicate 57	The box disappeared. If you added the words **of candy,** they would be part of the (*subject, predicate*). 58
V IO bought school DO equipment 277	**Mrs. Ray showed the ladies her beautiful garden.** S V IO DO _____ _____ _____ _____ 278
b 497	To modify a pronoun, an adjective must generally be in the subject complement position. **It was <u>beautiful</u>.** **He is very <u>tall</u>.** **They look <u>expensive</u>.** **Some were <u>green</u>.** In all these sentences, the adjectives come (*before, after*) the pronouns they modify. 498
good 717	**Lois has beautiful eyes, and she works for a bank.** Although both statements are about **Lois,** the two ideas have little to do with each other. Therefore, this is a (*good, poor*) compound sentence. 718
complex 937	Lesson **31** Using *–ing* Word Groups to Combine Ideas [Frames 939–978]
b 1157	a. **The next issue of our paper, therefore, will cost five cents more.** b. **The two essays were judged to be equally good, therefore the prize was divided equally between us.** Which sentence is correct? _____ 1158

risen 1377	The mayor's resignation has (*risen, raised*) much discussion. 1378
were 1596	Lesson **52** **Sentences Beginning with** *Here, There,* and *Where* [Frames 1598–1617]
apple 1815	a. **athlete** **employer** **instant** **olive** **untruth** b. **village** **shoulder** **family** **grape** **minute** Would you use the word **an** before the words in group *a* or *b*? ____ 1816
her 2034	**My young brother knows as much about cars as** (*I, me*). 2035
series 2253	We can also have a series of three or more verbs. **This dealer** *buys, sells,* **and** *trades* **used cars.** The third verb in this series of verbs is _____. 2254
babies' 2472	**baby** **babies** How would you write that the doctor kept a record of the birthday of only *one* baby? **The doctor kept a record of this _____ birthday.** 2473

subject 58	**The ball rolled.** If you added the words **into the street,** they would be a part of the (*subject, predicate*). 59
S V Mrs. Ray showed IO DO ladies garden 278	**The store gave each customer a souvenir.** S V IO DO _____ _____ _____ _____ 279
after 498	Some words can be used as either **adjectives** or **nouns.** If the word modifies a noun or pronoun, it is an **adjective.** If the word is the name of a person, place, thing, or an idea, it is a _____. 499
poor 718	**Lois has beautiful eyes, and her hair is most attractive.** Both statements in this compound sentence are about Lois's (*job, appearance*). 719
	green **leaves** *falling* **leaves** Both *green* and *falling* describe the noun _____. 939
a 1158	a. **Leslie arrived with his accordion, and then the fun began.** b. **Leslie arrived with his accordion, then the fun began.** Which sentence is correct? ____ 1159

raised 1378	**I have** (*risen, rose*) **early every day this week.** 1379
	We start many sentences with the words **There is** and **There are.** <div align="center">**There is no butter in this cake.**</div> <div align="center">(= **No butter is in this cake.**)</div> What noun is the subject of the verb **is?** _____ <div align="right">1598</div>
a 1816	a. **dollar** **theater** **raisin** **store** **minute** b. **action** **example** **Indian** **onion** **umpire** Would you use the word **an** before the words in group *a* or *b*? ____ <div align="right">1817</div>
I 2035	**Dad always feeds the dog, so it obeys him better than** (*she, her*). 2036
trades 2254	**Glen works** *after school, on Saturdays,* **and** *during the summer.* This series consists of three (*verbs, prepositional phrases*). <div align="right">2255</div>
baby's 2473	Copy the phrase in each frame. Then ask, "Who is the owner?" Underline the word that answers this question, and put an apostrophe after it; for example, **a dog's life—the girls' voices.** <div align="center">**my uncles coat**</div> <div align="center">*page 118*</div><div align="right">2474</div>

predicate	**A man came to the door.** If you added the words **tall and friendly,** they would be part of the (*subject, predicate*).
59	60

S V store gave IO customer DO souvenir	Lesson **10** Completing the Linking Verb [Frames 281–307]
279	

noun	a. **Our paper came late.** b. **We used paper spoons.** Is **paper** used as an adjective in sentence *a* or *b*? _____
499	500

appearance	a. **Lois has beautiful eyes, and she works for a bank.** b. **Lois has beautiful eyes, and her hair is most attractive.** Which compound sentence is better? _____
719	720

leaves	*green* **leaves** *falling* **leaves** Because both *green* and *falling* modify the noun **leaves,** both words are used as (*adjectives, adverbs*).
939	940

a	Lesson **38** Unit Review [Frames 1161–1193]
1159	

risen 1379	We went fishing before the sun had (*risen, rose, raised*). 1380
butter 1598	There <u>are</u> no <u>eggs</u> in this cake. (= No <u>eggs</u> <u>are</u> in this cake.) What noun is the subject of the verb **are?** _____ 1599
b 1817	**hour** **house** Both the above words begin with the consonant **h**. However, in one of these words the **h** is not sounded. The word that begins with a silent **h** is _____. 1818
her 2036	The Tigers made two more hits than (*them, they*). 2037
prepositional phrases 2255	a. **There are no telephones or electric lights on the island.** b. **There are no telephones, electric lights, or automobiles on the island.** Which sentence contains a series of nouns? ____ 2256
my <u>uncle's</u> coat 2474	Copy the phrase, underline the word that answers the question "Who is the owner?" and put an apostrophe after it. **several doctors opinions** 2475

subject 60	Most sentences have two parts. The naming part is called the _____, and the telling part is called the _____. 61

	Up to now, we have been working only with *action* verbs. There is another type of verb that shows *no action* at all.
	
	    a. **My mother** *hired* **a nurse.**
	    b. **My mother** *is* **a nurse.**
	
	In which sentence does the verb show *no action* of any kind? ____
	
	281

b 500	**We used paper spoons.** In this sentence, **paper** is an *adjective* because it modifies the noun _____. 501
b 720	a. **Dad rented the house on Monday, and we moved in on Wednesday.** b. **Dad rented the house on Monday, and it has three bedrooms.** Are the ideas more *similar* and more *equal in importance* in sentence *a* or *b*? ____ 721
adjectives 940	**Leaves fall.** This is a complete sentence. **Leaves** is the subject and _____ is the verb. 941
	While I was feeding the dog. Although this word group has a subject and a verb, it is not a (*sentence, clause*). 1161

risen 1380	Lesson **44** *Leave* **and** *Let* [Frames 1382–1406]
eggs 1599	**There is no butter in this cake.** **There are no eggs in this cake.** In sentences that begin with **There is** and **There are,** the subjects come (*before, after*) the verbs. 1600
hour 1818	**hour** The consonant **h** that starts this word is silent. The word **hour** is pronounced just like **our.** Since **hour** sounds as though it begins with the vowel **o,** we say (*a, an*) *hour.* 1819
they 2037	Possessive pronouns show ownership without the use of apostrophes. Underline the correct pronoun in each pair: **Does** (*your's, yours*) **work the same as** (*our's, ours*)? 2038
b 2256	a. **I'll have to beg or borrow a formal for Saturday's party.** b. **I'll have to beg, borrow, or steal a formal for Saturday's party.** Which sentence contains a series of verbs? ____ 2257
several <u>doctors'</u> opinions 2475	Copy the phrase, underline the word that answers the question "Who is the owner?" and put an apostrophe after it. **a childrens magazine** 2476

(naming part)
subject

(telling part)
predicate

The predicate makes a statement about the _____.

62

---

b

My mother *is* **a nurse.**

The verb *is* shows no action. Instead, it is used to tie up or *link* the word **nurse** with the subject _____.

281

282

---

spoons

a. **Tommy has a tin airplane.**
b. **Tin is a useful metal.**

Is **tin** used as an adjective in sentence *a* or *b*? _____

501

502

---

a

a. **Dad rented the house on Monday, and we moved in on Wednesday.**
b. **Dad rented the house on Monday, and it has three bedrooms.**

Which compound sentence is better? _____

721

722

---

fall

a. **Leaves fall.**
b. *falling* **leaves**

In *a*, **fall** is a verb because it makes a statement about its subject, **Leaves.**

In *b*, *falling* is an _____ because it describes the noun **leaves.**

941

942

---

sentence

While I was feeding the dog . . .

This word group is not a sentence because it leaves us wondering *"What happened?"*

A word group that has a subject and verb but does not make sense by itself is a _____.

1161

page 123

1162

To leave means (a) to go away from, (b) to place something and go away from it, (c) not to change or disturb something.

Which of the above meanings does the word **leave** have in the following sentence—*a*, *b*, or *c*? ____

Please take this note and leave it on Mr. Brown's desk.

1382

---

after

1600

a. **There is no butter in this cake.**
b. **There are no eggs in this cake.**

In sentence *a*, the singular verb **is** agrees with the singular subject **butter.**

In sentence *b*, the plural verb **are** agrees with the plural subject _____.

1601

---

an

1819

Before a word that begins with a vowel sound, use (*a*, *an*).

1820

---

yours, ours

2038

(*Its*, *It's*) **owner knows that** (*its*, *it's*) **vicious.**

2039

---

b

2257

Place commas *between* the items in a series—not before or after the series (unless they are needed for other reasons).

Punctuate this sentence:

His kindness patience and courtesy won him many friends.

2258

---

a children's magazine

2476

Copy the phrase, underline the word that answers the question "Who is the owner?" and put an apostrophe after it.

both neighbors lawns

2477

subject 62	The subject of a sentence usually comes (*before, after*) the predicate. 63
mother 282	**The weather** *was* **cold.** The verb *was* shows no action. It is used to tie up or *link* the word **cold** with the subject _____. 283
a 502	a. **The candy spoiled my appetite.** b. **The tree was decorated with candy canes.** Is **candy** used as an *adjective* in sentence *a* or *b*? ____ 503
a 722	a. **The car had no lights, and the accident occurred on our corner.** b. **The car had no lights, and its brakes were bad.** Are the ideas more *similar* and more *equal in importance* in sentence *a* or *b*? ____ 723
adjective 942	a. **Leaves fall.** b. *falling* **leaves** To make an adjective of the verb **fall**, we add the letters _____ to the verb. 943
clause 1162	**While I was feeding the dog . . .** Which word group could we add to make a complete sentence of this fragment? ____ a. **its evening meal** b. **on the back porch** c. **the telephone rang** *page 125* 1163

b 1382	**To leave** means (a) to go away from, (b) to place something and go away from it, (c) not to change or disturb something. Which of the above meanings does the word **leave** have in the following sentence—*a*, *b*, or *c*? _____ **I leave school at three o'clock.** 1383
eggs 1601	**There was a dent in the fender.** The singular verb **was** agrees with the singular subject _____. 1602
an 1820	In this and the following frames, copy the word before which the word **an** is required, and write **an** before it: **picture request audience** _____ _____ 1821
Its, it's 2039	(*Its, It's*) **collecting material for** (*it's, its*) **nest.** 2040
kindness, patience, 2258	Make a count to see how, in a series, the number of commas compares with the number of items: _____, _____, and _____ _____, _____, _____, and _____ The number of commas is always one (*more, less*) than the number of items in a series. 2259
both <u>neighbors'</u> lawns 2477	**a mans appearance** _____ 2478

before 63	Every word in a sentence generally belongs to either the subject or the predicate. (*True, False*) 64
weather 283	Verbs like **is** and **was** are called **linking verbs** because they connect or *link* a word that follows them with the subject. **The tire *was* flat.** The linking verb *was* links the word **flat** with the subject _____, which it describes. 284
b 503	a. **Amy wore a pretty cotton dress.** b. **Cotton grows in the South.** Is **cotton** used as a *noun* in sentence *a* or *b*? _____ 504
b 723	a. **The car had no lights, and the accident occurred on our corner.** b. **The car had no lights, and its brakes were bad.** Which compound sentence is better? _____ 724
–ing 943	a. **Faucets leak.** b. *leaking* **faucets** In *a*, **leak** is a verb because it makes a statement about its subject, **Faucets.** In *b*, *leaking* is an adjective because it describes the noun _____. 944
c 1163	**While I was feeding the dog, the telephone rang.** The adverb clause **While I was feeding the dog** modifies the verb _____ in the main statement. 1164

a 1383	**To leave** means (a) to go away from, (b) to place something and go away from it, (c) not to change or disturb something. Which of the above meanings does the word **leave** have in the following sentence—*a, b,* or *c*? _____ **Leave the window open a little longer.** 1384
dent 1602	**There was a dent in the fender.** If we changed the subject **dent** to **dents,** would we need to change the verb **was?** (*Yes, No*) 1603
an audience 1821	Copy the word before which **an** is required, and write **an** before it: **foot inch yard** _____ _____ 1822
It's, its 2040	(*Hers, Her's*) **is right next to** (*theirs, their's*). 2041
less 2259	In a series of *three* items, we would use *two* commas. In a series of *four* items, we would use _____ commas. 2260
a <u>man</u>'s appearance 2478	**the mens wages** _____ 2479

Lesson 3 The Simple Subject and the Verb

---

tire

284

Both **is** and **was** are forms of the linking verb **be**.

Be is by far the most common *linking verb*. It is important, therefore, to memorize its various forms.

FORMS OF *BE*: **is, am, are—was, were, been**

The verbs **is, am,** and **are** are (*present, past*) forms of the linking verb **be**.

285

---

b

504

Two or more adjectives can modify the same noun.
(*True, False*)

505

---

b

724

a. **My grandparents are old, but they have modern ideas.**
b. **My grandparents are old, and they live on a farm.**

Which compound sentence is better? _____

725

---

faucets

944

a. **Faucets leak.**

b. *leaking* **faucets**

To make an adjective of the verb **leak**, we add the letters _____ to the verb.

945

---

rang

1164

Grabbing the cat by its tail.

Does this **–ing** word group have a subject and a verb?
(*Yes, No*)

1165

c
 	
1384
	To let means "to permit" or "to allow."
	
	In which of the following sentences does this definition fit—*a* or *b*? ____
	
	     a. **Bob ... me use his book.**
	     b. **Bob ... his book at home.**
	
	     1385

Yes 1603	**There** (*was, were*) **dents in the fender.** The subject **dents** is plural. Therefore, we choose the verb _____. 1604

an inch
 	
1822
	Copy the word before which **an** is required, and write **an** before it:
	
	     honor hammer hotel
	
	   _____ _____
	
	     1823

Hers, theirs
 	
2041
	When using expressions like "*We* boys" and "*Us* girls," select the same pronoun that you would use if you omitted the noun *boys* or *girls*.
	
	     Some of (*we, us*) ~~**boys**~~ **have after-school jobs.**
	
	     2042

three 2260	**My collection of stamps, coins, and autographs is very large.** Do we use a comma before the first word or after the last word in a series? (*Yes, No*) 2261

the <u>men's</u>
wages
 	
2479
	Marys shoes
	
	   _____
	
	     2480

A little black dog with big ears   ran across our yard.

This sentence has two parts: first, it has a subject; second, it has a _____.

66

---

present

285

Keep repeating these six forms of the linking verb **be** until you remember them:

    FORMS OF *BE*: **is, am, are—was, were, been**

The verbs **was, were,** and **been** are (*present, past*) forms of the linking verb **be**.

286

True

505

An adjective must always come *before* the noun it modifies. (*True, False*)

506

---

a

725

a. **I did the problem several times, and my friends were waiting for me.**
b. **I did the problem several times, and I always got the same answer.**

Which compound sentence is better? _____

726

–ing

945

We can turn any verb into an adjective by adding the letters –*ing* to it (sometimes making a slight change in the spelling); for example, **jump—jumping, lose—losing, bat—batting.**

The adjective form of the verb **boil** is _____.

946

No

1165

Grabbing the cat by its tail . . .

Does this –**ing** word group make sense by itself? (*Yes, No*)

1166

a 1385	This is the main point to remember: When you mean **permit**, always use **let**, not **leave**. (*Leave, Let*) **me carry your books.** This means: **Permit** me to carry your books. Therefore, the correct verb is _____. 1386
were 1604	In sentences that begin **Here is, Here are, Where is,** and **Where are,** we also find the subject after the verb. **Here is your ticket.** (= **Your ticket is here.**) What noun is the subject of the verb **is?** _____ 1605
an honor 1823	Copy the word before which **an** is required, and write **an** before it: friend restaurant anecdote _____ _____ 1824
us 2042	(*We, Us*) **girls have been waiting for nearly an hour.** 2043
No 2261	a. **Every train, bus, and airplane was jammed with people.** b. **Every train, bus, and airplane, was jammed with people.** Which sentence is correctly punctuated? ____ 2262
<u>Mary's shoes</u> 2480	**both farmers corn** _____ 2481

predicate 66	**A little black dog with big ears ran across our yard.** Now let's look closely at just the *subject,* or *naming part,* of this sentence. The entire subject consists of _____ words. (How many?) 67
past 286	Supply the missing forms of the verb **be:** **is am _____ — was were _____** 287
False 506	An adjective used as a subject complement usually comes (*before, after*) the noun or pronoun it modifies. 507
b 726	a. **My shoulder was lame. All my muscles ached.** b. **My shoulder was lame. Our next game was on Friday.** Which pair of sentences could be combined into a good compound sentence? _____ 727
boiling 946	The adjective form of the verb **win** is _____. 947
No 1166	**Grabbing the cat by its tail . . .** This **–ing** word group is a (*fragment, sentence*). 1167

Let 1386	(*Leave, Let*) **the water run until it's cold.** This means: **Permit** the water to run until it's cold. Therefore, the correct verb is _____. 1387
ticket 1605	**Here is your ticket.** If we changed the subject **ticket** to **tickets,** would we need to change the verb **is?** (*Yes, No*) 1606
an anecdote 1824	Copy the word before which **an** is required, and write **an** before it: **union umbrella university** _____ _____ 1825
We 2043	**Why don't you give** (*we, us*) **fellows a chance to play?** 2044
a 2262	a. **Switzerland is bounded by, France, Germany, and Italy.** b. **Switzerland is bounded by France, Germany, and Italy.** Which sentence is correctly punctuated? ____ 2263
both <u>farmers'</u> corn 2481	**the womens club** _____ 2482

seven 67	**A little black dog with big ears . . .** These seven words are the **complete subject** of the sentence. There are no other words in the subject part of this sentence. These seven words are not just *part* of the subject. They are the entire or *com_____ subject.* <div align="right">68</div>
are, been 287	Supply the missing forms of the verb **be:** **is** _____ _____ **— was** _____ _____ <div align="right">288</div>
after 507	Some words can be used as either adjectives or nouns. (*True, False*) <div align="right">508</div>
a 727	**We won the football game, and my dad picked us up in his car.** This compound sentence is (*good, poor*). <div align="right">728</div>
winning 947	The adjective form of the verb **freeze** is _____. <div align="right">948</div>
fragment 1167	**And wiped his muddy shoes on the mat.** Is this a complete sentence with both a subject and a predicate? (*Yes, No*) <div align="right">1168</div>

Let 1387	Keep in mind that you always **let go**—never **leave go**—of an object like a rope, a hand, or a wheel. **Don't (*leave, let*) go of your end until I tell you.** 1388
Yes 1606	**Here (*is, are*) your tickets.** The subject **tickets** is plural. Therefore, we choose the plural verb _____. 1607
an umbrella 1825	Copy the word before which **an** is required, and write **an** before it: **hour harbor highway** _____ _____ 1826
us 2044	**(*We, Us*) students need to support our teams better.** 2045
b 2263	a. **My parents never coaxed, forced, or bribed, me to eat.** b. **My parents never coaxed, forced, or bribed me to eat.** Which sentence is correctly punctuated? ____ 2264

the <u>women's</u> club
 	
 2482
	Copy the correct form:
	
	     a ladie's voice
	     a lady's voice _____
	
	 2483

(com)plete 68	**A little black dog with big ears . . .** Now suppose that you were writing a telegram. You might have to reduce this **complete subject** to only one word. Which word would you choose as the most important word in the complete subject—**little, black, dog,** or **ears?** _____ 69
am, are, were, been 288	Supply the missing forms of the verb **be:** _____ _____ **are —** _____ _____ **been** 289
True 508	Lesson **18** And Now the Adverb [Frames 510–544]
poor 728	**I offered to help with the dinner, but Aunt May wouldn't let me.** This compound sentence is (*good, poor*). 729
freezing 948	An **–ing** word *by itself* cannot serve as a verb. **Our team winning.** This group of words (*is, is not*) a sentence. 949
No 1168	a. **and, but, or** b. **then, therefore** In which group are the words that do *not* have the power to connect two sentences into a compound sentence? ____ 1169

let	(*Leave, Let*) **go of my arm.**
1388	1389
are	a. **Where** (*was, were*) **her book?** b. **Where** (*was, were*) **her books?** Can we use the same verb in both sentences? (*Yes, No*)
1607	1608
an hour	Copy the word group before which **an** is required, and write **an** before it: **history course** **high tower** **honest man** ——————— ——————— ———————
1826	1827
We	Be careful not to use "–*self*" pronouns that do not exist. Write all "–*self*" pronouns as solid words without splitting them. Underline the correct word: **The sailors built** (*themselves, theirselves, their selves*) **a raft of logs.**
2045	2046
b	Supply the needed commas: **We made six hits three runs and two errors in the first inning.**
2264	2265
a lady's voice	Copy the correct form: **the ladies' voices** **the ladie's voices** —————————————
2483	2484

dog 69	A little black dog with big ears . . . It was not a **little** or **black** or **ears** that **ran across our yard.** It was a _____. 70
is, am, was, were 289	In a previous lesson, we saw that some *action verbs* can make complete statements about their subjects and that others cannot. a. **Sam** <u>**awoke.**</u> b. **Sam** <u>**fixed**</u> . . . In which sentence—*a* or *b*—does the *action verb* make a complete statement about its subject? _____ 290
	Adjectives can modify _____ and **pronouns,** but they cannot modify **verbs.** 510
good 729	Don't write two sentences together unless you use a **conjunction** to connect them. WRONG: **The lightning flashed, the thunder rumbled.** This sentence involves a serious error because there is no _____ to hold the two sentences together. 730
is not 949	An **–ing** word cannot serve as a verb unless it is used with some form of the verb **be (is, am, are—was, were, been).** Our <u>team</u> <u>was winning</u>. **Winning** is not an adjective in this sentence. It is part of the verb **was** _____. 950
b 1169	**The rug was rolled back,** *and* **then the dancing began.** If we removed the conjunction *and* from this sentence, this would be a (*correct, run-on*) sentence. 1170

Let	**PRESENT** **SIMPLE PAST** **PAST WITH HELPER**
	leave **left** **have left**
	let **let** **have let**
	Which verb means "to go away from"—**leave** or **let**?
	_____
1389	1390

	a. **Where was her book?**
	b. **Where . . . her books?**
No	In sentence *a*, the singular subject **book** requires the singular verb **was**.
	In sentence *b*, the plural subject **books** requires the plural verb _____.
1608	1609

an honest man	Copy the word before which **an** is required, and write **an** before it:
	opportunity **machine** **bakery**
	_____ _____
1827	1828

themselves	**I taught** (*myself, my self*) **to swim.**
2046	2047

hits, runs,	Supply the needed commas:
	The scouts hiked through the woods over a mountain and across a stream.
2265	2266

the ladies' voices	Lesson **80** Using Apostrophes— A Few Don'ts
	[Frames 2486–2527]
2484	

dog 70	**A little black dog with big ears . . .** The noun **dog** is the most important word in the *complete* (*subject, predicate*). 71
a 290	No linking verb, however, can ever make a complete statement about its subject. If a verb does make a complete statement about its subject, it (*is, is not*) being used as a linking verb. 291
nouns 510	There is another *class of words* that answers questions about **verbs** in the same way that _____ answer questions about **nouns** and **pronouns**. 511
conjunction 730	a. **I rang the doorbell, a child came to the door.** b. **I rang the doorbell, and a child came to the door.** Which sentence is wrong because the conjunction is missing—*a* or *b*? ____ 731
winning 950	a. **Our team** *was winning.* b. **The crowd cheered the** *winning* **team.** In which sentence is *winning* used as an adjective to modify a noun? ____ 951
run-on 1170	a. **The rug was rolled back,** *then* **the dancing began.** b. **The rug was rolled back.** *Then* **the dancing began.** Which is correct—*a* or *b*? ____ 1171

leave
 	
 1390
	Don't . . . a child play with matches.
	
	 In this sentence, do we want a verb that means *a* or *b*? _____
	
	       a. **to permit or allow**
	       b. **to go away from**
	
	 1391

were 1609	A word that is made by combining two words and omitting one or more letters is called a **contraction**. **There's = There is Here's = Here is Where's? = Where is?** **There's** is a short cut or contraction for two words: **There** and _____. 1610
an opportunity 1828	Copy the word group before which **an** is required, and write **an** before it: **useless part unusual trip useful tool** _____ _____ _____ 1829
myself 2047	**The dog didn't recognize** (*itself, it's self*) **in the mirror.** 2048
woods, mountain, 2266	Supply the needed commas: **My father mother and I will pick up Betty and Ruth at the station.** 2267
	If you know **to whom** or **to what** something belongs, you know exactly where to place the apostrophe. The owner is indicated by whatever comes before the _____. 2486

subject	**A little black dog with big ears . . .** We would have no idea of what **ran across our yard** if we dropped the word _____ from the complete subject.
71	72
is not	**Skippy <u>was</u> . . . (What?)** This sentence is not complete. Any word that completes it might be thought of as a *completer*. The grammar term for *completer* is **complement**. Any word that completes the meaning of this sentence would be a _____.
291	292
adjectives	**John swam recently.** Since the word **recently** tells **when** about **swam,** we say that it *mod*_____ the verb **swam.**
511	512
a	**The car stopped, a policeman stepped out.** This sentence is (*right, wrong*).
731	732
b	a. **I did not disturb the** *sleeping* **child.** b. **The child** *was sleeping* **on the sofa.** In which sentence is *sleeping* used as an adjective to modify a noun? ____
951	952
b	**The roads were icy, therefore traffic moved slowly.** Adding the conjunction **and** after the comma would make this sentence (*right, wrong*).
1171	1172

a 1391	**Don't . . . a child play with matches.** Because we want a verb that means "to permit" or "to allow," we should choose the verb _____. 1392
is 1610	a. **There's your brother.** b. **There's your parents.** Because **There's** means **There is,** which sentence is wrong— *a* or *b*? ____ 1611
an unusual trip 1829	Lesson **60** Unit Review [Frames 1831–1851]
itself 2048	**My oldest brother put** (*himself, his self*) **through college.** 2049
father, mother, 2267	Supply the needed commas: **The officer sounded his siren motioned me to the curb and asked to see my driver's license.** 2268
apostrophe 2486	**The boys room was untidy.** Until an apostrophe is inserted, we do not know whether the room belongs to one boy or to several. If we put the apostrophe after the **y** in **boy,** we show that the room belongs to (*one, more than one*) boy. 2487

dog 72	**A little black dog with big ears . . .** Just as the trunk of a tree supports all the branches, the word **dog** supports all the other words in the complete subject—no matter how many there may be. All the words in the **complete subject** are attached to the one word _____. <div align="right">73</div>
complement (*or* completer) 292	**Skippy <u>was</u> friendly.** The word **friendly** is a complement because it completes the meaning of the sentence. The complement **friendly** describes the subject _____. <div align="right">293</div>
(mod)ifies 512	a. **John swam <u>there</u>.** b. **John swam <u>yesterday</u>.** In which sentence does the underlined word tell **where** John swam? _____ <div align="right">513</div>
wrong 732	Don't use **and** where **but** would bring out the contrast more clearly. <div align="center">**We asked permission, _____ he refused.**</div> Which conjunction makes better sense in this sentence—**and** or **but**? _____ <div align="right">733</div>
a 952	a. **The car** *was speeding* **down the road.** b. **The police stopped the** *speeding* **car.** In which sentence is *speeding* used as an adjective? _____ <div align="right">953</div>
right 1172	a. **The roads were icy, and** *therefore* **traffic moved slowly.** b. **The roads were icy.** *Therefore* **traffic moved slowly.** Both *a* and *b* are (*right, wrong*). <div align="right">1173</div>

let
 	
1392
	Don't . . . matches where a child can get at them.
	
	In this sentence, do we want a verb that means *a* or *b*? ____
	
	    a. **to permit or to allow**
	    b. **to place something and go away from it**
	
	1393

b 1611	**There's (= There is) your parents.** This sentence is wrong because the subject **parents** is plural, and the contraction **There's** is _____. 1612
	a. **frankly regularly efficiently rapidly** b. **frank regular efficient rapid** Which group of words would you use to describe the action of a verb? ____ 1831
himself 2049	**We found** (*our selfs, ourselves*) **on the bus without any money.** 2050
siren, curb, 2268	It is not wrong to omit the comma before the **and** that connects the last two items of a series. However, without this comma a sentence may be confusing. **These ties come in green, blue, red and gray.** This might mean *either* three or four kinds of ties. With a comma after **red,** the sentence would mean _____ kinds. 2269
one 2487	**The boys room was untidy.** If we put the apostrophe after the **s** in **boys,** we show that the room belongs to (*one, more than one*) boy. 2488

dog 73	**A little black dog with big ears . . .** In grammar, the word **dog** is called the **simple subject** of the sentence. We call it the simple subject because one word is simpler than three or five or ten words. **A little black dog with big ears** is the *complete subject,* but the word **dog** is the _____ *subject.* 74
Skippy 293	**The roads were . . .** (What?) **The roads were muddy.** The complement **muddy** completes the meaning of the sentence and describes the subject _____. 294
a 513	a. **John swam away.** b. **John swam fast.** In which sentence does the underlined word tell **how** John swam? ____ 514
but 733	**We asked his permission, _____ he consented.** Which conjunction makes better sense in this sentence—**and** or **but?** _____ 734
b 953	We can use **–ing** words to make word groups that are used like adjectives to modify nouns and pronouns. **A girl** *carrying an umbrella* **was waiting for a bus.** The word group *carrying an umbrella* describes or modifies the noun _____. 954
right 1173	**The men pushed the truck.** *It* **wouldn't move an inch.** *It* and other pronouns can start a new sentence even though the meaning of the pronoun depends upon the previous sentence. (*True, False*) 1174

b 1393	**Don't . . . matches where a child can get at them.** We want a verb that means "to place something and go away from it." Therefore, we should choose the verb _____. 1394
singular 1612	a. **Where's my keys?** b. **Where's my key?** Is the contraction **Where's** correct in *a* or *b*? ____ 1613
a 1831	a. **Ward's apology was very . . . .** b. **Ward apologized very . . . .** The adverb **sincerely** should be used in sentence ____. 1832
ourselves 2050	UNIT 10: **HOW TO USE CAPITALS** Lesson **67** Capitalizing Geographical and Group Names [Frames 2052–2087]
four 2269	a. **She served coffee, ice cream, cookies ‸ and cake.** b. **She served coffee, ice cream, cheese ‸ and egg sand-wiches.** In which sentence would inserting a comma at the point indicated prevent a misunderstanding? ____ 2270
more than one 2488	a. **The boy's room was untidy.** b. **The boys' room was untidy.** Which sentence shows that more than one boy is the owner —*a* or *b*? ____ 2489

simple 74	**A little black dog with big ears . . .** The *complete subject* consists of seven words, but the *simple subject* consists of only _____ word(**s**). 75
roads 294	<u>Turtles **are** . . .</u> (What?) <u>Turtles **are** reptiles.</u> The complement **reptiles** completes the meaning of the sentence and *explains* or *identifies* the subject _____. 295
b 514	a. **John swam <u>frequently</u>.** b. **John swam <u>backward</u>.** In which sentence does the underlined word tell **how much** or **how often** John swam? ____ 515
and 734	**There was a stop sign at the corner, _____ Dick didn't see it.** Which conjunction makes better sense here—**and** or **but**? _____ 735
girl 954	**A girl** *carrying an umbrella* **was waiting for a bus.** Because the word group *carrying an umbrella* modifies the noun **girl**, it is used as an (*adverb, adjective*). 955
True 1174	In this and the following frames, label each item according to the following key: S = correct sentence: F = fragment; R–S = run-on sentence **During the five minutes between classes.** ____ 1175

leave 1394	**. . . the door open.** Suppose that a door is open, and you want it to remain that way. Which one of the following definitions would express your meaning—*a* or *b*? ____ a. **To leave** means "not to change or disturb something." b. **To let** means "to permit" or "to allow." 1395
b 1613	a. **Where's (= Where is) my keys?** b. **Where are my keys?** Sentence *b* is correct because the plural subject **keys** requires the plural verb _____. 1614
b 1832	Underline the correct word: **Raymond's reply to his dad's question seemed quite** (*disrespectful, disrespectfully*) **to his friends.** 1833
	man Moses Which one of the above nouns means one *particular* man? _____ 2052
b 2270	When you connect all the items in a series with **and**'s, no commas should be used. **Jerry sang <u>and</u> shouted <u>and</u> whistled until I was nearly deaf.** Does this sentence require any commas? (*Yes, No*) 2271
b 2489	Sometimes the thing owned is understood but not expressed. **Don's score was higher than Fred's.** We put an apostrophe in **Fred's** because it really means **Fred's** _____. 2490

one 75	In our grammar work, we shall be more concerned with the simple subject than with the complete subject. For convenience, therefore, we shall always refer to the simple subject as just the **subject.** From here on, the word **subject** will mean not the *complete subject* but the _____ subject. 76
Turtles 295	A complement that follows a linking verb and *describes* or *identifies* the subject is called a **subject complement.** It is called a **subject complement** because it *describes* or *identifies* the _____. 296
a 515	Words that tell **when, where, how, how much,** or **how often** about verbs are called **adverbs.** **Adjectives** modify **nouns** and **pronouns,** but **adverbs** can modify _____. 516
but 735	**The sign was too small, _____ many people failed to see it.** Which conjunction makes better sense here—**and** or **but?** _____ 736
adjective 955	**A girl** *carrying an umbrella* **was waiting for a bus.** **A girl** **was waiting for a bus.** When we omit the **–ing** word group from this sentence, do we have a complete sentence remaining? (*Yes, No*) 956
F 1175	S = correct sentence; F = fragment; R–S = run-on sentence **The roads were poorly marked, we therefore lost our way.** _____ 1176

a 1395	**. . . the door open.** Suppose that someone is blocking a door so that it can't open. You want the person to **permit** or **allow** the door to open. Which word would you choose—**leave** or **let?** _____ 1396
are 1614	a. **Here's my reason for refusing.** b. **Here's my reasons for refusing.** Is the contraction **Here's** correct in sentence *a* or *b?* ____ 1615
disrespectful 1833	Underline the correct word: **The commission studied the causes of crime very** (*scientific, scientifically*). 1834
Moses 2052	**Boston city** Which noun means one *particular* city? _____ 2053
No 2271	**Jerry sang <u>and</u> shouted <u>and</u> whistled until I was nearly deaf.** If you omitted the **and** after **sang,** would the sentence require commas? (*Yes, No*) 2272
score 2490	Suppose that we are writing about Dad's car and say— **Dads would not start.** Place an apostrophe in the above sentence even though the thing owned is not expressed. 2491

simple 76	**A little black dog with big ears ran across our yard.** To save words, we shall call the word **dog** not the *simple subject* of this sentence, but just the _____. <div align="right">77</div>
subject 296	**The box was . . .** (What?) **The box was empty.** Because the complement **empty** completes the meaning of the sentence and describes the subject **box,** it is a _____ *complement.* <div align="right">297</div>
verbs 516	Notice that the word **verb** occurs in the word **adverb.** This should help you to remember that there is a close connection between **adverbs** and _____. <div align="right">517</div>

and 736	Generally, it is not a good idea to begin a sentence with **and.**
	
	    a. **Ten years pass. And Paul is now a successful lawyer.**
	    b. **Ten years pass, and Paul is now a successful lawyer.**
	
	Which is better—*a* or *b?* ____ <div align="right">737</div>

Yes 956	**A girl** *carrying an umbrella* **was waiting for a bus.** The verb that makes a statement about the subject **girl** is not *carrying,* but _____ _____. (two words) <div align="right">957</div>
R–S 1176	S = correct sentence; F = fragment; R–S = run-on sentence **Before one selects a vocation, he should consider his interests and abilities.** ____ <div align="right">1177</div>

let 1396	PRESENT SIMPLE PAST PAST WITH HELPER **leave** **left** **have left** **let** **let** **have let** The two past forms of **leave** are (*alike, different*). The two past forms of **let** are (*alike, different*). <div align="right">1397</div>
a 1615	The apostrophe **s ('s)** in **There's, Here's,** and **Where's** stands for the verb (*is, are*), which is singular. <div align="right">1616</div>
scientifically 1834	Use the adverb **well,** not the adjective **good,** to describe how an action is performed. **This electric heater is** (*good, well*)**, and it heats the room very** (*good, well*). <div align="right">1835</div>
Boston 2053	**language** **Spanish** Which noun means one *particular* language? _____ <div align="right">2054</div>
Yes 2272	**The heat, the noise, and the crowd gave me a headache.** If you inserted an **and** after the word **heat,** how many commas would be necessary? _____ <div align="right">2273</div>
Dad's 2491	You have seen apostrophes used in such expressions as **a day's work** and **a dollar's worth of gas. A day's work** means the work belonging to one day. **A dollar's worth of gas** means the amount that can be bought for one dollar. Underline the two words that require apostrophes: **In five minutes time, it burns a dollars worth of gas.** <div align="right">2492</div>

subject 77	**A little black dog with big ears ran across our yard.** Now let's look at just the *predicate*, or *telling part*, of our sentence. The *complete predicate* consists of _____ words. (How many?) 78
subject 297	Among other verbs that can be used as *linking verbs* are **seem, become, appear, look, feel,** and **get** (when it means **become**). **The <u>room</u> <u>seems</u> dark.** The verb **seems** is a _____ *verb*. 298
verbs 517	**The dog ate <u>greedily</u>.** The adverb **greedily** tells (*how, when*) the dog **ate**. 518
b 737	a. **In those days people worked harder, and they needed more food.** b. **In those days people worked harder. And they needed more food.** Which is better—*a* or *b*? ____ 738
was waiting 957	**Bob,** *looking at the snow,* **saw rabbit tracks.** **Bob** **saw rabbit tracks.** The **-ing** word group *looking at the snow* modifies the noun **Bob.** The verb that makes a statement about **Bob** is not *looking,* but _____. 958
S 1177	*S, F,* or *R–S?* **Mr. Wetherby makes appointments, then he forgets to keep them.** ____ 1178

alike alike 1397	In this and the following frames, underline the correct verb in each pair. Remember always to choose **let** when you mean **permit** or **allow**. **Don't** (*leave, let*) **the toast burn.** 1398
is 1616	Do not use the contraction **There's, Here's,** or **Where's** unless you first look ahead in the sentence and see that a (*singular, plural*) subject is coming. 1617
good, well 1835	**We paid the carpenter** (*good, well*) **because his work was so** (*good, well*). 1836
Spanish 2054	A noun that names a *particular* person, place, or thing is called a **proper noun.** **Moses Boston Spanish** Each of the above nouns is a _____ noun. 2055
None 2273	a. **My face, and neck, and arms were covered with mosquito bites.** b. **My face and neck and arms were covered with mosquito bites.** Which sentence is correctly punctuated? ___ 2274
minutes, dollars 2492	We follow the usual rule for placing the apostrophe: TIME: **an hour's delay, two days' pay, a week's vacation** MONEY: **a nickel's worth, ten cents' worth, your money's worth** Supply the missing apostrophe: **After an hours delay, the plane finally took off.** 2493

. . . ran across our yard.

Here, too, we find a word that stands out from the others as the most important.

If you were writing a telegram, what one word in the *complete predicate* would you choose to tell what the dog did?

_____

---

linking

298

The room became dark.

The verb _____ is a linking verb.

299

---

how

518

The letter arrived today.

The adverb **today** tells (*where, when*) the letter **arrived**.

519

---

a

738

Two sentences should not be joined into a compound sentence unless their ideas are similar and are of (*equal, unequal*) importance.

739

---

saw

958

Sharon sat on the porch, *waiting for the mailman.*

An **–ing** word group can be some distance away from the word it modifies.

The word group *waiting for the mailman* modifies the noun (*Sharon, porch*).

959

R–S

1178

S, F, or *R–S?*

We drove up and down the street, looking for a place to park.

_____

let 1398	Don't (*leave, let*) **your books on the stairs.** 1399
singular 1617	Lesson **53** Unit Review [Frames 1619–1646]

well, good
 	
1836
	"Sense" words such as **look, taste,** and **feel** can be used as either action or linking verbs.
	    a. **The bleachers** *looked* **empty.**
	    b. **The golfers** *looked* **for the lost ball.**
	In which sentence is the verb *looked* used as a linking verb? ____
	    1837

proper
 	
2055
	A noun that might be applied to *any* one of a class or group of persons, places, or things is called a **common noun.**
	
	      man city language
	
	Each of the above nouns is a _____ noun.
	    2056

b
 	
2274
	In this and the following frames, insert the necessary commas. Several sentences require no commas at all. Remember that it takes at least three items to make a series.
	    Every hotel motel and tourist home was full.
	(In the answer box, parentheses around a comma mean that the comma is a matter of choice.)
	    2275

hour's
 	
2493
	a. **The dress cost Alice one <u>weeks</u> pay.**
	    b. **The dress cost Alice two <u>weeks</u> pay.**
	
	The word **weeks** requires an apostrophe in each sentence. In which sentence should the apostrophe come before the s? ____
	    2494

ran 79	...<u>ran across our yard.</u> The word **ran** is the most important word in the *complete* _____. 80
became 299	The <u>room</u> <u>looked</u> dark. Because the word **dark** completes the sentence and describes the subject **room**, it is a _____ _____. 300
when 519	This pen leaks <u>slightly.</u> The adverb **slightly** tells (*how much, where*) the pen **leaks.** 520
equal 739	**Cathy works in Mr. Daly's office. My dad bowls with Mr. Daly.** Combining these two sentences would produce a (*good, poor*) compound sentence. 740
Sharon 959	*Waiting for the mailman,* **Sharon sat on the porch.** **Sharon,** *waiting for the mailman,* **sat on the porch.** **Sharon sat on the porch,** *waiting for the mailman.* In the above sentences, the word group *waiting for the mailman* occupies _____ different positions. (How many?) 960
S 1179	*S, F,* or *R–S?* **The map is helpful, it shows the location of every trailer camp.** ____ 1180

leave 1399	**Please** (*leave, let*) **me off at Twenty-first Street. (= Permit** me to get off.) 1400
	Use **don't** only when you can put the two words **do not** in its place. **Steve's father** (*don't, doesn't*) **approve of his friends.** 1619
a 1837	Underline the correct word: **The lights of the city looked** (*beautiful, beautifully*) **from the plane.** 1838
common 2056	a. **month car country** b. **April Buick Mexico** Are the nouns in group *a* or *b* *proper* nouns? ____ 2057
hotel, motel(,) 2275	Insert commas where needed: **Dolores thinks looks and acts just like her mother.** 2276
a 2494	a. **He worked for <u>two days</u>.** b. **He got <u>two days</u> pay.** In which sentence does the word **days** require an apostrophe because it measures the noun that follows it? ____ 2495

predicate 80	↓ ↓ **A little black dog with big ears ran across our yard.** The word **ran** makes a statement about **dog**, which is the _____ . 81
subject complement 300	You can be sure that a verb is a *linking verb* if you can put some form of **be (is, am, are—was, were, been)** in its place. **The clothes feel** (= are) **damp.** In this sentence, **feel** is a *linking verb* because we can put the verb _____ in its place. 301
how much 520	**Tommy teases his sister continually.** The adverb **continually** tells (*how, how often*) Tommy teases. 521
poor 740	Can a comma without a conjunction be used to combine two separate sentences into a compound sentence? (*Yes, No*) 741
three 960	We can give interesting variety to our sentences if we learn to use **-ing** word groups. An **-ing** word group is built upon an adjective made by adding the letters **-ing** to a _____ . 961
R–S 1180	*S, F,* or *R–S*? **Sitting at his desk and doing nothing.** _____ 1181

let 1400	The doctor won't (*leave, let*) me play for another month. 1401
doesn't 1619	**"Rule of S":** When we add an *s* to the subject, we do not add an *s* to the verb. When we add an *s* to the verb, we do not add an *s* to the subject. Add one *s* to make this sentence singular: **The wheel____ squeak____.** 1620
beautiful 1838	The customer smelled the new perfume very (*dubious, dubiously*) before buying it. 1839
b 2057	a. **month** **car** **country** b. **April** **Buick** **Mexico** The nouns that begin with capital letters are (*common, proper*) nouns. 2058
thinks, looks(,) 2276	Insert commas where needed: **Children often don't realize that their slapping kicking and hair-pulling really hurt.** 2277
b 2495	a. **I had only ten cents.** b. **I bought ten cents worth of candy.** In which sentence does the word **cents** require an apostrophe because it measures the noun that follows it? ____ 2496

subject 81	**A little black dog with big ears ran across our yard.** We saw that the word **dog** supports all the other words in the *complete subject*. In the same way, the word **ran** supports all the other words in the *complete* _____. 82
are 301	**Arthur scolded his dog.** Try to put a form of the verb **be** in place of the verb **scolded**. The verb **scolded** (*is, is not*) a linking verb. 302
how often 521	**When? Where? How? How much? How often?** Words that answer these questions about **verbs** are called _____. 522
No 741	To bring out the contrast between two ideas, it is better to use the conjunction (*and, but*). 742
verb 961	To change a sentence to an **–ing** word group is simple. ~~We~~ *expected* a storm. We closed all the windows. ↓ *Expecting a storm*, **we closed all the windows.** To change the first sentence to an **–ing** word group, drop the **We,** and change the verb *expected* to _____. 962
F 1181	*S, F, or R–S?* **A plastic pen which shows the supply of ink.** ____ 1182

let 1401	We (*left*, *let*) everything just as we found it. 1402
(squeak)s 1620	Whenever a prepositional phrase follows the subject, select the verb that agrees with the subject, not with a noun in the prepositional phrase. **The spelling . . . very tricky.** **The spelling of some words . . . very tricky.** Would the verb **is** be correct in both sentences? (*Yes, No*) 1621
dubiously 1839	This bread tastes so (*fresh*, *freshly*)! 1840
proper 2058	a. **month** **car** **country** b. **April** **Buick** **Mexico** The nouns that begin with small letters are (*common*, *proper*) nouns. 2059
slapping, kicking (,) 2277	Insert commas where needed: **The Yanks and the Tigers will play a double-header.** 2278
b 2496	Supply one missing apostrophe: **For just nineteen cents, I got fifty cents worth of cookies.** 2497

predicate 82	**. . . ran across our yard.** The *complete predicate* consists of four words, but the *simple predicate* is only _____ word(s). 83
is not 302	**The engine became noisy.** Can we substitute **was** for the verb **became** in this sentence? The verb **became** (*is, is not*) a linking verb. 303
adverbs 522	**Floyd drove the car** _____. (How?) Underline the **adverb** that would fit in this sentence and answer the question printed in parentheses: **back cautiously regularly sometimes** 523
but 742	Starting sentences with the conjunction **and** (*is, is not*) a good idea generally. 743
Expecting 962	**He drove around the block. He** *looked* **for a place to park.** ↓ **He drove around the block,** *looking* **for a place to park.** To change the second sentence to an **–ing** word group, we must drop the subject **He** and change the verb *looked* to _____. 963
F 1182	*S, F, or R–S?* **Tickets to the telecast are free, they may be obtained by writing to the sponsor.** _____ 1183

left 1402	Greg (*left, let*) go of the ladder too soon. 1403
Yes 1621	**Each, every, either,** and **neither** are either singular them-selves or modify singular nouns or pronouns. In either case, they require singular verbs. **Each one of these sets** (*is, are*) **guaranteed.** 1622
fresh 1840	Form the second and third degree of short words such as **fast, high,** and **cold** by adding **–er** and **–est,** not by using the adverbs **more** and **most.** **It was the** (*most strong, strongest*) **coffee I have ever drunk.** 1841
common 2059	A capital letter is required at the beginning of every _____ noun. 2060
None 2278	**Many people have been killed because they didn't stop look and listen before crossing railroad tracks.** 2279
fifty cents' worth 2497	Supply two missing apostrophes: **Miss Young spent two years savings on a months travel in Europe.** 2498

one 83	A word that can be used as the *simple predicate* of a sentence is called a **verb**. A *simple predicate* and a *verb* are the same thing. <div align="center">**. . . <u>ran across our yard.</u>**</div> The verb in this complete predicate is _____. <div align="right">84</div>
is 303	<div align="center">**The <u>lettuce</u> <u>looks</u> fresh.**</div> See if you can put a form of **be** in place of the verb **looks**. If you can, **looks** is a linking verb. Is the verb **looks** a linking verb? (*Yes, No*) <div align="right">304</div>
cautiously 523	**Floyd drove the car** _____. (How often?) Underline the adverb that answers this question. <div align="center">**skillfully away frequently yesterday**</div> <div align="right">524</div>
is not 743	Lesson **25** Understanding the Adverb Clause <div align="right">[Frames 745–777]</div>
looking 963	<div align="center">**Rusty** *changed* **his mind. He ran back to third base.** ↓ *Changing his mind,* **he ran back to third base.**</div> In changing the first sentence to an –ing word group, we lost the subject of this sentence, which was _____. <div align="right">964</div>
R–S 1183	*S, F,* or *R–S*? **The driver tried to save a few minutes, but he lost his life.** <div align="right">1184</div>

let 1403	**Mother had** (*left, let*) **the iron on all night.** 1404
is 1622	Two singular nouns connected by **and** require a plural verb. Two singular nouns connected by **or** or **nor** require a singular verb. **The principal or his assistant** (*attends, attend*) **each game.** 1623
strongest 1841	**Each burst of fireworks seemed to be** (*wonderfuller, more wonderful*) **than the last.** 1842
proper 2060	a. **asia** **robert** **harvard** b. **hotel** **pupil** **kitchen** Which words require capital letters because they are *proper* nouns—those in group *a* or *b*? 2061
stop, look(,) 2279	**Dogs rats guinea pigs and other animals are used for medical experiments.** 2280

years', month's
 	
2498
	Don't insert an apostrophe wherever you see a final **s.** Some careless writers put apostrophes in ordinary plural nouns that don't show ownership at all.
	    a. **Rita bought some apple's and pear's.**
	    b. **Rita bought some apples and pears.**
	Which sentence is correct—*a* or *b*? ____
	page 168
	
	2499

ran 84	**A little black dog with big ears <u>ran across our yard</u>.** The verb tells us what the dog *did*. It didn't *bark* or *walk* or *jump*. The verb tells that the dog _____. 85

Yes
 	
304
	A few verbs can be used as either action or linking verbs.
	
	    a. **The coach** *felt* **my ankle.**
	    b. **The coach** *felt* **sorry for me.**
	
	In one sentence, *felt* is used as an *action* verb; in the other, as a *linking* verb.
	In which sentence can we substitute **was** for **felt?** _____ 305

frequently 524	**Myra looked** _____ **for her hat.** (Where?) Underline the adverb that answers this question. **everywhere again carefully quickly** 525
	Do you remember how adverbs answer such questions as **"When?"** and **"Where?"** and **"How?"** about verbs? WHEN? **Pete awoke** *early.* **Early** is an adverb because it modifies the _____ **awoke.** 745
Rusty 964	*Rusty changed his mind.* **He ran back to third base.** ↓ **Rusty** *Changing his mind,* ~~he~~ **ran back to third base.** To let the reader know who the sentence is about, we substitute **Rusty** for the pronoun _____ in the main statement of the sentence. 965
S 1184	*F, S,* or *R–S?* **The preface is important, it explains how the author collected his facts.** _____ 1185

page 169

left 1404	**You should have** (*left, let*) **the glue harden longer.** 1405
attends 1623	Before you choose between **There is** or **There are, Here is** or **Here are,** and so forth, look ahead in the sentence to see whether a singular or a plural subject is coming. **There** (*was, were*) **no electric lights in those days.** 1624
more wonderful 1842	Is it correct to use **more** with the adjective **taller,** and **most** with the adjective **cheapest?** (*Yes, No*) 1843

a
 	
2061
	Any ordinary noun becomes a proper noun when it is used as part of a particular name.
	
	    a. **The river was rising.**
	    b. **The Ohio River was rising.**
	
	In which sentence is **river** used as part of the name of a particular river? ____
	
	2062

Dogs, rats, guinea pigs (,) 2280	**I washed windows and dusted furniture and cleaned floors most of the day.** 2281
b 2499	Several nouns in the following sentence end in **s,** but only one shows ownership. Place the apostrophe in this word. **The dog always barks at and jumps on the familys visitors.** 2500

ran 85	**A little black dog with big ears <u>ran across our yard</u>.** Suppose that you were asked to reduce this sentence to only two words. Underline the two words which best "tell the story" of this sentence. **little dog big ears our yard dog ran** 86
b 305	a. **The coach** *felt* **my ankle.** b. **The coach** *felt* **sorry for me.** In which sentence is *felt* used as a linking verb? ____ 306
everywhere 525	**Miss Jones read the story _____. (How?)** Underline the adverb that answers this question. **often aloud again here** 526
verb 745	Prepositional phrases, too, can be used as adverbs. a. **Pete awoke** *early.* b. **Pete awoke** *in the morning.* The adverb phrase *in the morning* in sentence *b* does the same job as the adverb _____ in sentence *a.* 746
he 965	**George** *hoped* **to meet his dad. He went to the airport.** ↓ *Hoping to meet his dad,* **he went to the airport.** In changing the first sentence to an **–ing** word group, we lost the subject **George.** The reader won't know whom we are talking about unless we substitute _____ for the pronoun **he** in the new sentence. 966
R–S 1185	*F, S,* or *R–S?* **Which was not included in the price of the trip.** ____ 1186

let	**Ray's parents should have** (*left, let*) **him bring his friends home.**
1405	1406

were	From here on, the various types of subject-verb problems will be mixed. Don't put down your answer until you can give an exact reason for it.
	Underline the one subject among the three in parentheses that could be used as the subject of the verb:
	(*My shoes, The pails, The canoe*) **was full of water.**
1624	1625

No	**The water is** (*deeper, more deeper*) **on the other side of the raft.**
1843	1844

b	a. **Judy attends a small college.**
	b. **Judy attends Albion college.**
	In which sentence should **college** be capitalized because it is part of the name of a particular college? _____
2062	2063

None	**Cocker spaniels make lively friendly intelligent and obedient pets.**
2281	2282

family's	Supply any needed apostrophes:
	The missing nuts and bolts were in my brothers drawer.
2500	2501

dog ran 86	**A little black dog with big ears <u>ran across our yard.</u>** The two words **dog ran** do not give every detail of the sentence. However, they tell more about what happened than any other two words that you might choose. **Dog** is the *subject*, and **ran** is the *simple predicate* or _____. 87
b 306	**The coach felt my** *ankle.* **The coach felt** *sorry* **for me.** Only a linking verb can be followed by a subject complement. Which word is a subject complement—*ankle* or *sorry?* _____ 307
aloud 526	**I did my homework** _____ **last night.** (When?) Underline the adverb that answers this question. **eagerly quickly carelessly early** 527
early 746	WHEN? **Pete awoke** *in the morning.* The prepositional phrase *in the morning* modifies the verb by telling *when* Pete **awoke.** It is therefore called an (*adjective, adverb*) phrase. 747
George 966	**We went from door to door. We reminded people to vote.** **We went from door to door,** _____ *people to vote.* After combining the two sentences by using an **-ing** word group, what word will we have on the blank line? _____ 967
F 1186	*F, S,* or *R–S?* **The foreman blamed Rinehart, who should have tested his brakes.** ____ 1187

let 1406	Lesson **45** *Bring* **and** *Take* [Frames 1408–1432]
The canoe 1625	Underline the one subject that could be used as the subject of the verb: (*Our town, Schools, Cars*) **was much smaller in those days.** 1626
deeper 1844	**Maisie is the most** (*gentle, gentlest*) **horse that I have ever ridden.** 1845
b 2063	a. **The Crosby high school was completed last year.** b. **The high school was completed last year.** In which sentence should the words **high school** be capitalized because they are part of a proper noun? ____ 2064
lively, friendly, intelligent (,) 2282	**Two or three coyotes will team together to hunt rabbits antelope and other game.** 2283
brother's 2501	Another careless mistake is to put apostrophes in verbs that end in **s.** A verb, of course, cannot possibly show ownership. a. **Martha sings while she cleans the house.** b. **Martha sing's while she clean's the house.** Which sentence is correct—*a* or *b*? ____ 2502

verb 87	**A little black dog with big ears ran across our yard.** The framework upon which this entire sentence is built is the subject _____ and the verb _____. <div align="right">88</div>
sorry 307	Lesson **11** **The Subject Complement Pattern** <div align="right">[Frames 309–328]</div>
early 527	**Don pushed the car _____. (Where?)** Underline the adverb that answers this question. <div align="center">**forward easily often slightly**</div> <div align="right">528</div>
adverb 747	WHEN? **Pete awoke** *when I called him.* The word group *when I called him* is not an adverb phrase. It is a different kind of word group. Because the word group *when I called him* also tells *when* Pete **awoke**, it does the same job as an (*adjective, adverb*). <div align="right">748</div>
reminding 967	In this and the following frames, combine each pair of sentences by changing the italicized sentence to an **–ing** word group. Write the full sentence. <div align="center">*We heard a crash.* **We rushed to the window.**</div> _____ <div align="right">968</div>
S 1187	*F, S,* or *R–S*? **The sky was cloudy, therefore the eclipse was not visible.** <div align="right">1188</div>

Bring, like **come,** is a movement **toward** the person speaking.

Come over tonight and bring your accordion with you.

The movement in this sentence is (*toward, away from*) the person speaking.

1408

Our town

1626

(*The sandwiches, Two boys, My coat*) **was in the other car.**

1627

---

gentle

1845

Use only a single negative word to make a negative statement.

Our family didn't go (*anywhere, nowhere*) **last summer.**

1846

---

a

2064

Capitalize all geographical names, such as the names of particular countries, states, and cities.

Japan   North Carolina   New York

Write the name of the country in which you live.

_____

2065

---

rabbits, antelope(,)

2283

Our beds and our clothes and our food were full of sand.

2284

---

a

2502

Five words in the following sentence end in **s,** but only one shows ownership. Place the apostrophe in this word.

My friends mother grows and cans most of her own fruits and vegetables.

2503

(subject) dog (verb) ran 88	**The car ahead of us <u>skidded on the ice.</u>** The framework upon which this sentence is built is the subject _____ and the verb _____. 89
	A **linking verb** (_does, does not_) show action. 309
forward 528	Many **adverbs**—especially those that tell **how** about the verb—end in **–ly.** **Scotty argued firmly but politely with the umpire.** Does this sentence contain one or two adverbs? _____ 529
adverb 748	Now let's remove this word group from the sentence and look at it more closely: _when I <u>called</u> him_ Unlike a prepositional phrase, this word group has both a subject, _____, and a verb, _____. 749
Hearing a crash, we rushed to the window. 968	**Sandra took the wrong coat.** _She thought it was hers._ _____ _____ 969
R–S 1188	_F, S,_ or _R–S?_ **The tornado, destroying everything in its path.** ____ 1189

toward <div align="right">1408</div>	**Take,** like **go,** is a movement **away from** the person speaking. **Go to the game and take your camera along.** The movement in this sentence is (*toward, away from*) the person speaking. <div align="right">1409</div>
My coat <div align="right">1627</div>	(*My sisters, He, Rosemary*) **don't like movies.** <div align="right">1628</div>
anywhere <div align="right">1846</div>	**If I were you, I wouldn't buy** (*neither, either*) **of these two suits.** <div align="right">1847</div>
the United States <div align="right">2065</div>	Write the name of the state in which **Chicago** is located. _____ <div align="right">2066</div>
None <div align="right">2284</div>	**Eggs may be used as a substitute for meat fish or cheese in planning meals.** <div align="right">2285</div>
friend's *or* friends' <div align="right">2503</div>	Supply any needed apostrophes: **The way Stanley teases his younger sisters and brothers gets on his mothers nerves.** <div align="right">2504</div>

(subject) car (verb) skidded 89	**A small fire often spreads to a large area.** **Fire** is the _____ of the sentence, and **spreads** is the _____. 90
does not 309	A **linking verb** with its subject (*can, cannot*) form a complete sentence. 310

Two
 	
529
	Many words have two forms—the **adjective** form without **–ly** and the **adverb** form with **–ly**.
	
	    EXAMPLES: **eager—eagerly** **polite—politely**
	                 simple—simply **serious—seriously**
	
	Write the *adverb* form of the *adjective* **prompt.** _____
	
	530

(subject) I (verb) called 749	*when I called him* Although this word group has both a subject and a verb, does it form a complete sentence by itself? (*Yes, No*) 750
Sandra took the wrong coat, thinking it was hers. 969	*The planes fly low.* **They drop emergency supplies.** _____ _____ (Remember to put back the lost subject *planes*.) 970
F 1189	*F, S,* or *R–S?* **They made a down payment, then they discovered that they couldn't keep up the monthly payments.** ____ 1190

away from

1409

The difference between **bring** and **take** is a difference in the direction of the movement.

If you mean *come with*, use _____.

If you mean *go with*, use _____.

1410

My sisters

1628

(*The bread, The pie, The cookies*) **don't taste fresh.**

1629

---

either

1847

The fog was so thick that we (*could, couldn't*) **hardly see ten feet ahead of the car.**

1848

Illinois

2066

Write the name of the **capital** of the United States.

_____

2067

---

meat, fish (,)

2285

Lesson **74** Commas in Compound Sentences

[Frames 2287–2320]

---

mother's

2504

Be careful when you use apostrophes with people's names that end in **s,** like **Jones** and **Burns.**

First, you need to know how to form the ordinary plurals of these names.

Mr. Jones (one person)   the **Joneses** (the whole family)

What is the plural of the name **Burns?** _____

2505

page 180

(fire) subject (spreads) verb 90	In this and the following frames, underline the simple subject with one line and the verb with two lines. These are the two words that "tell the story" of the sentence better than any other two words. **Some people worry about very silly things.** 91
cannot 310	To complete the meaning of the sentence, every **linking verb** must be followed by a _____ *complement.* 311
promptly 530	Write the adverb form of these two adjectives: **frequent** _____ **courteous** _____ 531
Nc 750	*when* I *called him* Word groups like this are called **clauses.** A **clause** is a group of words which has a subject and a verb but (*does, does not*) form a complete sentence by itself. 751
Flying low, the planes drop emergency supplies. 970	**He explained the problem.** *He made each step clear.* _____ _____ 971
R–S 1190	*F, S, or R–S?* **If the weather is good, a dog team can cover eleven miles in an hour.** ____ 1191

(come with) bring (go with) take 1410	When you are puzzled, try to fit in the words *come with* or *go with*. **My brother often . . . a friend home from college.** (= *comes with* a friend) The correct word is (*brings, takes*). 1411
The cookies 1629	**Don't** (*Mr. Crane, Shirley, the Carters*) **live on your street?** 1630
could 1848	Use the word **an** before any word that begins with a (*vowel, vowel sound*). 1849
Washington 2067	Capitalize, too, the complete names of oceans, rivers, lakes, mountains, parks, etc. **Arctic Ocean Ohio River Duck Lake Hyde Park** Write the capital letters you would need to use in writing **zion national park.** _____ 2068
	A sentence that consists of two (or more) sentences joined by the conjunction **and, but,** or **or** is called a **compound sentence.** In a compound sentence, there is a complete sentence both before and after the _____. 2287

Burnses
 	
2505
	Mr. Jones (one person) **the Joneses** (the whole family)
	      a. **Our dog was in <u>Mr. Jone's</u> car.**
	      b. **Our dog was in <u>Mr. Jones's</u> car.**
	Which is correct because the apostrophe comes after the full name of the owner—*a* or *b*? ____
	
	2506

<u>people</u> <u><u>worry</u></u> 91	Underline the simple subject with one line and the verb with two lines: **Heavy black smoke blew back over the deck.** 92
subject 311	A **subject complement** is a word that describes or identifies the _____ of the sentence. 312
frequently courteously 531	A final **–ly** is often, though not always, the sign of an _____. 532
does not 751	a. **Pete awoke** *early*. b. **Pete awoke** *when I called him*. Both the clause *when I called him* and the adverb *early* tell *when* Pete **awoke**. Because the clause modifies the verb **awoke**—just like any adverb—we call it an (*adverb, adjective*) clause. 752
He explained the problem, making each step clear. 971	In this and the following frames, eliminate the *and* in each sentence by changing the italicized part to an **–ing** word group. Write the full sentence. *I thought the envelope was empty,* **and I threw it away.** _____ _____ 972
S 1191	*F, S,* or *R–S*? **Although Frances has many admirable qualities.** ____ 1192

brings 1411	We usually . . . our car to Miller's garage. (= *go with* our car) The correct word is (*bring, take*). 1412
the Carters 1630	In this and the following frames, underline the correct verb: **Either of these roads** (*leads, lead*) **to the park.** 1631
vowel sound 1849	Write **a** or **an** in each blank: **I spent _____ hour looking over _____ history book.** 1850
Z N P 2068	In this and the following frames, copy the words that require capitals. If no capitals are required, write *None*. (Do not copy the first word of the sentence, which must always be capitalized.) **The family moved from sweden to this country.** _____ 2069
conjunction 2287	a. **The chairman** <u>rapped on the table</u> **and** <u>waited for order.</u> b. **The chairman** <u>rapped on the table,</u> **and** <u>the audience quieted down.</u> Which sentence is compound? _____ 2288
b 2506	a. **Our dog was in** <u>Mr. Jone's</u> **car.** b. **Our dog was in** <u>Mr. Jones's</u> **car.** Sentence *a* is wrong because the man's name is not **Mr. Jone,** but **Mr. _____.** 2507

smoke <u>blew</u>

92

Underline the simple subject with one line and the verb with two lines:

The bright headlights blinded the approaching driver.

93

---

subject

312

Underline the *three* words that are forms of the linking verb **be:**

    is   can   seems   are   was   will

313

---

adverb

532

The rain started suddenly.

Because the word **suddenly** modifies the verb **started,** it is an _____.

533

---

adverb

752

Think of an **adverb clause** as a "stretched-out" adverb of several words that modifies a verb, like any ordinary

_____.

753

Thinking the envelope was empty, I threw it away.

972

We sauntered down the street *and looked in the shop windows.*

_____

_____

973

F

1192

F, S, or *R–S?*

There were very few flies or mosquitoes, the swamp had been recently drained. ____

1193

take 1412	**I asked my brother to . . . in the newspaper.** If you are outside and want your brother "to *go* in with the paper," use _____. 1413
leads 1631	**The janitor or an older pupil** (*help, helps*) **the younger children cross the street.** 1632
an (hour) a (history) 1850	Write **a** or **an** in each blank: **Dad belongs to** _____ **union that has** _____ **unusual record.** 1851
Sweden 2069	Copy and capitalize the words that require capitals: **The park is on pine lake.** _____ 2070
b 2288	<u>The chairman</u> <u>rapped on the table</u>, and <u>the audience</u> <u>quieted down</u>. This is a **compound sentence** because there is a complete sentence both before and after the conjunction **and**. What punctuation mark comes after the first statement and before the conjunction? _____ 2289

Jones
 	
2507
	Now suppose that we want to write about the car of the whole family, the **Joneses.**
	
	      a. **Our dog was in the <u>Joneses'</u> car.**
	      b. **Our dog was in the <u>Jones's</u> car.**
	Which is correct because the apostrophe comes after the name of the whole family—*a* or *b*? ____
	
	2508

headlights <u>blinded</u> 93	Underline the simple subject with one line and the verb with two lines: **Two big salty tears streamed down the little boy's face.** 94
is, are, was 313	Underline the *three* words that are forms of the linking verb **be:** **were shall might am do been** 314
adverb 533	<u>Suddenly</u> the rain started. The rain <u>suddenly</u> started. The rain started <u>suddenly</u>. These sentences consist of the same words. However, one word occupies a different position in each sentence. This word is the adverb _____. 534
adverb 753	Now let's look at modifiers that answer the question **"Where?"** about the action of the verb. WHERE? **Connie works** *there.* WHERE? **Connie works** *on the third floor.* Both the adverb *there* and the adverb phrase *on the third floor* modify the verb _____. 754
We sauntered down the street, looking in the shop windows. 973	*The lady turned around* **and asked us not to talk.** _____ _____ (Be sure to put back the lost subject *lady*.) 974
R–S 1193	UNIT 6: **USING VERBS CORRECTLY** Lesson **39** **Overcoming the Dangerous Six** [Frames 1195–1236] *page 187*

take 1413	**I asked my brother to . . . in the newspaper.** If you are inside and want your brother "to *come* in with the paper," use _____. 1414
helps 1632	**Here** (*are, is*) **the names for the honor roll.** 1633
a (union) an (unusual) 1851	UNIT 9: **USING PRONOUNS CORRECTLY** Lesson **61** The Subject Form of Pronouns [Frames 1853–1891]
Pine Lake 2070	Copy and capitalize the words that require capitals: **Sibley park is on a lake.** _____ 2071
comma 2289	In a compound sentence, the comma is placed at the point where you would pause if you were speaking the sentence. Put a comma where you would naturally pause in saying this sentence: **We didn't want the picture but Mom couldn't refuse it.** 2290
a 2508	a. **Our dog was in the Joneses' car.** b. **Our dog was in the Jones's car.** Sentence *a* is correct because the car belongs not to the **Jones,** but to the _____. 2509

<u>tears</u> <u><u>streamed</u></u>	Underline the simple subject with one line and the verb with two lines: **The chairman of the committee resigned because of the criticism.**
94	95
were, am, been	If we can substitute **is, was,** or some other form of **be** for a verb, this verb (*is, is not*) used as a linking verb.
314	315
suddenly	Now let's return, for one frame, to **adjectives.** The <u>wet</u> pavement caused a <u>serious</u> accident. Can either adjective—**wet** or **serious**—be moved from its present position before the noun it modifies to any other position in the sentence? (*Yes, No*)
534	535
works	WHERE? **Connie works** *where* <u>*Mother*</u> *shops*. Because *where Mother shops* has a subject and a verb but does not form a complete sentence by itself, it is a (*phrase, clause*).
754	755
Turning around, the lady asked us not to talk.	**Dad went on a vacation** *and left me in charge of the shop.* _____ _____
974	975
	PRESENT: **I collect stamps.** PAST: **I collected stamps.** What letters do we add to change the verb **collect** from present to past time? _____
	1195

bring 1414	PRESENT SIMPLE PAST PAST WITH HELPER **bring** **brought** **have brought** **take** **took** **have taken** Both past forms of the verb _____ are alike. <div align="right">1415</div>
are 1633	**The hinges of the door** (*needs, need*) **oiling.** <div align="right">1634</div>
	Jerry wants Jerry's friends to go with Jerry. This sentence sounds very monotonous because of the repetition of the noun _____. <div align="right">1853</div>
Park 2071	**It is the largest island in the pacific ocean.** _____ <div align="right">2072</div>
picture, 2290	Without a comma to indicate the pause, the reader might get the wrong idea. In the sentence below, suppose the reader were to pause at the vertical line: **Earl painted the porch and his father | paid him for the job.** To prevent misreading, put a comma after _____. <div align="right">2291</div>
Joneses 2509	a. **Charle's story won a prize.** b. **Charles's story won a prize.** Which is correct because the apostrophe comes after the full name of the owner—*a* or *b*? ____ <div align="right">2510</div>

Lesson **4** Finding the Verb

[Frames 97–128]

---

a. **The <u>driver</u> <u>looked</u> angry.**
b. **The <u>driver</u> <u>looked</u> at his speedometer.**

is

In which sentence can we substitute **was** for **looked?**

The verb **looked** is used as a linking verb in sentence _____.

315

316

No

Adjectives can seldom be moved to another position in the sentence. **Adverbs,** on the contrary, can sometimes be shifted from one position to another.

Adverbs are (*more, less*) movable than **adjectives.**

535

536

---

clause

WHERE? **Connie works** *where Mother shops*.

Because the clause *where Mother shops* modifies the verb **works,** it is an (*adverb, adjective*) clause.

755

756

Dad went on a vacation, leaving me in charge of the shop.

We can form an adjective from any verb by adding the letters _____ to it.

975

976

–ed

The simple past form of most verbs ends in **–ed.**

The simple past form of the verb **collect** is **collected.**

The simple past form of the verb **jump** is _____.

1195

1196

bring 1415	Mother said, "You forgot to . . . your books to school this morning." (= *go* to school with) The movement of the books would be (*toward, away from*) the mother, who is speaking. 1416
need 1634	Any one of these boys (*know, knows*) where the office is. 1635

Jerry
 	
1853
	Once we make it clear that we are talking about **Jerry,** we can avoid repetition and save time by using *pronouns* in place of the noun **Jerry.**
	
	    a. <u>Jerry</u> wants <u>Jerry's</u> friends to go with <u>Jerry</u>.
	    b. <u>Jerry</u> wants <u>his</u> friends to go with <u>him</u>.
	
	In sentence *b*, **his** and **him** are (*nouns, pronouns*). 1854

Pacific Ocean 2072	There is not a single large city on this river. 2073
porch, 2291	Put a comma at the end of the first statement in a compound sentence—that is, just before the conjunction **and, but,** or **or.** Supply the necessary comma: The gate must be kept closed or the dog will run away. 2292
b 2510	In an earlier lesson, you learned that pronouns have special forms that show ownership **without** apostrophes. Don't put an apostrophe before the final **s** in any possessive pronoun. Underline the two possessive pronouns in this sentence: Yours are better than theirs. 2511

The verb is the most important word in the (*subject*, *predicate*).

97

---

a

The sky . . . cloudy.

Underline *two* of the following verbs that could be used as linking verbs in the above sentence to show that **cloudy** describes **sky.**

looked   believed   grew   lived

316

317

---

more

The new pitcher stepped confidently to the mound.

The adjective **new** cannot be moved, but the adverb _____ can be moved to another position.

536

537

---

adverb

Adverb clauses, just like adverbs, can also answer the question **"How?"** about the action of the verb.

HOW? **Tom ate** *greedily.*
HOW? **Tom ate** *as though* <u>*he*</u> <u>*were*</u> *starved.*

Both the adverb *greedily* and the adverb clause *as though he were starved* modify the verb _____.

756

757

–ing

An **–ing** word by itself (*can, cannot*) serve as a verb.

976

977

---

jumped

a. **I collected stamps.**
b. **I have collected stamps.**

The verbs in both of these sentences show past time. In *a*, the verb that shows past time consists of one word.

In *b*, the verb that shows past time consists of ____ word(s).

1196

1197

away from 1416	Mother said, "You forgot to (*bring, take*) your books to school this morning." The movement of the books would be **away from** the speaker. Therefore, the correct verb is _____. 1417
knows 1635	The speed and power of the boat (*were, was*) remarkable. 1636
pronouns 1854	**Pronouns** are words used in place of nouns. Pronouns can do the same work in a sentence that _____ do. 1855
None 2073	Chesapeake bay divides maryland into two parts. _____ 2074
closed, 2292	The comma makes a compound sentence easier to read. The reader can take it in two small bites instead of one big bite. a. **Urban areas are constantly growing in population and rural areas are diminishing.** b. **They won and we lost.** In which sentence would a comma be more helpful? _____ 2293

Yours, theirs
 	
2511
	POSSESSIVE PRONOUNS: **his, hers, yours**
	                          its (belonging to **it**), **ours, theirs**
	      Hers was parked behind Johns.
	The above sentence contains a possessive noun and a possessive pronoun. How many apostrophes are needed? _____
	
	2512

predicate 97	Most verbs are *action words*. Verbs like **break, swim, build,** and **write** represent actions that we see going on around us. **apple stumbled shirt** Which one of these words is an *action verb?* _____ 98
looked, grew 317	**Washington . . . our first President.** Underline *two* verbs that could be used as linking verbs to show that **President** identifies **Washington.** **chose was became has** 318
confidently 537	**A serious accident occurred there.** An adverb in this sentence tells **where** the accident occurred. This *adverb* is _____. 538
ate 757	Although single adverbs cannot answer the question **"Why?"** about verbs, **adverb clauses** can. WHY? **Bobby cried** *because he bumped his head.* In the clause *because he bumped his head,* the subject is *he,* and the verb is _____. 758
cannot 977	An **–ing** word is useful for forming word groups that are used as (*adjectives, adverbs*). 978
two 1197	a. **I collected stamps.** b. **I have collected stamps.** In *b,* the past form of the verb consists of two words: the main verb **collected** and the helping verb _____. 1198

take 1417	The teacher asked, "Why didn't you ... your books to school today?" (= *come* to school with) The movement of the books would be (*toward, away from*) the teacher, who is speaking. <div align="right">1418</div>
were 1636	(*Was, Were*) **the refreshments as good as usual?** <div align="right">1637</div>
nouns 1855	a. **Joe liked Sue.** b. **Sue liked Joe.** In sentence *a*, **Joe** is the subject, and **Sue** is the direct object. In sentence *b*, **Sue** is the subject, and **Joe** is the _____ _____. <div align="right">1856</div>
Bay, Maryland 2074	**The most densely populated country in europe is belgium.** _____ <div align="right">2075</div>
a 2293	**They won and we lost.** This sentence is so short and simple that it doesn't need a comma. The reader can take it comfortably in a single bite. A comma is not necessary and is usually omitted in a (*long, short*) compound sentence. <div align="right">2294</div>
one (John's) 2512	**Hers was parked behind John's.** Only one apostrophe is needed because an apostrophe should not be used in a possessive (*noun, pronoun*). <div align="right">2513</div>

stumbled 98	**painted grass teacher** Which one of these words is an *action verb*? _____ 99
was, became 318	A word that completes a linking verb and *describes* or *identifies* the subject is called a _____ _____. 319
there 538	**The children soon spent all their money.** An adverb in this sentence tells **when** about the verb **spent**. This *adverb* is _____. 539
bumped 758	An adverb clause can also tell **on what condition** an action will occur. ON WHAT CONDITION? **Jim will go** *if he can get a ticket.* The adverb clause *if he can get a ticket* explains **on what condition** Jim _____ _____. 759
adjectives 978	Lesson **32** **Using Appositives to Combine Ideas** [Frames 980–1012]
have 1198	**Joe has collected stamps for a long time.** In this sentence, the past form of the verb consists of two words: the main verb **collected** and the helping verb _____. 1199

toward 1418	The teacher asked, "Why didn't you (*bring, take*) your books to school today?" The movement of the books would be **toward** the speaker. Therefore, the correct verb is _____. 1419
Were 1637	**One of my front teeth** (*is, are*) **loose.** 1638
direct object 1856	a. Joe liked <u>Sue</u>. b. <u>Sue</u> liked <u>Joe</u>. Do the nouns **Joe** and **Sue** change in form or spelling when their use in the sentence changes? (*Yes, No*) 1857
Europe, Belgium 2075	**Our town is in cook county.** _____ 2076
short 2294	a. Hot air rises but cold air falls. b. You can lead a horse to water but you cannot make him drink. Which compound sentence does not require a comma? ____ 2295
pronoun 2513	In this and the following frames, insert the necessary apostrophes, remembering the various don'ts in this lesson. Several frames require no apostrophes. **This girls job is to check the ladies wraps.** 2514

painted	Some verbs like **decide, remember, think, hope,** and **understand** represent *actions of the mind*. These actions can't be seen by an outsider. **planted planned** Which verb represents an action of the mind? _____
99	100
subject complement	PATTERN 4: *Subject—Linking Verb ← Subject Complement* This is another common sentence pattern. The three other patterns we studied contained action verbs. The verb in this pattern is always a _____ verb.
319	320
soon	**Tommy reads well for his age.** The word _____ is an *adverb* because it tells **how** Tommy **reads.**
539	540
will go	Learn to recognize the **clause signals** that tell us that an adverb clause is beginning. They are grouped according to the kind of information that the clauses supply. WHEN? **while when whenever as** **before after since until** The clause signals (*begin, end*) adverb clauses.
759	760
	Suppose that someone should say to us— **"Archibald bit me."** We wouldn't know whether **Archibald** is a dog, a turtle, or a neighbor's child. To be clear, this sentence needs some words to explain *who* or *what* _____ is.
	980
has	**Joe had collected many stamps.** Here the main verb is **collected,** and the helping verb is _____.
1199	1200

bring 1419	→ **Take these flowers to Mrs. Smith, but** <u>bring</u> **back the vase.** ← Which verb shows a movement **away from** the speaker— **take** or **bring?** _____ . 1420
is 1638	(*Doesn't, Don't*) **this knob turn on the radio?** 1639
No 1857	Now let's change the nouns **Joe** and **Sue** to pronouns: a. **He liked her.** b. **She liked him.** Although these sentences concern only two persons, **Joe** and **Sue,** how many different pronouns are used? _____ 1858
Cook County 2076	**Denver is situated at the very foot of the rocky mountains.** _____ 2077
a 2295	Don't mistake a sentence with two (compound) *predicates* for a compound sentence. Their punctuation is different. a. _____ _____ , and _____ _____ . b. _____ _____ and _____ . One diagram represents a compound sentence. Which diagram represents a compound predicate? ____ 2296
girl's, ladies' 2514	Insert any necessary apostrophes: **Bobby complains about his headaches only on school days.** 2515

planned 100	In each line, underline *one* verb that represents an action of the mind: **regretted pushed departed** **crossed erased disliked** 101

linking
 	
320
	In this and the following frames, write in the missing words of the sentence framework. (S = Subject, V = Verb, SC = Subject Complement)
	
	The road through the woods is much shorter.
	
	       S V SC
	     road is _____ 321

well 540	**Dad never eats between meals.** The word _____ is an *adverb* because it modifies the verb **eats**. 541

begin
 	
760
	There are only two **clause signals** which can start adverb clauses that answer the question **"Where?"**
	
	WHERE? **where, wherever**
	    a. **The days get longer** *as the summer advances.*
	    b. **Gloria was sitting** *where we couldn't see her.*
	
	In which sentence does the clause tell **where?** ____ 761

Archibald 980	**"Archibald, *our cat,* bit me."** Now we know that **Archibald** is a *cat.* The noun *cat* comes (*before, after*) the noun **Archibald**, which it explains. 981

had
 	
1200
	Most verbs show past time in these two ways:
	
	    1. By the simple past form that ends in **–ed.**
	    2. By this same simple past form combined with the
	
	             _____*ing* verb **have, has,** or **had.**
	
	                                    1201

take 1420	← → **Dad brought home a visitor and took him to the airport after dinner.** Which verb shows a movement **toward** the speaker— **brought** or **took?** _____ <div align="right">1421</div>
Doesn't 1639	**Each of these girls** (*have, has*) **a part in the play.** <div align="right">1640</div>
four 1858	a. **He liked her.** b. **She liked him.** The two pronouns that refer to **Joe** are **He** and **him.** The two pronouns that refer to **Sue** are **She** and _____. <div align="right">1859</div>
Rocky Mountains 2077	Capitalize the words **street, avenue, road, boulevard,** etc., when they are parts of particular names. **Beacon Street Fifth Avenue Salem Road** Continue to copy the words that require capitals: **This avenue crosses jackson boulevard.** _____ 2078
b 2296	a. _____ _____ , and _____ _____ . b. _____ _____ and _____ . Diagram *b* represents a compound predicate since only a predicate—not a subject and a predicate—follows the **and.** Does a sentence with a compound predicate require a comma? (*Yes, No*) <div align="right">2297</div>
None 2515	Insert any necessary apostrophes: **Joyce made hers with only ten cents worth of materials.** <div align="right">2516</div>

regretted, disliked 101	Verbs are the only words that can show by a change in spelling whether they mean *present* or *past* time; for example, **shout—shouted, play—played, take—took, give—gave.** <div align="center">**washes washed**</div> Which verb means *past* time? _____ <div align="right">102</div>
SC shorter 321	<div align="center">**Mr. White became a partner in the business.**</div> S V SC _____ became _____ <div align="right">322</div>
never 541	<div align="center">**Dad does not eat between meals.**</div> The word _____ is an *adverb* because it modifies the verb **does eat,** which it interrupts, as adverbs often do. <div align="right">542</div>

b
 	
761
	Several clause signals can start adverb clauses that answer the question **"Why?"**
	
	WHY? **because, since, as, so that**
	     a. **The bag tore** *when I picked it up.*
	     b. **The bag tore** *because it was wet.*
	
	Which sentence explains **why** the bag tore? ____
	
	<div align="right">762</div>

after 981	<div align="center">**"Archibald,** *our cat,* **bit me."**</div> A noun or pronoun that is set *after* another noun or pronoun to explain it is called an **appositive.** In the above sentence, the noun _____ is an **appositive.** <div align="right">982</div>

help(ing)
 	
1201
	With most verbs, we use the same form with **have, has,** or **had** that we use for the simple past.
	
	   SIMPLE PAST PAST WITH HELPER
	      look<u>ed</u> have look<u>ed</u>
	      walk<u>ed</u> have walk<u>ed</u>
	      play<u>ed</u> have _____
	
	<div align="right">1202</div>

brought 1421	In this and the following frames, underline the correct verb in each pair. Remember always to choose **take** when the movement is **away from** the speaker. **Why don't you** (*bring, take*) **this souvenir home to your children?** (= *go* home with this souvenir) 1422
has 1640	**Either Harry or his brother** (*has, have*) **a pocket radio.** 1641
her 1859	a. **He liked Sue.** b. **Sue liked him.** When the pronoun takes the place of the subject **Joe,** we use **He.** When the pronoun takes the place of the direct object **Joe,** we use _____. 1860
Jackson Boulevard 2078	**We live three streets beyond miller road.** _____ 2079
No 2297	a. <u>I put the cake into the oven</u>, and <u>I forgot it completely.</u> b. <u>I put the cake into the oven</u> and <u>forgot it completely.</u> Which sentence requires a comma because it is a compound sentence with both a subject and a predicate after the conjunction **and?** ____ 2298
cents' 2516	**All the pupils parents met in the schools auditorium.** 2517

washed

102

---

writes   wrote

Which verb means *present* time? _____

103

S
Mr. White

SC
partner

322

The book was a great success on the screen.

S   V   SC

_____ was _____

323

---

not

542

The river often overflows in the spring.

The adverb in this sentence is _____.

543

---

b

762

Ellen's parents bought her a typewriter . . . *she would learn to type.*

Underline the clause signal you would add to explain **why** Ellen's parents bought the typewriter.

while   as if   so that   although

763

---

cat

982

The word **appositive** has four syllables.

ap-pos-i-tive

You will spell it correctly if you will write the letters **ap** in front of the word _____.

983

---

played

1202

SIMPLE PAST   PAST WITH HELPER
    earn<u>ed</u>   have earn<u>ed</u>
    paint<u>ed</u>   have paint<u>ed</u>
    chang<u>ed</u>   have chang<u>ed</u>

The form of the verb used with the helper and the form used without the helper are (*different, alike*).

1203

take 1422	**Dad often** (*brought, took*) **us foreign stamps from the office.** (= *came* home with foreign stamps) 1423
has 1641	**There** (*was, were*) **no zeroes in the Roman numbering system.** 1642
him 1860	a. **She liked Joe.** b. **Joe liked her.** When the pronoun takes the place of the subject **Sue,** we use **She.** When the pronoun takes the place of the direct object **Sue,** we use _____. 1861
Miller Road 2079	**Woodward avenue is our main business street.** _____ 2080
a 2298	**I put the cake into the oven, and <u>I</u> forgot it completely.** If we omitted the underlined **I** from this sentence, would we still keep the comma? (*Yes, No*) 2299
pupils', school's 2517	**Theirs always runs and barks after passing cars.** 2518

writes 103	What is the *past* form of the verb **walks?** _____ 104
S SC book success 323	**My friend seemed very unhappy about something.** S V SC friend _____ _____ 324
often 543	**Adverbs** are a class of words that can tell **when, where, how much,** and **how often** about _____ . 544

so that
 	
763
	There are only two clause signals which can start adverb clauses that answer the question **"How?"**
	HOW? **as if, as though**
	    a. **Bobby cried** *when his toy balloon broke.*
	    b. **Bobby cried** *as if his heart would break.*
	Which sentence tells **how** Bobby cried? ____
	764

positive 983	**Jerry,** *my locker partner,* **lost his key.** The appositive is the noun _____. 984

alike
 	
1203
	When we use the same **–ed** form of a verb with **have, has,** or **had** that we use for the simple past, the verb is said to be **regular.**
	    a. **We talked to the principal.**
	    b. **We have talked to the principal.**
	The verb **talk** is a(n) *(regular, irregular)* verb.
	1204

brought 1423	Whenever I went to the hospital, I (*brought, took*) **candy along for Donnie.** (= *went* with candy) 1424
were 1642	Neither of these coats (*seem, seems*) warm enough for winter. 1643
her 1861	a. He liked her. b. She liked him. Do the pronouns change when their use in the sentence changes? (*Yes, No*) 1862
Avenue 2080	Capitalize the names of particular nationalities, languages, races, and religions. Italian Negro Chinese Catholic American Indian Jewish Protestant Supply the missing letter: A citizen of Canada is called a ____anadian. 2081
No 2299	Paul drove to the side of the road and ‸ let the other car pass. If we added **he** at the point indicated, would we need to insert a comma after the word **road**? (*Yes, No*) 2300
None 2518	The boys gym holds more people than our girls study hall. 2519

walked

104

What is the *present* form of the verb **took?** _____

105

V   SC
seemed unhappy

324

A good driver is always ready for emergencies.

S   V   SC

_____ _____ ready

325

---

verbs

544

Lesson **19** A Special Kind of Adverb

[Frames 546–579]

---

b

764

The dog was limping . . . *it had been hurt.*

Underline the clause signal you would add to explain **how** the dog was limping.

unless   as though   since   although

765

---

partner

984

Jerry, *my locker partner,* **lost his key.**

The noun *partner* is an appositive because it is set *after*

another noun, _____, to explain it.

985

---

regular

1204

Most verbs, fortunately, are regular. However, there are a number of verbs that do not follow the usual pattern.

PRESENT: **I see Donna every day.**
PAST: **I saw Donna every day.**

The past form of **see** does not end in _____, as all regular verbs do.

1205

took 1424	The milkman (*brought, took*) us our milk too late for break-fast. 1425
seems 1643	The air and the water (*were, was*) perfect for swimming. 1644
Yes 1862	a. **I** **he** **she** **we** **they** b. **me** **him** **her** **us** **them** **. . . drove the car.** Which pronouns could be used as the subject of the little sentence above—those in group *a* or *b*? ____ 1863
C (capital) 2081	A citizen of Japan speaks ____apanese. 2082
Yes 2300	a. **We must raise the price of our paper, or we shall have to reduce its size.** b. **We must raise the price of our paper, or reduce its size.** From which sentence should the comma be omitted? ____ 2301
boys', girls' 2519	**Childrens haircuts cost less than mens.** 2520

take *or* takes
 	
105
	When you change a sentence from *present* to *past* or from *past* to *present*, only one word changes—the verb.
	
	      PRESENT: **The girls wash the dishes.**
	      PAST: **The girls washed the dishes.**
	
	The word **wash** is a verb because it is the only word that
	
	_____ . 106

S V driver is 325	**They were the only Italians in this little town.** S V SC They _____ _____ 326
	We have studied two classes of words that modify other words: (1) **adjectives** and (2) **adverbs**. **Adjectives** modify _____ and **pronouns**. 546
as though 765	Four signal words can start adverb clauses that answer the question **"On what condition?"** ON WHAT CONDITION? **if, unless, though, although** **Jerry will play** *if he can be the pitcher.* This clause explains **on what condition** Jerry _____ _____ . 766
Jerry 985	Although an appositive is usually a single noun or pronoun, we generally add other words to modify it. a. **Jerry,** *my locker* <u>partner</u>**, lost his key.** b. **Jerry,** *my careless locker* <u>partner</u> *with the red hair*, **lost his key.** Does the appositive have more modifiers in *a* or *b*? ____ 986

–ed
 	
1205
	Underline one of the following verbs whose past form does not end in **–ed:**
	
	      follow **bring** **cook**
	
	           1206

brought 1425	Henry must have (*brought, taken*) his blue suit to the cleaner. 1426
were 1644	One of us (*have, has*) to stay home with the baby. 1645
a 1863	her he him Which pronoun can be used as the subject of a sentence and is, therefore, in the subject form? _____ 1864
J (capital) 2082	The Pope is the spiritual leader of the ____atholics. 2083
b 2301	a. This is a powerful engine but runs very quietly. b. This is a powerful engine but it runs very quietly. In which sentence should a comma be inserted after en-gine? ____ 2302
Children's, men's 2520	I got twenty-five cents worth of cookies for only ten cents. 2521

changes *or changed* 106	PRESENT: **I often see my uncle.** PAST: **I often saw my uncle.** The word _____ is a verb because it is the only word that changes. 107
V SC were Italians 326	**The tires on the car looked quite new.** S V SC _____ looked _____ 327
nouns 546	The **adverbs** that we studied in the previous lesson modified only _____. 547
will play 766	a. **This chair will collapse** *if you sit on it.* b. **This chair will collapse** *because it is broken.* Which sentence explains **on what condition** the chair will collapse? ____ 767
b 986	**Mr. Davis,** *our new coach,* **is very strict.** The noun *coach* comes after the noun **Mr. Davis** and explains it. The noun **coach,** therefore, is an _____. 987
bring 1206	Verbs like **bring, see,** and **go** whose past forms do not end in **–ed** are called **irregular verbs.** **I saw Donna every day.** **See** is an **irregular** verb because its past form, **saw,** does not end in _____. 1207

taken 1426	We (*brought, took*) our dog to the vet last week. 1427
has 1645	Only two customers (*were, was*) in the store at the time. 1646
he 1864	**they us me I them her** Which two pronouns are in the subject form? _____ and _____ 1865
C (capital) 2083	Marian Anderson is a great ____egro singer. 2084
b 2302	This sentence has two **and**'s. Only one of them, however, is used to connect the two parts of this compound sentence. **Larry has worked after school <u>and</u> on Saturdays <u>and</u> he has saved up nearly $500.** A comma is needed before the (*first, second*) **and**. 2303
cents' worth 2521	This post shows where theirs leaves off and ours begins. 2522

see *or* saw 107	Now let's change a sentence from *past* to *present* time and see which word changes. 　　　　PAST:　　**This job took too much time.** 　　PRESENT: **This job takes too much time.** The word _____ is a verb because it is the only word that changes. 108
S　　SC tires　new 327	**A warm sweater feels cozy on a chilly day.** 　　S　　　　　　　　V　　　　　　　SC _____　_____　_____ 328
verbs 547	Both **adjectives** and **adverbs** modify or change the pictures or ideas we get from words by making their meaning (*more, less*) clear and exact. 548
a 767	**We placed the notice** *so that everyone would see it.* The clause signal consists of two words: _____　_____. 768
appositive 987	**Mr. Davis,** *our new coach,* **is very strict.** **Mr. Davis** is the *coach,* and the *coach* is **Mr. Davis.** An appositive and the noun it explains are always the _____ person, place, or thing. 988
–ed 1207	a. **I saw Donna every day.** 　　b. **I have seen Donna every day.** Compare the past form of the verb **see** in *a* with the form used in *b*. The simple past form and the form used with the helper **have** are (*alike, different*). 1208

took 1427	We (*brought*, *took*) our dog home from the vet's today. 1428
were 1646	UNIT 8: **CHOOSING THE RIGHT MODIFIER** Lesson **54** **Words That Describe Actions** [Frames 1648–1682]
they, I 1865	a. **You like it.** b. **It likes you.** Do the pronouns **you** and **it** change in form when their use in the sentence changes? (*Yes, No*) 1866
N (capital) 2084	Adjectives that are formed from proper nouns should also be capitalized. **French bread Russian dressing Asiatic flu** **Julius Caesar was a ____oman general.** 2085
second 2303	The three conjunctions that can connect the two parts of a compound sentence are _____, _____, _____. 2304
None 2522	**Paul did a weeks work in three days time.** 2523

took *or* takes 108	The temperature usually dropped in the evening. Which word would change if you changed this sentence from *past* to *present?* _____ 109

S   V
sweater feels
     SC
     cozy
 	
328
	Lesson **12** **Recognizing Basic Sentence Patterns**
	[Frames 330–363]

more 548	The weather is <u>cold</u>. The weather is <u>very cold</u>. In both sentences, the adjective **cold** modifies the noun _____. 549
so that 768	The fire wouldn't start because our wood was wet. The adverb clause starts with the clause signal _____ and ends with the word _____. 769
same 988	An appositive with its modifiers should be set off from the rest of the sentence by commas. The commas are missing below. **Mr. Davis** *our new coach* **is very strict.** One comma is needed after **Mr. Davis,** and another after _____. 989
different 1208	Most irregular verbs have two different past forms: one for the simple past and one to be used with **have, has,** or **had.** Underline one of the following verbs that is irregular because it has two different past forms: **escape return take** 1209

brought 1428	Would you please (*bring, take*) this report to Mr. Brown. 1429
	There are hundreds of words that have two forms: an adjective form without **–ly** and an adverb form with **–ly**. a. **bad** **lazy** **polite** **careful** **foolish** b. **badly** **lazily** **politely** **carefully** **foolishly** Which group of words consists of adverbs? ____ 1648
No 1866	**she you we I it they** Which two pronouns could be used as either a subject or an object without changing their form? _____ and _____ 1867
R (capital) 2085	The styles from Paris are called ____arisian styles. 2086
and, but, or 2304	In this and the following frames, supply the necessary commas. Several sentences do not require commas because they are not compound. **We talked to the animal trainer and we asked him many questions.** 2305
week's, days' 2523	**Mothers parakeet was not in its cage.** 2524

dropped

All my friends go to church.

Which word would change if you changed this sentence from *present* to *past?* _____

109   110

We have now studied *four* basic sentence patterns.

PATTERN I: *Subject—Action Verb*

EXAMPLES: **His grades improved.**

             The lake freezes in the winter.

The verbs in these sentences make (*complete, incomplete*) statements about their subjects.

330

---

weather

a. **The weather is cold.**
b. **The weather is very cold.**

Which sentence gives you the idea of greater coldness? _____

549   550

---

because,
wet

Ralph jumped from the bus before it came to a stop.

The adverb clause starts with the clause signal _____

and ends with the word _____.

769   770

---

coach

Mr. Davis *our new football* underline{coach} *from Evanston* **is very strict.**

One comma is needed after **Mr. Davis,** and another after

_____.

989   990

---

take

PRESENT	SIMPLE PAST	PAST WITH HELPER
see	**saw**	**have seen**

We ∧ *saw* **several porpoises.**

If you added the helping verb *have* at the point marked by the caret, you would need to change the verb *saw* to _____.

1209   1210

take	**The salesman urged us to** (*bring, take*) **the set home for a free trial.**
1429	1430
b	To modify a noun or a pronoun, we use an (*adjective, adverb*).
1648	1649
you, it	When a single pronoun is the subject of a sentence, it is almost impossible to make a mistake. Only a small child would say, "*Us* want a drink" or "*Her* took a cookie." (*Her, She*) **saw the accident.** Which is the correct pronoun? ____
1867	1868
P (capital)	**Tom-toms are a kind of ____frican drum.**
2086	2087
trainer,	Insert any necessary commas: **The product must be advertised or the public will never ask for it.**
2305	2306
Mother's	**After Phil borrowed yours, he borrowed Elmers.**
2524	2525

go

The milk in our refrigerator sometimes freezes.

The verb in this sentence is _____.

110   111

---

complete

a. **The other <u>team</u> always <u>wins</u>.**
b. **The other <u>team</u> always <u>wins</u> the game.**

In which sentence does the verb complete the meaning of the sentence without requiring an additional word? _____

330   331

---

b

a. **The weather is cold.**
b. **The weather is very cold.**

The added word which gives you the idea of greater coldness in sentence *b* is _____.

550   551

---

before,
stop

Don't drink the water unless it has been boiled.

The adverb clause starts with the clause signal _____
and ends with the word _____.

770   771

Evanston

Yosemite, *the famous national park,* **is in California.**
We spent a week at Yosemite, *the famous national park.*

An appositive word group that comes in the middle of a sentence requires two commas.

How many commas does an appositive word group require when it comes at the end of a sentence? _____

990   991

---

seen

PRESENT   SIMPLE PAST   PAST WITH HELPER
  take   **took**   **have taken**

The simple past form of this verb is **took.**

The form that must be used with **have, has,** or **had** is (*took, taken*).

1210   1211

take 1430	The librarian said, "You should have (*brought, taken*) this book back yesterday." 1431
adjective 1649	To describe the action of a verb, we use an (*adjective, adverb*). 1650

She
 	
1868
	When a sentence has a compound subject—either two pronouns or a noun and a pronoun—mistakes sometimes occur.
	    a. **She saw the accident.**
	    b. **Ken and (*her, she*) saw the accident.**
	
	In sentence *b*, which pronoun is correct? _____
	1869

A (capital) 2087	Lesson **68** **Using Capitals for Organizations and Institutions** [Frames 2089–2123]
advertised, 2306	Insert any necessary commas: **The sailor looked out over the water and pointed to a small speck in the distance.** 2307
Elmer's 2525	Copy the correct words in this sentence: (*Charles's, Charle's*) **dog was in the** (*Jones's, Joneses'*) **yard.** _____ 2526

freezes 111	**An empty bottle rolled down the basement stairs.** The verb in this sentence is _____. 112
a 331	PATTERN 2: *Subject—Action Verb → Direct Object* EXAMPLES: **Jim changed the tire.** **The baby swallowed the button.** In these sentences, the action passes from the *subjects* to the *direct* _____, as the arrows show. 332
very 551	**The weather is very cold.** The word **very** modifies the adjective _____. 552
unless, boiled 771	**Mr. Curtis treated Roy as though he were his own son.** The adverb clause starts with the two-word clause signal _____ _____ and ends with the word _____. 772
One 991	**Andy,** *the best hitter on our team,* **sprained his wrist.** **Andy** **sprained his wrist.** If we omit the appositive word group from this sentence, do we have a complete sentence remaining? (*Yes, No*) 992

taken
 	
1211
	Irregular verbs cause many errors because people some-times confuse the two past forms.
	
	PRESENT SIMPLE PAST PAST WITH HELPER
	   do **did** **have done**
	Which past form is required in the following sentence?
	    I should have _____ better on the test.
	
	1212

brought 1431	Walter should have (*brought, taken*) his problem to the principal. 1432
adverb 1650	**Pete's report was accurate.** **Accurate** modifies the noun **report.** It is, therefore, an _____. 1651
she 1869	**Ken and she saw the accident.** The subject form **she** is correct because **she,** as well as **Ken,** is the subject of the verb _____. 1870
	A noun that names a *particular* person, place, or thing is a (*common, proper*) noun. 2089
None 2307	**The coat was a bargain but I had spent all my money.** 2308
Charles's, Joneses' 2526	Copy the correct words in this sentence: (*Mrs. Jone's, Mrs. Jones's*) **cakes are better than** (*hers, her's*). _____ _____ 2527

rolled 112	When looking for the *subject* and *verb* in a sentence, always find the *verb* first. Look for the verb (*before, after*) you find the subject. 113
objects 332	PATTERN 3: *Subject—Action Verb→Indirect Object—Direct Object* EXAMPLES: **The company sent us a sample.** (to us) 　　　　　　**Dad built us a workshop.** (for us) Before the *direct object* we find an _____ *object.*　　　　　　　　　　　　　　　　　333
cold 552	**very cold**　　　**so cold**　　　**rather cold** **extremely cold**　**quite cold**　**slightly cold** **terribly cold**　　**too cold**　　**somewhat cold** All the underlined words give a more exact idea of *how* **cold** something is. We say, therefore, that these words *mod*_____ the adjective **cold.**　　　553
as though, son 772	To be a clause, a word group must have both a _____ and a **verb.** 773
Yes 992	a. **Andy the best hitter on our team made a home run.** b. **A home run was made by Andy the best player on our team.** Which sentence requires only one comma because the appositive word group comes at the end of the sentence— *a* or *b*? ____　　　　　　　　　　　　　　　993
done 1212	PRESENT　　　SIMPLE PAST　　PAST WITH HELPER 　**do**　　　　　　**did**　　　　　　**have done** Which past form is required in the following sentence? 　　**George** _____ **the problem twice.** 1213

---

adjective

1651

Pete reported the game accurately.

Accurately describes *how* Pete **reported** the game.

Because **accurately** modifies the verb **reported,** it is an

_____.

1652

---

saw

1870

When two pronouns (or a noun and a pronoun) are used as subjects, choose the same form of each pronoun that you would choose if the pronoun were used alone.

a. **He missed the bus. I missed the bus.**
b. **He and (***I, me***) missed the bus.**

In sentence *b,* which pronoun is correct? ____

1871

---

proper

2089

Every proper noun and adjective should begin with a (*capital, small*) letter.

2090

---

bargain,

2308

Columbus had expected to make a fortune but died a pauper.

2309

Mrs. Jones's,
hers

2527

Lesson **81** Pronouns and Contractions
—Avoiding Confusion

[Frames 2529–2567]

before 113	After you find the verb, find the subject in this way: If, for example, the verb is **ran,** ask yourself, "Who or what **ran?**" The answer to this question always tells you the subject. **The plane from Nashville arrives at six.** What **arrives?** The _____ arrives. 114
indirect 333	a. **They <u>gave</u> the winner a car.** b. **They <u>gave</u> a car to the winner.** Which sentence contains an indirect object? ____ 334
(mod)ify 553	**The car was going <u>fast</u>.** **The car was going extremely <u>fast</u>.** In both sentences, the adverb **fast** modifies the _____ **was going.** 554
subject 773	a. **We postponed the picnic** *because of bad weather.* b. **We postponed the picnic** *because the weather was bad.* Although both italicized word groups begin with *because,* only one has a subject and a verb. Which sentence contains an adverb clause? ____ 774
b 993	**St. Augustine the oldest city in the United States is in Florida.** (Commas are missing.) This sentence contains an appositive word group. One comma is needed after **St. Augustine,** and another after the word _____. 994
did 1213	a. **Dad done all the painting himself.** b. **Dad did all the painting himself.** Which sentence is wrong because the helper form of the verb is used without a helper? ____ 1214

PRESENT   SIMPLE PAST   PAST WITH HELPER
call   called   have called
take   took   have taken

Which verb is irregular—**call** or **take**? _____

1434

---

adverb

Pete reported the game (*accurate, accurately*).

To describe *how* Pete **reported,** we should choose the adverb _____.

1652   1653

I

You would never say, "*Him* missed the bus" or "*Me* missed the bus"; so don't make the same mistake by saying, "*Him* and *me* missed the bus."

(*He, Him*) **and I share the same locker.**

1871   1872

---

capital

Capitalize the names of companies, organizations, buildings, hotels, theaters, etc.

Logan Drug Company   Red Cross   Bayview Hotel
Union Bank Building   Curtis Garage   Hollywood Theater

Write the capital letters you would need to use in writing **empire state building.** _____

2090   2091

None

The weather was cold and rainy or we would have walked to the library.

2309   2310

Apostrophes are also used to show where letters have been omitted from words.

EXAMPLE: **We've** (= *We have*) **won the game.**

The apostrophe in **We've** takes the place of the missing letters _____.

2529

plane 114	**The plane from Nashville arrives at six.** The subject of the verb **arrives** is _____. 115
a 334	PATTERN 4: *Subject—Linking Verb ← Subject* *Complement* EXAMPLES: **The apples are ripe.** (describes subject) **Tom became an officer.** (identifies subject) In these sentences, the subject complements *describe* or *identify* the _____, as the arrows show. 335
verb 554	a. **The car was going fast.** b. **The car was going extremely fast.** Sentence *b* gives an idea of greater speed than sentence *a*. The added word which gives the idea of greater speed in sentence *b* is _____. 555
b 774	Unlike a sentence, a clause (*does, does not*) form a com- plete sentence by itself. 775
States 994	Learn the difference between an **appositive word group** and an **adjective clause.** An adjective clause has both a subject and a verb. An appositive is just a _____, often with modifiers. 995
a 1214	a. **Dad did all the painting himself.** b. **Dad has did all the painting himself.** Which sentence is wrong because the simple past form of the verb, instead of the helper form, is used with the helper **has?** ____ 1215

take 1434	**Walter wrote a letter of apology.** If you added *should have* to the verb, you would need to change **wrote** to _____. 1435
accurately 1653	**Ellen's voice is very pleasant.** **Pleasant** is an adjective because it modifies the noun _____. 1654
He 1872	<u>They</u> are at the top of the league. <u>We</u> are at the top of the league. Underline the correct pronouns: (*They, Them*) **and** (*we, us*) **are at the top of the league.** 1873
E S B 2091	a. **a fence company** b. **the Master Fence Company** Which item could mean *any* fence company at all? ____ 2092
rainy, 2310	**He went his way and I went mine.** 2311
ha 2529	**I'll** (= *I will*) **tell you a secret.** In this sentence, the apostrophe takes the place of the two letters _____. 2530

plane 115	**The man at the desk refused.** Who **refused?** The answer to this question is not **desk** but _____. 116
subjects 335	It is easy to see the difference between a direct object and a subject complement. A direct object can follow only an *action verb,* but a subject complement always follows a _____ *verb.* 336
extremely 555	**The car was going <u>extremely</u> fast.** The word **extremely** modifies the adverb _____. 556
does not 775	An adverb clause does the work of a single (*adjective, adverb*). 776
noun 995	a. **Tom,** *our talented pianist,* **got us a radio engagement.** b. **Tom,** *who <u>is</u> our talented pianist,* **got us a radio engagement.** One sentence contains an adjective clause and the other an appositive. Which sentence contains the appositive? ____ 996
b 1215	PRESENT SIMPLE PAST PAST WITH HELPER **give** **gave** **have given** Which past form of the verb is required in the following sentence? **The coach has _____ Earl another chance.** 1216

written 1435	The verb in one of the following sentences is wrong: a. **I saw Don yesterday.** c. **The mail come late today.** b. **Their dog ran away.** d. **The painter did a good job.** The incorrect verb is in sentence ____. 1436
voice 1654	**Ellen speaks very pleasantly over the phone.** **Pleasantly** describes *how* Ellen **speaks.** Because **pleasantly** modifies the verb **speaks,** it is an _____. 1655
They, we 1873	Be just as careful to choose the correct pronoun when the pronoun is paired with a noun. Use the same pronoun that you would choose if the pronoun were used alone. **Rita and** (*her, she*) **reported on the same book.** 1874
a 2092	a. **a fence company** b. **the Master Fence Company** Which item names a particular company? ____ 2093
None 2311	**We had no use for the old picture but Mother couldn't re-fuse it.** 2312
wi 2530	**They're going to New York.** The apostrophe takes the place of the letter ____. 2531

man 116	**The man at the desk refused.** The subject of the verb **refused** is _____. 117

linking
 	
336
	If a verb is a linking verb, we can always put **is, was,** or some other form of **be** in its place.
	
	      The teacher *corrected* **the papers.**
	      The teacher *seemed* **happy.**
	
	For which verb can we substitute **was**—*corrected* or *seemed?* _____
	
	337

fast 556	very fast so fast rather fast extremely fast quite fast slightly fast terribly fast too fast somewhat fast All the underlined words increase or decrease the "power" of the adverb _____. 557
adverb 776	The first word of an adverb clause is generally the (*clause signal, subject*). 777
a 996	a. **Rayon, which is an artificial silk, is made from wood.** b. **Rayon, an artificial silk, is made from wood.** Which sentence contains an appositive? ____ 997

given
 	
1216
	PRESENT SIMPLE PAST PAST WITH HELPER
	  give gave have given
	
	    The coach has given Earl another chance.
	
	The helper form **given** is correct because it is used after the helping verb _____.
	
	1217

c 1436	**Our landlord had given us notice.** If you omitted the helper **had,** you would need to change **given** to _____. 1437
adverb 1655	**Ellen speaks very** (*pleasant, pleasantly*) **over the phone.** To describe *how* Ellen **speaks,** we need to use the adverb _____. 1656
she 1874	**Rita and she reported on the same book.** This sentence is correct because if we used each subject separately, we would say: **Rita reported on the same book.** (*Her, She*) **reported on the same book.** 1875
b 2093	a. **The Keystone lumber company owns the property.** b. **A lumber company owns the property.** In which sentence should the words **lumber company** be capitalized because they are part of a particular company's name? ____ 2094
picture, 2312	**You must be completely satisfied or your money will be cheerfully refunded.** 2313
a 2531	*To contract* means *to shorten*. The shortening of words by omitting letters is called **contraction.** The word **doesn't** is a contraction of _____ _____. 2532

man

117

The keys to our car disappeared last night.

The subject of the verb **disappeared** is _____.

118

---

seemed

337

The teacher *corrected* the papers.
The teacher *seemed* (*was*) **happy.**

Because we can put *was* in its place, *seemed* is a _____ verb.

338

---

fast

557

---

very fast   **so** fast   **rather** fast
extremely fast   **quite** fast   **slightly** fast
terribly fast   **too** fast   **somewhat** fast

All the underlined words give a more exact idea of the adverb **fast.** We say, therefore, that these words _____ the adverb **fast.**

558

---

clause signal

777

Lesson **26**   **How to Make Adverb Clauses**

[Frames 779–813]

---

b

997

When one sentence explains something mentioned in the previous sentence, we can sometimes use an appositive to combine the two sentences.

I felt sorry for Dick. He was the only boy in the class.

The second sentence explains something about _____ in the first sentence.

998

---

has

1217

PRESENT	SIMPLE PAST	PAST WITH HELPER
go	went	have gone

Which past form of the verb is required?

The Johnsons had _____ to their cottage.

1218

---

gave 1437	The "past with helper" form of many irregular verbs ends with **–en** or **–n**. This form should be used after all forms of **be** and _____. 1438
pleasantly 1656	a. **Your solution of this problem was . . . .** b. **You solved this problem . . . .** The adverb **differently** should be used in sentence ____. 1657
She 1875	(*They, Them*) **were on the same plane.** **The Seeleys and** (*they, them*) **were on the same plane.** Would you choose the same pronoun in both the above sentences? (*Yes, No*) 1876
a 2094	a. **Paul works at a garage.** b. **Paul works at the Fuller garage.** In which sentence should **garage** be capitalized because it is part of the name of a particular business? ____ 2095
satisfied, 2313	**I had heard about the Dodgers and the White Sox and wanted to see them play.** (Look at this sentence carefully before you make your decision.) 2314
does not 2532	The use of the apostrophe to take the place of missing letters has nothing to do with ownership. a. **We'll call for you at seven.** b. **You can use anyone's ticket.** Is the apostrophe used for a contraction in sentence *a* or *b*? ____ 2533

keys 118	In this and the following frames, find the verb first and underline it with two lines. Then find the subject and underline it with one line. **The lock on our back door often sticks.** 119
linking 338	**The <u>teacher</u> <u><u>seemed</u></u> (was) happy.** **Seemed** is a *linking verb*. Therefore the word **happy,** which follows it and completes the meaning of the sentence, is a (*direct object, subject complement*). 339

modify
 	
558
	MODIFY ADJECTIVES MODIFY ADVERBS
	  <u>very</u> sudden **<u>very</u> suddenly**
	  <u>quite</u> steady **<u>quite</u> steadily**
	  <u>more</u> convenient **<u>more</u> conveniently**
	
	The same special words that modify adjectives can also modify _____.
	
	559

	In one way, a **clause** is like a sentence because it has both a _____ and a verb. 779
Dick 998	**I felt sorry for Dick. (He was)** *the only <u>boy</u> in the class.* By omitting the words **He was,** we change the second sentence into an appositive phrase. **I felt sorry for Dick,** *the only <u>boy</u> in the class.* The noun *boy* has now become an _____. 999
gone 1218	**The Johnsons had gone to their cottage.** If you omitted the helper **had,** what word would you need to put in place of **gone?** _____ 1219

have 1438	a. **break** c. **sell** e. **fly** b. **drive** d. **fall** f. **cry** Two of the above verbs do not have an **–en** or **–n** form. They are _____ and _____. 1439
b 1657	a. **prompt** skillful careless courteous b. **promptly** skillfully carelessly courteously Which group of words would you use to describe how an action was performed? _____ 1658
Yes 1876	In this and the following frames, select the correct pro- nouns. Always choose the same form of the pronoun that you would use if the pronoun were used by itself. **My dad and** (*I, me*) **are building a sailboat.** 1877
b 2095	a. **The bank was closed.** b. **The Wabash bank was closed.** In which sentence should **bank** be capitalized? _____ 2096
None 2314	**Ross must make up this test or lose credit for the entire course.** 2315
a 2533	In contractions, the apostrophe always goes in where the letters come out. **it i̸s = it's** **we wi̸ll = we'll** **I ha̸ve = I've** **who i̸s = who's** **you a̸re = you're** **I wou̸l̸d = I'd** The contraction of **they are** would be _____. 2534

<u>lock</u> <u>sticks</u> 119	First find and underline the verb; then find and underline the subject: **The huge trailer swayed along behind the car.** 120
subject complement 339	**The <u>teacher</u> <u>seemed</u> (was) happy.** **The <u>teacher</u> <u>corrected</u> the papers.** **Seemed is a** *linking verb*, but **corrected** is an _____ *verb*. 340
adverbs 559	We have been working with special words that control the "power" of other modifiers. These words are **adverbs**. These special adverbs can modify both _____ and other _____. 560
subject 779	In another way, a clause is **not** like a sentence because it (*does, does not*) form a complete sentence by itself. 780

appositive
 	
999
	In combining sentences, put the appositive word group next to the noun it explains.
	
	    a. **Dick was absent,** *the only boy in the class.*
	    b. **Dick,** *the only boy in the class,* **was absent.**
	
	Which sentence is correct because the appositive word group comes right after the noun it explains? _____
	
	1000

went 1219	PRESENT SIMPLE PAST PAST WITH HELPER **come** **came** **have come** The simple past form of **come** is not **come** but _____. 1220

c, f
 	
1439
	The verb in one of the following sentences is wrong:
	
	    a. **Dave give me his ticket.**
	    b. **The gale had broken many windows.**
	    c. **The driver was thrown through the windshield.**
	
	The incorrect verb is in sentence _____.
	
	1440

b 1658	In the case of a few words, the adjective form without **–ly** can also serve as an adverb. Here are several examples: **Drive slow** or **slowly.** **He works steady** or **steadily.** **Don't talk so loud** or **loudly.** **He plays fair** or **fairly.** The words **slow, loud, fair,** and **steady** are both adjectives and adverbs. (*True, False*) 1659
I 1877	**The Potters and** (*us, we*) **shop at the same market.** 1878
b 2096	**The ⌃ company has opened several branches.** If you inserted the name **C. K. Jensen** before the word **company,** would you need to capitalize the noun **company?** (*Yes, No*) 2097
None 2315	**The train had started to move and we couldn't find Jimmie anywhere in the station.** 2316
they're 2534	Many contractions end with **n't,** which is a shortened form of the adverb **not.** **doesn't isn't shouldn't wasn't** The apostrophe in **n't** takes the place of the missing _____. 2535

<u>trailer</u> <u>swayed</u> 120	First find and underline the verb; then find and underline the subject: **Gloria's friends often phoned at inconvenient times.** 121
action 340	**The <u>teacher</u> <u>corrected</u> the papers.** The noun **papers** shows what *received the action* of the verb **corrected**. **Papers,** therefore, is a (*direct object, subject complement*). 341
adjectives, adverbs 560	Although certain adverbs like **very, quite,** and **extremely** modify adjectives and other adverbs, most adverbs modify _____ . 561
does not 780	a. **The store closed.** b. *When the store closed* Which word group does not form a complete sentence by itself? ____ 781
b 1000	**The dessert was the big treat of the meal. (It was)** *a fluffy lemon pie.* To change the second sentence to an appositive word group, drop the subject _____ and the verb _____ . 1001
came 1220	Select the correct form of the verb **come:** **The package (***come, came***) by express.** 1221

a
 	
1440
	The verb in one of the following sentences is wrong:
	
	    a. **These tomatoes were grown under glass.**
	    b. **Ripe figs are eaten raw.**
	    c. **Much English is spoke in Japan.**
	
	The incorrect verb is in sentence ____.
	
	      1441

True
 	
1659
	a. **Frank doesn't play** (*fair, fairly*).
	    b. **Frank doesn't play** (*honest, honestly*).
	
	In which sentence are both forms of the word correct—*a* or *b*? ____
	
	      1660

we 1878	**Either you or** (*her, she*) must stay with the baby. 1879
Yes 2097	**The Lennox Hotel was full.** If you dropped the name **Lennox** from this sentence, would you still write **Hotel** with a capital letter? (*Yes, No*) 2098
move, 2316	In a compound sentence, the comma comes *after* the conjunction **and, but,** or **or.** (*True, False*) 2317

o
 	
2535
	People sometimes misplace the apostrophe in writing words that end with **n't.** The apostrophe is not used to separate **nt** from the verb, but to take the place of the missing **o.**
	    a. **was'nt, should'nt, have'nt, does'nt**
	    b. **wasn't, shouldn't, haven't, doesn't**
	Which group of words is correct—*a* or *b*? ____
	      2536

<u>friends</u> <u>phoned</u> 121	First find and underline the verb; then find and underline the subject: **The drugstore on our corner never closes before midnight.** 122
direct object 341	The *subject* and the *direct object* are usually two *different* things, and the action passes from the first to the second. 1 ⟶ 2 **Eileen raises cats.** **Eileen** and **cats** are (*one, two*) thing(s). 342
verbs 561	Adjectives can modify only *two* different classes of words—nouns and pronouns, but adverbs can modify (*two, three*) different classes of words. 562
b 781	a. **The store closed.** b. <u>*When*</u> *the store closed* Which word group is a clause? ____ 782
It, was 1001	a. **The dessert was the big treat of the meal,** *a fluffy lemon pie.* b. **The dessert,** *a fluffy lemon pie,* **was the big treat of the meal.** In which sentence is the appositive word group correctly placed right after the noun it explains? ____ 1002
came 1221	**The package came by express.** If you added the helper **has** to the verb, what word would you need to put in place of **came?** _____ 1222

c
 	
1441
	The verb in one of the following sentences is wrong:
	
	    a. **The Hills have gone back to Pasadena.**
	    b. **A light snow had fell during the night.**
	    c. **Eleanor has written a humorous poem.**
	
	The incorrect verb is in sentence ____.
	
	1442

a 1660	**Frank doesn't play** (*fair, fairly*). Although both **fair** and **fairly** are correct in this sentence, we should, as a general rule, choose the adverb form (*with, without*) **-ly** to modify a verb. 1661
she 1879	**My cousins and** (*he, him*) **are going to Silver Lake.** 1880
No 2098	Capitalize the complete names of particular schools, colleges, churches, clubs, libraries, hospitals, etc. **Todd High School** **Trinity Church** **Parkman Library** **Oberlin College** **Rotary Club** **Lakeside Hospital** Write the capital letters you would need to use in writing **stevens memorial hospital.** _____ 2099
False 2317	In a compound sentence, there are *both* a subject and a predicate *after* the conjunction. (*True, False*) 2318
b 2536	Write out the two words for which each contraction stands: **I'll** (_____) **go if you're** (_____) **willing.** 2537

<u>drugstore closes</u> 122	Many sentences are built upon the framework of a *subject* and a _____. 123
two 342	A subject complement refers back to the subject, which it *describes* or *identifies*. When the subject complement *identifies* the subject, both words mean the *same* person or thing. 1 ←————— 2 **Mr. Jones <u>is</u> our postman.** **Mr. Jones** and the **postman** are (*one, two*) person(s). 343
three 562	We can now define **adverbs** as words that modify _____, **adjectives,** and **other adverbs.** 563
b 782	a. **The store closed.** b. *When the store closed* One of these word groups is one word longer than the other. The word group with the added word is the (*sentence,* *clause*). 783
b 1002	**Dr. Seldin calls his farm "Tooth Acres." Dr. Seldin is a dentist.** The second sentence can be changed to an appositive word group of (*one, two, three*) word(s). 1003
come 1222	The form of **come** that should be used after **have, has,** or **had** is _____. 1223

b
 	
1442
	The verb in one of the following sentences is wrong:
	
	    a. **Someone had drove a nail into the tree.**
	    b. **We must have known half the people in town.**
	    c. **Our neighbors have flown to Miami.**
	
	The incorrect verb is in sentence _____.
	
	1443

with 1661	a. **Colette's dresses are very** (*stylish, stylishly*). b. **Colette dresses very** (*stylish, stylishly*). In which sentence shall we use the adjective **stylish** because it modifies the *noun* **dresses?** ____ 1662
he 1880	**The Angelos and** (*they, them*) **organized a neighborhood club for teenagers.** 1881
S M H 2099	a. **A new high school is needed.** b. **Martin high school won the cup.** In which sentence should the words **high school** be capitalized because they are part of the name of a particular school—*a* or *b*? ____ 2100
True 2318	A sentence with a *compound predicate* requires a comma just like a compound sentence. (*True, False*) 2319
I will *or* I shall, you are 2537	Write out the two words for which each contraction stands: **He's (_____) sure that we've (_____) taken it.** 2538

verb 123	The verb is the most important word in the (*subject*, *predicate*). 124
one 343	a. **Ralph called the usher.** b. **Ralph is an usher.** In which sentence are the **usher** and **Ralph** two different persons? ____ 344
verbs 563	Since adjectives and adverbs are **modifiers,** we can simplify our definition in this way: **Adverbs** modify **verbs** and **other modifiers.** By **"other modifiers"** we mean adjectives and _____. 564
clause 783	a. **The store closed.** b. *When the store closed* When we put a signal word before a sentence, it is no longer a sentence. The added word changes the sentence to a _____. 784
two 1003	**Dr. Seldin calls his farm "Tooth Acres." (Dr. Seldin is)** *a dentist.* The words *a dentist* should be placed in the first sentence right after (*Dr. Seldin, Acres*). 1004
come 1223	PRESENT SIMPLE PAST PAST WITH HELPER **run** **ran** **have run** The simple past form of **run** is not **run** but _____. 1224

a	Be careful not to write **of** when you mean **have**.
	
	    a. **Most of the food was left over.**
	    b. **We should of started earlier.**
	    c. **They printed a picture of our team.**
	
	In which sentence should **of** be changed to **have?** ____

1443	1444
a	a. **Colette's dresses are very** (*stylish, stylishly*). b. **Colette dresses very** (*stylish, stylishly*). In which sentence shall we use the adverb **stylishly** because it modifies the *verb* **dresses?** ____
1662	1663
they	**You and** (*me, I*) **can't do this alone.**
1881	1882
b	a. **The meeting will be held in our High School.** b. **The meeting will be held in Galesburg High School.** Which sentence contains errors in capitalization? ____
2100	2101
False	Commas are generally omitted in short compound sentences. (*True, False*)
2319	2320
he is, we have	Write the contraction of each pair of underlined words. Remember that the apostrophe goes in where the letters come out. **Where is** (_____) **the pen that does not** (_____) **write?**
2538	2539

predicate 124	The verb makes a statement about the _____. 125
a 344	1 ——————→ 2 **Ralph called the usher.** Because the **usher** and **Ralph** are two different persons, **usher** is a (*direct object, subject complement*). 345
adverbs 564	**an <u>extremely</u> hot day** **Hot** is an adjective because it modifies the noun **day.** Does **extremely** modify the adjective **hot** or the noun **day?** 565
clause 784	SENTENCE: **Dad needed the car.** CLAUSE: *Because Dad needed the car* The clause has one more word than the sentence. The added word is a (*preposition, clause signal*). 785
Dr. Seldin 1004	**Edison's next invention astonished the world,** *and* **it was the phonograph.** To eliminate the *and*, which noun in the second part of the sentence could be used as an appositive to explain **invention?** _____ 1005

ran
 	
1224
	PRESENT SIMPLE PAST PAST WITH HELPER
	  run **ran** **have run**
	    a. **Yesterday I run into an old friend.**
	    b. **Yesterday I ran into an old friend.**
	Which sentence is wrong because the helper form of the verb *run* is used without a helper? ____
	
	1225

b 1444	a. **lie, sit, rise** b. **lay, set, raise** Which verbs would you use to state that you put, place, or change the position of something—those in *a* or *b*? ____ 1445
b 1663	In this and the following frames, choose the **–ly** word (adverb) when there is action in the sentence, and the word describes this action. Choose the word *without* **–ly** (adjective) where there is no action in the sentence, and the word describes the subject. Underline the correct choice. **Peggy does everything** (*perfect, perfectly*). 1664
I 1882	(*She, Her*) **and her mother look alike.** 1883
a 2101	a. **I plan to attend Colby College.** b. **I must get good grades for College.** Which sentence contains an error in capitalization? ____ 2102
True 2320	Lesson **75** **Commas After Introductory Phrases and Clauses** [Frames 2322–2356]
Where's, doesn't 2539	Write the contraction of each pair of underlined words: **I am** (_____) **sure that we must not** (_____) **sign in pencil.** 2540

subject 125	When you change a sentence from present to past or from past to present time, the only word that changes is the _____. 126
direct object 345	1 ←——— 1 **Ralph is an usher.** Because, in this sentence, the **usher** and **Ralph** are the same person, **usher** is a (*direct object, subject complement*). 346
hot 565	**an <u>extremely</u> hot day** Because **extremely** modifies the adjective **hot,** it is an _____. 566
clause signal 785	In this and the following frames, capitals and periods are omitted to avoid revealing the answers. a. **the ice is melting** b. **if the ice is melting** Which of the above word groups is a clause? ____ 786
phonograph 1005	**Edison's next invention astonished the world,** *and* **(it was)** *the phonograph.* The words *the phonograph* should be placed right after the word _____, which it explains. 1006
a 1225	Underline the correct verb in each of the two pairs: I (*ran, run*) **to see who had** (*ran, run*) **through the corridor.** 1226

b 1445	Write in the missing forms: PRESENT SIMPLE PAST PAST WITH HELPER **lie** (in bed) _____ **have lain** **lay** (put) _____ **have laid** 1446
perfectly 1664	**Miss Dean usually treats her customers very** (*courteous, courteously*). 1665
She 1883	**The Moodys and** (*we, us*) **took turns in driving the children to school.** 1884

b
 	
2102
	a. **a Baptist church**
	    b. **Calvary Baptist Church**
	
	Which item could mean *any* Baptist church at all? ____
	
	                                2103

	I wanted to be a cowboy when I was five years old. One of these word groups makes the *main statement* of the sentence; the other is an *adverb clause* that does not make complete sense by itself. The main statement in this sentence comes (*first, last*). 2322
I'm, mustn't 2540	Write the contraction of each pair of underlined words: **<u>It is</u>** (_____) **not too late if <u>you are</u>** (_____) **ready now.** 2541

verb	Most, but not all, verbs show actions that one can see.
	
	    a. **threw, walked, pushed, arrived, laughed, turned**
	    b. **thought, hoped, expected, decided, remembered**
	
	Which group of verbs represents actions that one might *not* be able to see? ____

126	127

subject complement	a. **The <u>lemon</u> <u>improved</u> the punch.** b. **The <u>lemon</u> <u>was</u> sour.** Which sentence concerns only one thing? ____
346	347

adverb	**a <u>very</u> sharp pain** Does **very** modify the adjective **sharp** or the noun **pain?**
566	567

b	a. **after the sun went down** b. **the sun went down** Which word group is a clause? ____
786	787

invention	a. **Edison's next invention astonished the world, and it was the phonograph.** b. **Edison's next invention, the phonograph, astonished the world.** Which sentence is more direct and better organized? ____
1006	1007

ran, run	Underline the correct verb in each of the two pairs: **This explorer** (*saw, seen*) **something that few people ever have** (*saw, seen*).
1226	1227

(lie) lay (lay) laid 1446	Underline the correct verb in each pair: **I** (*laid, lay*) **my book aside and** (*laid, lay*) **down for a nap.** 1447
courteously 1665	**Miss Dean is usually very** (*courteous, courteously*) **to her customers.** 1666
we 1884	**Neither the Webbs nor** (*them, they*) **own a dog.** 1885
a 2103	a. **a Baptist church** b. **Calvary Baptist Church** Which item names a *particular* church? ____ 2104
first 2322	a. **I wanted to be a cowboy when I was five years old.** b. **When I was five years old, I wanted to be a cowboy.** In which sentence does the main statement of the sentence come ahead of the adverb clause? ____ 2323
It's, you're 2541	There are several pairs of words that sound alike but have entirely different meanings. **your you're** Copy the contraction that means **you are.** _____ 2542

b

127

In analyzing a sentence, always look for the verb first. If the verb is **fell,** find its subject by asking yourself, "_____ or _____ **fell?"**

128

---

b

347

1 ←‾‾‾‾‾‾‾⌐
The lemon was sour.

Sour is not a different thing, apart from the **lemon.**

Sour describes the subject **lemon.**

Sour, therefore, is a _____ _____.

348

---

sharp

567

a very sharp pain

The word **very** is an (*adjective, adverb*).

568

---

a

787

a. **although West High lost the game**
b. **West High lost the game**

Which word group is a clause? ____

788

---

b

1007

In this and the following frames, change the italicized part of each sentence to an appositive word group. Then put it after the word it explains in the other sentence.

We visited the Grand Canyon. *It is one of the great sights of the world.* _____

_____

1008

---

saw, seen

1227

Underline the correct verb in each of the two pairs:

This morning I (*done, did*) **the work that I should have** (*done, did*) **last night.**

1228

laid, lay 1447	Underline the correct verb in each pair: **Uncle Ray had** (*lain, laid*) **some newspapers on the grass and had** (*lain, laid*) **down to relax.** 1448
courteous 1666	**The mechanic fixed the car** (*satisfactory, satisfactorily*). 1667
they 1885	**Peggy and** (*she, her*) **are always together.** 1886
b 2104	a. **a Baptist Church** b. **Calvary Baptist Church** Which item contains an error in capitalization? ____ 2105
a 2323	a. **I wanted to be a cowboy when I was five years old.** b. **When I was five years old, I wanted to be a cowboy.** Only one of the above sentences contains a comma. The comma is used when the main statement comes (*first, last*). 2324
you're 2542	**your you're** Copy the possessive pronoun that means **belonging to you.** ____ 2543

Lesson 5 Here Comes the Noun!

[Frames 130–163]

---

subject complement

348

1 ←⟍

The water felt cold.

Cold is not a different thing, apart from the **water.**

Cold describes the subject **water.**

Cold, therefore, is a (*direct object, subject complement*).

349

---

adverb

568

an unusually hard test

The word **unusually** is an (*adjective, adverb*).

569

---

a

788

although West High lost the game

The adverb clause signal that starts this clause is

_____.

789

We visited the Grand Canyon, one of the great sights of the world.

1008

Mr. Hill made many changes. *He is the new principal.*

_____

_____

1009

---

did, done

1228

Underline the correct verb in each of the two pairs:

Mother (*give, gave*) **me the ring which her father had** (*gave, given*) **her.**

1229

laid, lain 1448	**Why would anyone want to** (*sit, set*) **where he** (*sat, set*). 1449
satisfactorily 1667	**Bruce takes his work quite** (*serious, seriously*). 1668
she 1886	In this and the following frames, underline the two correct pronouns in each sentence: (*They, Them*) **and** (*we, us*) **are tied for first place.** 1887
a 2105	**The** ∧ **Lutheran church has been completed.** If you inserted the name **Hillside** at the point indicated, would you need to capitalize the noun **church?** (*Yes, No*) 2106
last 2324	**At the end of the game the fans swarmed over the field.** One of these word groups makes the *main statement;* the other consists of two *prepositional phrases.* The main statement of this sentence comes (*first, last*). 2325
your 2543	**your you're** Write the word that fits in the following sentence: **I know that _____ joking.** 2544

Words—just like tools—can be grouped according to the jobs they do. There are *eight* different kinds, or classes, of words. Each kind does a different job in the sentence.

We have already met one class of words—the words that make statements about subjects. These words are called

_____ .

130

---

subject
complement

349

1 ——————→ 2
Ann knitted a sweater.

Ann and **sweater** are two different things. **Sweater,** therefore, is a (*direct object, subject complement*).

350

---

adverb

569

The lake suddenly grew extremely rough.

One adverb modifies the verb; the other modifies an adjective.

Which adverb modifies an adjective? _____

570

---

although

789

a. **he knew everything about planes**
b. **as though he knew everything about planes**

Which word group is a clause? _____

790

Mr. Hill, the new
principal, made
many changes.

1009

Ellen was walking with her dog. *It is a frisky French poodle.*

_____

_____

1010

---

gave, given

1229

If you had (*gone, went*), **I would have** (*gone, went*), **too.**

1230

sit, sat 1449	The young man (*sat, set*) his suitcase in the aisle of the bus and (*set, sat*) **down on it.** 1450
seriously 1668	The company's answer to my letter was very (*prompt, promptly*). 1669
They, we 1887	(*Him, He*) **and** (*me, I*) **caught most of the fish.** 1888
Yes 2106	a. **I joined the Woodlawn camera club.** b. **I joined a camera club.** In which sentence should the words **camera club** be capitalized? ____ 2107
last 2325	a. **At the end of the game, the crowd swarmed over the field.** b. **The crowd swarmed over the field at the end of the game.** The comma is used when the main statement of the sentence comes (*first, last*). 2326
you're 2544	Here is another confusing pair: **their they're** Copy the word that means **they are.** _____ 2545

verbs 130	We can't talk about anything unless it has a name, can we? We therefore need a class of words to name the persons, places, and things we talk about. These words are called **nouns.** A **noun** is the _____ of a person, place, or thing. 131
direct object 350	1 ——————————→ 2 _____ **sold his** _____. If you were to complete this sentence, the word in the space that follows the verb would be a (*direct object, subject complement*). 351
extremely 570	**Don spoke <u>quite</u> <u>frankly</u> about his problems.** Which of the two underlined adverbs modifies the verb **spoke?** _____ 571
b 790	a. **while we were waiting impatiently for the bus** b. **we were waiting impatiently for the bus** Only one of these word groups could be used by itself as a complete sentence. The sentence contains one (*more, less*) word than the clause. 791
Ellen was walking with her dog, a frisky French poodle. 1010	**Sam struck out.** *He was the first boy at bat.* _____ _____ 1011
gone, gone 1230	**Earl** (*came, come*) **home early, but Vic hasn't** (*came, come*) **home yet.** 1231

set, sat 1450	The company's prices (*raised, rose*) **soon after it** (*raised, rose*) **the workers' wages.** 1451
prompt 1669	**The company answered my letter very** (*prompt, promptly*). 1670
He, I 1888	(*She, Her*) **and** (*he, him*) **attended the same college.** 1889

a
 	
2107
	Do not capitalize the word **the** or any short preposition **(of, in, for, to)** when it is part of a name.
	    Boy Scouts of America
	    Daughters of the American Revolution
	Underline the words you would capitalize in this name:
	    society for the preservation of democracy
	2108

last 2326	A group of words that comes ahead of the main statement is called an **introductory word group.** Just as a speaker's introductory remarks lead into his main speech, an introductory word group leads into the main statement. Underline the introductory word group: **Sitting down on a log, Jeff took off his shoes.** 2327
they're 2545	**their** **they're** Copy the word that fits in this sentence: **Don't walk on** _____ **grass.** 2546

name 131	Miami office Mexico restaurant These nouns are the names of (*persons, places, things*). 132
direct object 351	1 ←————— 1 **Manhattan is an island.** **Island** and **Manhattan** are one and the same thing. **Island,** therefore, is a (*direct object, subject complement*). 352
frankly 571	**Don spoke <u>quite</u> <u>frankly</u> about his problems.** Which of the two underlined adverbs modifies another adverb? _____ 572

less
 	
791
	Adverb clauses are useful for combining sentences. They can make the relationship between two facts much clearer.
	  a. **The game was close. We finally won.**
	  b. <u>*Although*</u> *the game was close,* **we finally won.**
	Which arrangement shows more clearly how the two facts are related? ____
	792

Sam, the first boy at bat, struck out. 1011	Get rid of the *and* by changing the italicized part of this sentence to an appositive phrase. **Archie was the next batter,** *and he was a strong hitter.* _____ _____ 1012
came, come 1231	**Dunlap** (*ran, run*) **for the same office for which his father had** (*ran, run*). 1232

rose, raised 1451	The cost of automobile insurance is (*raising, rising*) because the accident rate has (*rose, risen*). 1452
promptly 1670	Ann types more (*rapid, rapidly*) than Eleanor. 1671
She, he 1889	Neither (*them, they*) nor (*us, we*) made a touchdown in the first quarter. 1890
<u>Society</u> for the <u>Preservation</u> of <u>Democracy</u> 2108	The injured fireman was taken to the ˄ hospital. If you inserted the name **Lexington** at the point indicated, would you need to capitalize the noun **hospital**? (*Yes, No*) 2109
Sitting down on a log, 2327	An introductory word group is generally an *adverb clause*, an *–ing word group*, or one or two *prepositional phrases*. An introductory word group always modifies something in the main statement of the sentence. Could an introductory word group make sense by itself—apart from the sentence? (*Yes, No*) 2328
their 2546	**their they're** Copy the word that fits in this sentence: Tell me when _____ ready to eat. 2547

places 132	**Henry doctor uncle Mr. Smith** These nouns are the names of (*persons, places, things*). 133
subject complement 352	1 ⟵————————— 1 _____ **was a** _____. If you were to complete this sentence, the word in the space that follows the verb would be a (*direct object, subject complement*). 353
quite 572	**I had a <u>very</u> strange experience <u>today</u>.** Which of the two underlined adverbs modifies an adjective? _____ 573
b 792	a. **We didn't hear the doorbell** *because the radio was turned on.* b. **We didn't hear the doorbell. The radio was turned on.** Which arrangement shows more clearly how the two facts are related? ____ 793
Archie, a strong hitter, was the next batter. 1012	Lesson **33** Unit Review [Frames 1014–1041]
ran, run 1232	The past forms of most verbs end in **–ed**. These verbs are called (*regular, irregular*) verbs. 1233

rising, risen 1452	This is the main point to remember about the use of **leave** and **let**: Always use (*let, leave*) when you mean "to permit" or "to allow." 1453
rapidly 1671	**The wooden bridge is only** (*temporary, temporarily*). 1672
they, we 1890	(*Her, She*) **and** (*me, I*) **can make the posters.** 1891
Yes 2109	**Our club meets weekly in the Whittier library.** The noun that needs to be capitalized in this sentence is (*club, library*). 2110
No 2328	Use a comma after an introductory word group—especially if it is more than a few words in length. a. <u>When something disappears</u> they always blame Ralph. b. <u>When some article disappears around the house</u> they always blame Ralph. Which sentence requires a comma? ____ 2329
they're 2547	**whose who's** Copy the contraction that means **who is.** _____ 2548

persons 133	**peach pencil automobile book** These nouns are the names of (*persons, places, things*). 134
subject complement 353	a. **The other team always wins the game.** b. **The other team is much heavier.** Which sentence contains a *subject complement* which describes the subject **team?** ____ 354
very 573	**Too many cooks spoil the broth.** One of the underlined modifiers is an adjective because it modifies a noun; the other is an adverb because it modifies an adjective. Which word is the adverb? _____ 574

a
 	
793
	Now let's look in this frame at a single adverb:
	
	    Finally Bert got the right answer.
	    Bert **finally** got the right answer.
	    Bert got the right answer **finally.**
	
	The adverb **finally**—like many adverbs—(*can, cannot*) be moved from one position to another in a sentence.
	
	794

  	In a compound sentence, there are a subject and a verb before (*and also, but not*) after the conjunction. 1014
regular 1233	The simple past form and the helper form of regular verbs such as **look** and **open** are (*the same, different*). 1234

let 1453	The Burdicks (*leave, let*) their friends use their pool. 1454
temporary 1672	How do you comb your hair so (*neat, neatly*)? 1673
She, I 1891	Lesson **62** **The Object Form of Pronouns** [Frames 1893–1933]
library 2110	Our club meets weekly in the Whittier Library. If you dropped the name **Whittier** from this sentence, would you still write **Library** with a capital letter? (*Yes, No*) 2111
b 2329	a. **In some schools, several grades are taught in the same classroom.** b. **In some of the country schools of our state, several grades are taught in the same classroom.** In which sentence might we omit the comma after the introductory word group? ____ 2330
who's 2548	**whose** **who's** Copy the possessive pronoun that means **belonging to whom.** _____ 2549

things 134	Underline the noun that is the name of a *person:* money church teacher kitchen 135

b
 	
354
	In one sentence, the verb **broke** is complete; in the other, it requires a word to show what *receives the action.*
	
	    a. **The strain broke the chain.**
	    b. **The chain between the two cars broke.**
	
	Which sentence contains a *direct object?* ____
	
	355

Too 574	**I eat a <u>fairly</u> <u>big</u> breakfast.** Which one of the two modifiers is an adverb? _____ 575
can 794	a. **A dog walked on the cement** *before it had hardened.* b. *Before it had hardened,* **a dog walked on the cement.** In which sentence has the adverb clause been moved from the end to the beginning of the sentence? ____ 795
and also 1014	a. **Sherry was my own horse, and I felt very proud of my possession.** b. **I had my own horse and felt very proud of my possession.** Which sentence is compound? ____ 1015
the same 1234	Verbs whose past forms do not end in **-ed** are called (*regular, irregular*) verbs. 1235

let 1454	When Marlene came over last night, she (*took, brought*) her guitar along. 1455
neatly 1673	Uncle Will eats rather (*hearty, heartily*) for a sick person. 1674
	a. Joe liked Sue. b. Sue liked Joe. In sentence *a*, **Joe** is the subject, and **Sue** is the direct object. In sentence *b*, **Sue** is the subject, and **Joe** is the _____ _____. 1893
No 2111	lake club church hotel river company school college Words like these should not be capitalized unless they are part of a proper noun. (*True, False*) 2112
a 2330	Use a comma even after a short introductory word group if there is any danger that your sentence might be confusing. a. **Whenever I eat my dog begs for food.** b. **Whenever I eat I use a napkin.** In which sentence would a comma help to prevent confusion? _____ 2331
whose 2549	whose who's Don't use the word **who's** unless the words **who is** would fit in. a. **. . . bike is on our sidewalk?** b. **. . . ringing our doorbell?** In which sentence would **Who's** be correct? _____ 2550

teacher 135	Underline the noun that is the name of a *place:* **soldier** **piano** **Paul** **hospital** 136
a 355	a. **The band played** *poorly.* b. **The band played a** *march.* In which sentence is the italicized word a direct object? _____ 356
fairly 575	**Miss Hagerty** <u>sometimes</u> **becomes** <u>impatient</u> **with us.** Which one of the two modifiers is an adverb? _____ 576
b 795	An adverb clause can frequently be moved from one position to another, just like an (*adjective, adverb*). 796
a 1015	**I had my own horse and felt very proud of my possession.** This is *not* a compound sentence because a (*subject, verb*) is missing after the conjunction **and.** 1016
irregular 1235	When an irregular verb is used with **have, has,** or **had,** the (*simple past, helper*) form of the verb should be used. 1236

brought 1455	Everyone who goes to Mexico should (*take, bring*) his camera with him. 1456
heartily 1674	This tie will go (*nice, nicely*) with your blue suit. 1675
direct object 1893	He liked Sue. Sue liked him. Which form of the pronoun is used for the direct object—he or him? _____ 1894

True
 	
2112
	Capitalize all nouns and pronouns that refer to God.
	    God Almighty Lord His mercy
	Copy each word that requires capitals, adding the needed capitals:
	    We thanked the lord for his many blessings.
	_____
	2113

a 2331	a. **As she slipped she grabbed the railing.** b. **As she turned the car got out of control.** After which of the short introductory word groups is a comma necessary for clearness? ____ 2332
b 2550	Underline the correct word: **Where's the man (*whose, who's*) car was wrecked?** 2551

hospital 136	Underline the noun that is the name of a *thing:* onion **Europe** **farmer** **Ohio** 137
b 356	**The bright headlights blinded the approaching driver.** The noun **driver** is a (*direct object, subject complement*). 357
sometimes 576	Any word that modifies a noun or a pronoun is an _____. 577
adverb 796	**Our sales increased** *when we lowered our price.* Can the adverb clause *when we lowered our price* be moved to the beginning of the sentence? (*Yes, No*) 797
subject 1016	The conjunctions commonly used to connect the two parts of a compound sentence are **and,** _____, and _____. 1017
helper 1236	Lesson **40** Thirteen Irregular Verbs [Frames 1238–1277]

Lesson 47 — Was and Were; Don't and Doesn't

[Frames 1458–1495]

take

1456

---

nicely

The patient's temperature is now (*normal, normally*) **again.**

1675   1676

---

a. **I**   **he**   **she**   **we**   **they**
b. **me**   **him**   **her**   **us**   **them**

him

Joe liked . . . .

Which pronouns could be used as the direct object of the verb **liked** in the little sentence above—those in group *a* or *b*? _____

1894   1895

Lord, His

In this and the following frames, cross out each capital letter that is not correct; for example, **a Catholic $chool.**

The new High School will be on Fuller Avenue.

2113   2114

---

b

To Ellen Stuart was very attentive.

Would you recommend a comma after the name **Ellen?**
(*Yes, No*)

2332   2333

---

its (= *belonging to it*)   **it's** (= *it is*)

whose

No two words cause more trouble than these. Try hard not to confuse them.

Write the word that fits in this sentence:

_____ **your turn to play.**

2551   2552

onion 137	A noun is the name of a person, _____, or _____. 138
direct object 357	**Some of us felt dizzy after the ride.** The word **dizzy** is a (*direct object, subject complement*). 358
adjective 577	To explain **how** sweet an apple is or **how** quietly a motor runs, we would need to use an _____. 578
Yes 797	a. **Our sales increased** *when we lowered our price.* b. *When we lowered our price,* **our sales increased.** A comma is needed when the adverb clause comes (*before, after*) the main statement of the sentence. 798
but, or 1017	a. **My grandmother doesn't care for housework, and her years of experience have taught her many short cuts.** b. **Whales reach their full size in about 12 years, and live for about 40 years.** Because it is not a compound sentence, the comma should be omitted from sentence ____. 1018
	Most verbs are **regular.** They have only a single past form that ends in **–ed.** We use the same **–ed** form with **have, has,** or **had** that we use for the simple past. a. **Tony** *pitched* **as he never** *had pitched* **before.** b. **Leo** *gave* **me the ticket that the coach** *had given* **him.** Which sentence contains a regular verb? ____ 1238

Singular means **one**; plural means **more than one**.

apple apples

To change a noun from singular to plural, we usually add the letter ____.

1458

---

normal

1676

The patient was breathing (*normal, normally*) **again.**

1677

---

b

1895

The form of a pronoun that can be used as the object of a verb or a preposition is called the **object form.**

a. **I**	**he**	**she**	**we**	**they**
b. **me**	**him**	**her**	**us**	**them**

Which pronouns are in the object form—those in group *a* or *b*? ____

1896

~~H~~igh ~~S~~chool

2114

Continue to cross out each capital letter that is not correct:

The Stanford Inn is the best Hotel in our City.

2115

Yes

2333

It began to rain at the very beginning of the game.

Is a comma needed after the word **rain?** (*Yes, No*)

2334

It's

2552

Its (no apostrophe) is a possessive pronoun—just like **ours, yours, theirs.** Apostrophes are needed to make nouns possessive. Pronouns show ownership *without* apostrophes.

The violin is in _____ case.

2553

place, thing 138	Most of the things that we talk about can be *seen* or *touched*—just like the things in this room. But we sometimes talk about something that we can't *see* or *touch*. Underline the word that names something we can't see or touch: **grass** **freedom** **brother** 139
subject complement 358	**The explosion shook the entire neighborhood.** In this sentence, the *direct object* is _____. 359
adverb 578	A word that modifies a verb, an _____ or another _____ is an adverb. 579
before 798	**A salesman will call** *if you leave your name.* No comma is needed in this sentence because the adverb clause comes (*before, after*) the main statement. 799
b 1018	Only *similar* ideas *of equal importance* should be combined into a compound sentence. a. **The lake was rough, and our boat was very small.** b. **The lake was rough, and my two cousins were in the boat with me.** Which is the better sentence? ____ 1019

a
 	
1238
	PRESENT SIMPLE PAST PAST WITH HELPER
	  take **took** **have taken**
	
	    This job has taken too much time.
	
	Because **has** is part of the verb, we use the (*simple past, helper*) form of the verb **take**.
	
	1239

s 1458	Although we form the plural of most nouns by adding **s** to the singular, there are some exceptions: **man** **men** **woman** **women** **tooth** **teeth** **child** _____ <div align="right">1459</div>
normally 1677	**Students often write** (*bad, badly*) **when they are not interested in their subject.** <div align="right">1678</div>
b 1896	<div align="center">**Joe liked . . . .**</div>The pronouns like **I, we,** and **she** that do *not* fit after the verb are in the (*subject, object*) form. <div align="right">1897</div>
Hotel, City 2115	**The Carson Insurance Company has an Office in the Scott Building.** <div align="right">2116</div>
No 2334	<div align="center">**It began to rain <u>at the very beginning of the game.</u>**</div>If the underlined word group were moved to the beginning of the sentence, would a comma be needed? (*Yes, No*) <div align="right">2335</div>
its 2553	Do not use the contraction **it's** unless you can put the two words _____ _____ in its place. <div align="right">2554</div>

freedom 139	Words like **freedom, strength, truth,** and **imagination** are also nouns because they are the names of *ideas* that we have in our minds. Underline the noun that is the name of an *idea:* **wallet actor honesty** 140
neighborhood 359	**Mother felt _____ about Bob's grades.** The missing word in this sentence would be a (*direct object, subject complement*). 360
adjective, adverb 579	Lesson **20** Learning to Recognize Prepositions [Frames 581–614]
after 799	*If you leave your name,* **a salesman will call.** Now a comma is needed because the adverb clause comes at the (*beginning, end*) of the sentence. 800
a 1019	As a general rule, it is not a good idea to begin a sentence with the conjunction **and.** a. **It was a hot July day, and all the windows were open.** b. **It was a hot July day. And all the windows were open.** Which is better—*a* or *b*? _____ 1020

helper
 	
1239
	When an irregular verb has two past forms, one form is used for the simple past, and the other with a helping verb.
	
	      The job . . . too much time.
	      The job has . . . too much time.
	
	Can the same past form of the verb **take** be used in both sentences? (*Yes, No*)
	
	1240

children 1459	Underline the one noun that is plural: **boy** **doctor** **women** **student** 1460
badly 1678	**The management of the hospital seemed quite** (*bad, badly*) **to me.** 1679
subject 1897	We use one set of pronouns *before* verbs as their sub- jects and another set of pronouns *after* verbs as their _____. 1898
Ⱥffice 2116	**You will pass a new Methodist Church on the way to the** **Library.** (This sentence does not give the name of a particular church building.) 2117
Yes 2335	**Although they spoke different languages the children played** **well together.** Is a comma needed after the word **languages?** (*Yes, No*) 2336
it is 2554	a. **It's time to eat.** b. **It's meal is ready.** Which sentence is wrong because you cannot substitute **it is** for **it's?** ____ 2555

honesty 140	Underline the noun that is the name of an *idea:* **friendship** **theater** **airplane** 141
subject complement 360	**Dorothy peeled the _____ for dinner.** The missing word in this sentence would be a (*direct object, subject complement*). 361
	Look at these two unrelated nouns: **man** **car** No word stands between them to tell us whether the man is **in, by, under, behind, beside,** or **near** the _____. 581
beginning 800	a. *Unless you have good grades* **a college will not accept you.** b. **A college will not accept you** *unless you have good grades.* In which sentence should a comma be added? ____ 801
a 1020	A clause that tells *when, where, how,* and so forth, about the action of the verb is an (*adjective, adverb*) clause. 1021
No 1240	You have seen that the helper form of the verb is used with **have, has,** and **had.** It is also used with all forms of the verb **be (is, am, are—was, were, been).** Besides being used after **have, has,** and **had,** the helper form is also used after all forms of the verb _____. 1241

women 1460	The noun **women** is plural even though it does not end in _____ . 1461
bad 1679	a. **angry** **loose** **strict** **thorough** b. **angrily** **loosely** **strictly** **thoroughly** Which group of words would you use to describe the action of a verb? _____ 1680
objects 1898	**she** **him** **he** Which one of these pronouns can be used after a verb as its object and is, therefore, in the object form? _____ 1899
Church, Library 2117	**The Knights Of Columbus is a Society for men of the Catholic faith.** 2118
Yes 2336	**Although they spoke different languages, the children played well together.** If the underlined word group were moved to the end of the sentence, would the comma still be needed? (*Yes, No*) 2337
b 2555	a. **It's time to eat.** b. **It's meal is ready.** Which sentence is right because you can substitute **it is** for **it's**? _____ 2556

friendship 141	The noun **truth** is not the name of a *person*, *place*, or *thing*. It is the name of an _____ that exists in people's minds. 142
direct object 361	**The coat looked too _____ for me.** The missing word in this sentence would be a _____ _____. 362
car 581	**man** **car** There is no word to tell us the **relationship** between the _____ and the _____. 582
a 801	*Unless you have good grades,* **a college will not accept you.** Because the adverb clause comes at the beginning of this sentence, the comma is (*right, wrong*). 802
adverb 1021	a. **who (whom, whose), which, that** b. **because, when, if, unless, although** In which group can the words be used as signals for adverb clauses? ____ 1022

be
 	
1241
	PRESENT SIMPLE PAST PAST WITH HELPER
	  take **took** **have taken**
	    These pictures were (*took, taken*) **last year.**
	Which past form of the verb is right?
	
	1242

s 1461	In grammar, we speak of **singular** and **plural** as **number**. The number of a noun tells us whether it means *one* or *more than one*. The noun **tree** is singular in number; the noun **trees** is plural in _____. 1462
b 1680	Does a student study his lesson **thorough** or **thoroughly?** _____ 1681
him 1899	**them** **we** **I** **they** **me** Which two pronouns are in the object form? _____ and _____ 1900
∅f, $ociety 2118	In this and the following frames, copy only the words that now lack required capitals, adding the needed capitals: **The Ferndale stamp club has a display of rare american stamps in the Wilson library.** 2119

No
 	
2337
	In most of our writing, we generally put our main statements first, not last.
	
	    a. **Our dog begins to howl whenever it hears a siren.**
	    b. **Whenever it hears a siren, our dog begins to howl.**
	Which sentence begins with the main statement, not with the adverb clause? ____
	
	2338

a
 	
2556
	The contraction **Let's** (= *Let us*) combines a verb and a pronoun. **Lets**—without an apostrophe—is just an ordinary verb like **talks** or **runs**.
	
	    a. **. . . go to the game.**
	    b. **Dad . . . Peggy drive the car.**
	In which sentence would **let's** (= *let us*) fit? ____
	
	2557

idea 142	We have now become acquainted with two kinds or *classes* of words: **verbs** and **nouns.** The class of words that makes, or helps to make, statements about subjects is called _____. 143
subject complement 362	**We carried the _____ to the attic.** The missing word in this sentence would be a _____ _____. 363
man, car 582	**man** $\begin{cases} in \\ by \\ with \end{cases}$ **car** **man** $\begin{cases} near \\ behind \\ under \end{cases}$ **car** Each italicized word standing between **man** and **car** shows (*the same, a different*) **relationship** between the two nouns. 583
right 802	*Whenever I pass their home,* **their dog barks at me.** If we move the adverb clause *whenever I pass their home* to the end of the sentence, the sentence will require no comma. (*True, False*) 803
b 1022	**All members approve this change.** To change this sentence to an adverb clause, we would need to (*add, drop*) a word. 1023
taken 1242	**These pictures were taken last year.** We use **taken,** rather than **took,** because the verb is used with the helper _____. 1243

number 1462	**car pen room shoe** These nouns are all of the same number because they are all (*singular, plural*). 1463
thoroughly 1681	**fair—fairly loud—loudly** **slow—slowly cheap—cheaply** **quick—quickly steady—steadily** These are examples of a small number of words that can be used either with or without **-ly** to modify verbs. (*True, False*) 1682
them, me 1900	**she you we I it they** Which two pronouns could be used as either subjects or objects without changing their forms? _____ and _____ 1901
Stamp Club, American, Library 2119	Copy the words that require capitals: **Catholics, protestants, and jews all worship the same god.** 2120

a
 	
2338
	For the sake of variety, it's a good idea now and then to begin a sentence with an introductory word group.
	    a. **The job will take all day if I have to do it alone.**
	    b. **If I have to do it alone, the job will take all day.**
	If you had written several sentences beginning with the main statement, which sentence would add more variety? ___
	2339

a 2557	In the next sentences, choose the correct word from the two words printed in parentheses, and write this word on the blank line. Don't choose a contraction unless the two words for which it stands would make sense in the sentence. _____ **color changes when** _____ **ripe.** (It's, Its) (it's, its) 2558

verbs 143	The class of words that names persons, places, things, and ideas is called _____. 144
direct object 363	Lesson **13** **Sentences with Compound Parts** [Frames 365–392]

man $\begin{cases} in \\ by \\ with \end{cases}$ car   man $\begin{cases} near \\ behind \\ under \end{cases}$ car

a different 583	Each time we change the word between **man** and **car,** we change the *rela_____* between the two nouns. 584
True 803	It is important to select the right clause signal. **We placed the electric razor _____** *Dad would be sure to see it.* Underline the adverb clause signal that shows the relationship between the two ideas most clearly: **if because while where** 804
add 1023	**If all members approve this change, we should make it.** In this sentence, the adverb clause begins with the clause signal _____ and ends with the word _____. 1024
were 1243	In this lesson, we shall study the two past forms of thirteen irregular verbs that we use constantly. Here are the helper forms of eight of these verbs: **have broken have eaten have given have taken** **have driven have fallen have spoken have written** The last two letters of each helper form are _____. 1244

singular 1463	streets cloud cookies window Because two of these nouns are singular and two are plural, we say that they are not alike in n_____. 1464
True 1682	Lesson **55** **Choosing Between** *Good* **and** *Well* [Frames 1684–1704]
you, it 1901	<u>You</u> liked <u>it</u>. <u>It</u> liked <u>you</u>. The subject and object forms of the pronouns **you** and **it** are (*alike, different*). 1902
Protestants, Jews, God 2120	Members of St. Andrew's church may use the parking lot of the Studio theater. 2121
b 2339	In this and the following frames, supply the necessary commas. Some of the sentences do not require commas. **Ever since Lois was a little girl she has wanted to be a nurse.** 2340
its, it's 2558	_____ the girl _____ story won first prize? (Who's, Whose) (who's, whose) 2559

nouns 144	It is hard to talk about anything unless it has a name. For this reason, the subject of a sentence is very often a **noun.** **The <u>rain</u> <u>stopped</u>.** In this sentence, the subject **rain** is a _____. 145
	We can talk about more than one thing at a time. A sentence, therefore, can have more than one subject. EXAMPLE: **The <u>smoke</u> and <u>water</u> <u>caused</u> much damage.** This sentence has two subjects—**smoke** and _____. 365
(rela)tionship 584	Here we have the verb **rushed** and the noun **hospital:** **rushed hospital** There is no word between them to tell us whether someone **rushed** *to, from, past* or *around* the _____. 585
where 804	_____ *it was a sunny day,* **Uncle Pete was wearing a raincoat.** Underline the adverb clause signal that shows the relationship between the two ideas most clearly: **although because until wherever** 805
If, change 1024	A comma is needed in a sentence when the adverb clause comes (*first, last*). 1025
–en 1244	Here are the helper forms of five more irregular verbs: **have flow<u>n</u> have know<u>n</u> have throw<u>n</u>** **have grow<u>n</u> have see<u>n</u>** Each one of these helper forms ends with the letter ____. 1245

(n)umber 1464	Verbs, too, sometimes—though not always—show number. Some verb forms are singular, and other verb forms are plural. **The house** *is* **new.** **The houses** *are* **new.** Which verb is plural—*is* or *are*? _____ <div align="right">1465</div>
	The aim of this lesson is to teach you not to use the *adjective* **good** in place of the *adverb* **well.** **These pens are good.** **Good** is an adjective because it modifies the noun _____. <div align="right">1684</div>
alike 1902	a. **I** **he** **she** **we** **they** b. **me** **him** **her** **us** **them** **Joe looked at . . . .** Which pronouns could be used as the object of the preposition **at**—those in group *a* or *b*? _____ <div align="right">1903</div>
Church, Theater 2121	**The Clayton parents' club bought uniforms for our school band.** <div align="right">2122</div>
girl, 2340	Insert any necessary commas: **Lois has wanted to be a nurse ever since she was a little girl.** <div align="right">2341</div>
Who's, whose 2559	_____ **heart beats faster when** _____ **running.** (You're, Your) (you're, your) <div align="right">2560</div>

noun 145	Any word that is a noun can be used as the subject of a verb. If a word can't be used as the subject of a verb, it is not a _____. 146
water 365	**The car and the trailer went into the ditch.** This sentence also has two subjects. The second of the two subjects is _____. 366
hospital 585	**rushed hospital** There is no word to tell us the **relationship** between the noun **hospital** and the verb _____. 586
although 805	**We protect the young plants** _____ *frost will not injure them.* Underline the adverb clause signal that shows the relationship between the two ideas most clearly: **since while so that as if** 806
first 1025	a. **Unless you have had rain, you can't have a rainbow.** b. **You can't have a rainbow, unless you have had rain.** The comma should be omitted from sentence ____. 1026
–n 1245	**have broken have given have flown have seen** **have driven have spoken have grown have thrown** **have eaten have taken have known** **have fallen have written** All the helper forms of these thirteen verbs end either with the letters _____ or the letter ____. 1246

are 1465	**The houses are new.** We know that the verb **are** is plural because its subject **houses** is (*singular, plural*). 1466
pens 1684	**These pens write well.** **Well** is an adverb because it describes the action of the verb _____. 1685
b 1903	The object form is also used for any pronoun that is the object of a preposition. Here are the nine most common prepositions: **in to of at on by for from with** A pronoun that follows any of these prepositions should be in the (*subject, object*) form. 1904
Parents' Club 2122	**The Vollmer Baking company supplies bread to the Weldon Children's hospital and to the Clifton high school.** 2123
None 2341	Insert any necessary commas: **With icy shivers in my spine I reached for my flashlight.** 2342
Your, you're 2560	_____ **find out why Mr. Carr** _____ (Let's, Lets) (let's, lets) **some students go home early.** 2561

noun 146	**The . . . disappeared.** Underline the word that could be used as the subject of the verb **disappeared:** often against letter 147
trailer 366	We can also make two (or more) statements about the same subject by using two (or more) verbs. EXAMPLE: <u>**Bert**</u> <u>**dived**</u> into the water and <u>**disappeared.**</u> Both verbs—**dived** and **disappeared**—make statements about the subject _____. 367
rushed 586	**rushed** $\begin{cases} to \\ from \\ toward \end{cases}$ **hospital** **rushed** $\begin{cases} past \\ around \\ through \end{cases}$ **hospital** Each time we change the word between **rushed** and **hospital**, we change the _____ _ship between the verb and the noun. 587
so that 806	**Mother always spoke to us children** _____ _we were adults._ Underline the adverb clause signal that shows the relationship between the two ideas most clearly. **because as if although unless** 807
b 1026	Eliminate the **and** in this sentence by changing the italicized part to an adverb clause. Write the full sentence. _Noreen took vocal lessons,_ **and her singing improved a great deal.** _____ _____ 1027
–en, –n 1246	Whenever you are doubtful about which verb form to use after the various forms of **have** or **be**, look for a form that ends with **–en** or **–n.** If there is one, use it. **We had . . . since early morning.** Is there a form of the verb **drive** that ends with **–en** or **–n?** _(Yes, No)_ 1247

plural 1466	**The <u>house</u> <u>is</u> new.** We know that the verb **is** is singular because its subject **house** is (*singular, plural*). 1467
write 1685	**good well** Which of these words can be used to modify a verb? _____ 1686
object 1904	Other prepositions you will need to recognize are— about among beside near above before between over after behind except toward against below like without Be sure to use the object form for objects of verbs and _____. 1905
Company, Hospital, High School 2123	**Lesson 69** **Various Other Uses of Capitals** [Frames 2125–2163]
spine, 2342	**Seeing nothing ahead of me on the road I increased my speed.** 2343
Let's, lets 2561	_____ **house looks as if** _____ **not at home.** (They're, Their) (they're, their) 2562

letter 147	**The letter <u>disappeared</u>.** **Letter,** the subject of the verb **disappeared,** is a _____. 148
Bert 367	**A blue jay swooped down and pecked at our cat.** The two verbs in this sentence are **swooped** and _____. 368
relation(ship) 587	A word that **relates** a noun or pronoun which follows it to some other word in the sentence is called a **preposition.** Learn to spell **preposition** correctly. Just write **pre** in front of the word **position** and you have the word _____. 588
as if 807	In this and the following frames, combine each pair of sentences by changing the italicized sentence to an adverb clause. Write the full sentence. Be sure to put a comma after each adverb clause that begins a sentence. *I was taking his picture.* **He suddenly moved.** _____ 808
After (Because, When) Noreen took vocal lessons, her singing improved a great deal. 1027	A clause that is used to modify a noun or pronoun is an _____ clause. 1028
Yes 1247	The form of the verb **drive** that ends with **–en** or **–n** is _____. 1248

singular 1467	a. **This sweater** *is* **warm.** b. **These sweaters** *are* **warm.** Which sentence contains a plural verb? _____ 1468
well 1686	WRONG: **These pens write good.** This sentence is wrong because the adjective **good** cannot be used to modify the verb _____. 1687
prepositions 1905	When a single pronoun is the object of a verb or preposition, mistakes are very rare. We are not likely to hear such mistakes as "Paul invited *I*" or "Dad is waiting for *we*." **The dog followed** (*she, her*) **home.** 1906
	Capitalize the names of particular brands of products. **Wheaties Chrysler Listerine Rinso** **I brush my teeth with** (*freshie, Freshie*). 2125
road, 2343	**More than half the Pilgrims had died by the end of the first winter.** 2344
Their, they're 2562	_____ **the neighbor who** _____ **his dog** (Who's, Whose) (let's, lets) **run loose on the street?** 2563

noun 148	**The loud noise suddenly stopped.** The noun in this sentence is _____. 149
pecked 368	Two or more subjects with the same verb are called a **compound subject.** The word *compound* means "having more than one part." **All the <u>doors</u> and <u>windows</u> <u>were</u> locked.** This sentence has a _____ subject. 369
preposition 588	**The grass <u>under</u> the tree was dead.** The **grass** was not *above, beyond,* or *around* the **tree.** The **grass** was _____ the **tree.** 589
As (When, While) I was taking his picture, he suddenly moved. 808	*Jane can speak French.* **She can't speak it well.** _____ _____ 809
adjective 1028	a. **who (whom, whose), which, that** b. **because, when, if, unless, although** In which group can the words be used as signals for adjective clauses? _____ 1029
driven 1248	**We had driven since early morning.** We use **driven** rather than **drove** because the verb follows the helping verb _____. 1249

b 1468	An important rule of English is that a subject and a verb must **agree** (be alike) in number. This rule means that with a singular subject we must use a singular verb, and that with a plural subject we must use a _____ verb. 1469
write 1687	**The pitcher was good. He pitched well.** **Good** modifies the noun **pitcher,** but **well** modifies the verb _____. 1688
her 1906	When a verb or preposition has compound objects—either two pronouns or a noun and a pronoun—mistakes often occur. a. **The dog followed her home.** b. **The dog followed Al and** (*she, her*) **home.** In sentence *b*, which pronoun is correct? _____ 1907
Freshie 2125	**Don't use ordinary paint—use** (*Durex, durex*). 2126
None 2344	**By the end of the first winter more than half the Pilgrims had died.** 2345
Who's, lets 2563	_____ **going to raise** _____ **price again.** (They're, Their) (it's, its) 2564

noise 149	The _____ of this child surprises me. Underline the word that is a noun and that could therefore be used as the subject of this sentence: **lazy lazily laziness** 150
compound 369	Two or more verbs that make statements about the same subjects are called **compound verbs**. **The blazing <u>fire</u> <u>crackled</u> and <u>snapped</u>.** This sentence has _____ verbs. 370
under 589	**The grass <u>under</u> the tree was dead.** The preposition **under** shows the relationship between the noun **tree,** which follows it, and the noun _____, which comes before it. 590
Although Jane can speak French, she can't speak it well. 809	*Pure gold is soft.* **It is generally mixed with a harder metal.** _____ _____ 810
a 1029	Do not use the pronoun **which** as a clause signal to refer to (*persons, things, animals*). 1030
had 1249	**Many windows were . . . by the explosion.** Is there a form of the verb **break** that ends with **–en** or **–n**? (*Yes, No*) 1250

plural
 	
1469
	When the subject and verb are of the **same** number, as they should be, we say that they **agree** in number.
	
	    a. **Tom** *was* **absent.**
	    b. **Tom** *were* **absent.**
	
	The verb agrees with its subject in sentence ____.
	
	<div align="right">1470</div>

pitched 1688	**The driver was good.** **He drove well.** Which word is an adverb—**good** or **well?** _____ <div align="right">1689</div>
her 1907	**The dog followed Al and her home.** The object form **her** is correct because **her,** as well as **Al,** is the object of the verb _____. <div align="right">1908</div>
Durex 2126	**Your dog will just love** (*krunchies, Krunchies*). <div align="right">2127</div>
winter, 2345	**If the Yankees win another game will be played.** <div align="right">2346</div>
They're, its 2564	**I can guess** _____ **manners** _____ **discussing.** (who's, whose) (you're, your) <div align="right">2565</div>

laziness 150	**My wild** _____ **worried my parents.** Underline the word that is a noun and that could therefore be used as the subject of this sentence: **imagine imagination imaginary imagined** 151
compound 370	Direct objects, indirect objects, and subject complements can also be compound. **Dale quickly changed his** _shirt_ **and** _tie_. The words _shirt_ and _tie_ are compound (_direct objects, subject complements_). 371
grass 590	**The children played under the tree.** The **children** didn't play _in, near, behind,_ or _above_ the **tree.** They played _____ the **tree.** 591
Because (Since, As) pure gold is soft, it is generally mixed with a harder metal. 810	_We were eating dinner._ **Some company arrived.** _____ _____ 811
persons 1030	Which kind of clause can be farther away from the word it modifies—an adverb clause or an adjective clause? An _____ _clause_ can be farther away. 1031
Yes 1250	The form of the verb **break** that ends with **–en** or **–n** is _____. 1251

a 1470	**Tom** *were* **absent.** This sentence is wrong because the subject and verb do not agree in number. The subject **Tom** is singular, but the verb **were** is _____. <div align="right">1471</div>
well 1689	WRONG: **He drove good.** This sentence is wrong because **good** is an adjective, and an adjective cannot modify the verb _____. <div align="right">1690</div>
followed 1908	When two pronouns (or a noun and a pronoun) are used as objects, choose the same form of the pronoun that you would choose if the pronoun were used alone. **Betty showed <u>him</u> her gifts. Betty showed <u>me</u> her gifts.** **Betty showed <u>him</u> and (***I, me***) her gifts.** <div align="right">1909</div>
Krunchies 2127	Notice that although brand names are capitalized, the products that they identify are *not* capitalized. **Ford station wagon Esterbrook pens Speed King skates** Write the capital letters you would need to use in writing **red arrow batteries.** _____ <div align="right">2128</div>
win, 2346	**Looking for a place to park we drove around the block several times.** <div align="right">2347</div>
whose, you're 2565	_____ **meet at** _____ **house.** (Let's, Lets) (you're, your) <div align="right">2566</div>

imagination 151	A word is printed in parentheses after each sentence that follows. This word is not a noun. Write the *noun form* of this word that would fit in as the subject of the sentence. EXAMPLE: **His** *strength* **surprised everyone. (strong)** **The** _____ **started over a nickel. (argue)** 152
direct objects 371	**The Holdens lent** *Howard* **and** *me* **their boat.** Two words in this sentence show *to whom* something was done. The words **Howard** and **me** are compound (*direct objects, indirect objects*). 372
under 591	**The children played <u>under</u> the tree.** The preposition **under** shows the relationship between the noun **tree,** which follows it, and the verb _____, which comes before it. 592
While (When, As) we were eating dinner, some company arrived. 811	**The actor wore dark glasses.** *People would not recognize him.* _____ _____ 812
adverb 1031	Combine these two sentences by changing the italicized sentence to an adjective clause. Write the full sentence. **Dean has several savings bonds.** *He is keeping them for his education.* _____ _____ 1032
broken 1251	**Many windows were . . . by the explosion.** We use **broken** rather than **broke** because the verb follows the helping verb _____. 1252

plural 1471	**The car** *stopped.* **The plane** *disappeared.* The verbs in these sentences show (*present, past*) time. 1472
drove 1690	The main point to remember is that the adjective **good** should never be used to describe *how an action is performed.* An adjective cannot modify a (*noun, verb*). 1691
me 1909	**You can ride with them. You can ride with us.** Choose the correct pronouns in the following sentence: **You can ride with** (*them, they*) **or** (*us, we*). 1910
R, A 2128	a. **These cookies were made with Tastee Peanut Butter.** b. **These cookies were made with Tastee peanut butter.** Which sentence is correctly capitalized? ____ 2129
park, 2347	**You should always wash your hands before you handle food.** 2348
Let's, your 2566	_____ **car looks good when** _____ **cleaned up.** (Their, They're) (it's, its) 2567

argument 152	Write the *noun form* of the word in parentheses that will fit in as the subject of this sentence: His _____ came to a sudden end. (happy) 153
indirect objects 372	**The pears were** *small* **but very** *sweet*. The two words—*small* and _____—describe the subject **pears**. 373
played 592	A **preposition** can relate a noun or pronoun that follows it to a **noun, pronoun,** or _____ in some other part of the sentence. 593
The actor wore dark glasses so that people would not recognize him. 812	*I put down the right answer.* **I foolishly changed it.** _____ _____ 813
Dean has several savings bonds which (*or* that) he is keeping for his education. 1032	After each sentence, write *adverb* or *adjective* to show what kind of clause the sentence contains: a. **Bananas are always harvested when they are green.** _____ b. **Most people who have seen the movie recommend it highly.** _____ 1033
were 1252	PRESENT SIMPLE PAST PAST WITH HELPER eat ate have eaten **The entire cake was** _____ **last night.** Which form of the verb is required? 1253

past 1472	The car *stopped.* The plane *disappeared.* The subjects of these sentences are singular. Now read these sentences again, substituting the plural subjects **cars** and **planes.** Did you need to change the verbs to make them agree with the plural subjects? (*Yes, No*) 1473
verb 1691	**Well** is the word to use if you want to say that something is done *in a good or satisfactory manner.* a. **The water is good.** b. **The motor runs good.** In which sentence is the adjective **good** wrong? ____ 1692
them, us 1910	Be just as careful to choose the correct pronoun when the pronoun is paired with a noun. Choose the same pronoun that you would choose if the pronoun were used alone. **The car splashed mud over <u>Grace</u> and (*I, me*).** 1911
b 2129	a. **I removed the stain with Zippo spot remover.** b. **I removed the stain with Zippo Spot Remover.** Which sentence is correctly capitalized? ____ 2130
None 2348	**When we first met Harvey was a sophomore in high school.** 2349
Their, it's 2567	Lesson **82** **Quotation Marks to Make Words Talk** [Frames 2569–2610]

happiness 153	Write the *noun form* of the word in parentheses that will fit in as the subject of this sentence: **My _____ improved a great deal. (spell)** 154
sweet 373	**The pears were** *small* **but very** *sweet.* *Small* and *sweet* are compound (*direct objects, subject complements*). 374
verb 593	Many prepositions show relationships in **position.** POSITION: *in, on, under, beneath, below, over, above, by, beside, across, behind, between,* etc. **The fog** <u>over</u> **the airport was very thick.** The preposition **over** shows the *pos_____* of the **fog** with reference to the **airport.** 594
After I put down the right answer, I foolishly changed it. 813	**Lesson 27 Using Adverb Clauses to Improve Sentences** [Frames 815–839]
a. adverb b. adjective 1033	Adverb or adjective clause? a. **People seldom like foods which they are not accustomed to eating.** _____ b. **All food seems to taste better when it is eaten out-of-doors.** _____ 1034
eaten 1253	PRESENT SIMPLE PAST PAST WITH HELPER **fall** **fell** **have fallen** **The brush has _____ into the paint.** Which form of the verb is required? 1254

SINGULAR

The car *stopped.*
The plane *disappeared.*

PLURAL

The cars *stopped.*
The planes *disappeared.*

The same simple past verb is used whether the subject is singular or plural. (*True, False*)

---

a. **I always sleep good.**
b. **I always sleep well.**

Which sentence is correct? _____

The car splashed mud over Grace and me.

In the above sentence, the object form **me** is correct because if we used each object separately, what would we say?

The car splashed mud over Grace.
The car splashed mud over (*I, me*).

---

a. **the Chrysler Building**
b. **a Chrysler Car**

Which item is incorrect because the type of product, as well as the brand name, is capitalized? _____

From the beginning of recorded time men have observed strange objects in the sky.

To quote means to report what a person said *in his own words*.

a. **The child replied that his name was Martin.**
b. **The child replied, "My name is Martin."**

Which sentence reports directly the child's own words? _____

spelling 154	Write the *noun form* of the word in parentheses that will fit in as the subject of this sentence: _____ **increases in stormy weather. (tardy)** 155
subject complements 374	**Chris and Dad built a small sailboat.** What *connecting word* connects the two parts of the compound subject? 375
(pos)ition 594	Some prepositions show **direction.** DIRECTION: *from, to, toward, down, up, at* **Mark walked toward the corner.** The preposition **toward** shows that Mark **walked** in the direction of the _____. 595
	a. **and, but, or** b. **when, because, if, before, unless, although** Which words can be used as adverb clause signals—those in group *a* or *b*? ____ 815
a. adjective b. adverb 1034	a. **Don worked there for two weeks, and he decided to find a better job.** b. **After Don worked there for two weeks, he decided to find a better job.** Which sentence brings out more clearly the relationship between the two ideas? ____ 1035
fallen 1254	PRESENT SIMPLE PAST PAST WITH HELPER **fly** **flew** **have flown** **Food and medicine were _____ to the flooded area.** 1255

True 1474	When we use simple past verbs, there is almost no problem of making verbs agree with their subjects. The only exception is the verb **be.** Unlike all other verbs, the verb **be** has two simple past forms—**was** and **were.** **Was** is singular, and **were** is _____. 1475
b 1693	**I always sleep** (*good, well*). To describe *how* you **sleep,** you should choose the adverb _____. 1694
me 1912	Be especially careful not to say, **"for you and *I*."** This is probably the most widespread of all pronoun blunders. Since you would never say, **"for *I*,"** do not say, **"for you and *I*,"** which is the same mistake. **Mother left some lunch for you and** (*me, I*). 1913
b 2131	Capitalize the names of the days of the week, months, holidays, and special days. **Wednesday February Thanksgiving Day** Write the capital letters you would need to use in writing **fourth of july.** _____ 2132
time, 2350	**I found a dollar bill at the very bottom of the wastebasket.** 2351
b 2569	a. **The child replied that his name was Martin.** b. **The child replied, "My name is Martin."** Which sentence reports indirectly in someone else's words what the child said? ____ 2570

Tardiness 155	**careless carelessly carelessness** Which one of these words is the *noun form*? _____ 156
and 375	**Andy caught but dropped the ball.** What *connecting word* connects the compound verbs? _____ 376
corner 595	**The space between the two cars was small.** The preposition **between** shows (*position, direction*). 596
b 815	**The plane took off.** To change this simple sentence to an adverb clause, we would need to (*drop, add*) a word. 816
b 1035	A sentence that contains an adverb clause or an adjective clause is a (*compound, complex*) sentence. 1036
flown 1255	Is there a form of the verb **speak** that ends with **–en** or **–n**? (*Yes, No*) 1256

plural
 	
1475
	The verb **be** has two simple past forms—**was** for singular subjects and **were** for plural subjects.
	    a. **talked** **saw** **laughed** **gave**
	    b. **was** **were**
	Which simple past verbs *cannot* be used with both singular and plural subjects—those in *a* or *b*? ____
	                                          1476

well
 	
1694
	a. **Shake the bottle well.**
	        b. **Shake the bottle good.**
	Which sentence is correct because an adverb modifies the verb **Shake?** ____
	                                          1695

me 1913	**Mother left some lunch for you and me.** The object form **me** is correct because **me** is the object of the preposition _____. 1914
F, J 2132	Fill each blank with a small or capital letter, as the word requires: **Schools will open on the ____uesday after Labor ____ay.** 2133
None 2351	**When Mother returned to the store her purse was still on the counter.** 2352
a 2570	**The child replied,** *"My name is Martin."* Because the italicized words quote directly the child's *own words*, we call them a **direct quotation.** We surround the quotation with quotation marks—or **quotes,** for short. We use quotes only when we quote a person's _____ words. 2571

carelessness 156	**announces announcement announced** Which one of these words is the *noun form*? _____ 157
but 376	**Linda or Gail has your purse.** What *connecting word* connects the compound sub-jects? _____ 377
position 596	**We flew to Miami.** The preposition **to** shows (*position, direction*). 597
add 816	An adverb clause can come before or after the main state-ment of a sentence. (*True, False*) 817
complex 1036	A **suffix** is an ending added to a word to make a new word. Underline the suffix that makes the following statement true: We can turn any verb into an adjective by adding the suf-fix (*–ful, –ing, –ous*) to it. 1037
Yes 1256	**The customer had _____ to the manager.** Which form of the verb **speak** is required? 1257

b 1476	A very serious error is the use of the singular verb **was** with a plural subject. WRONG: **The roads was good. Was the roads good?** The subject and verb do not agree in number. The subject **roads** is plural; the verb **was** is _____. 1477
a 1695	A person or thing is **good,** but an action is performed _____. 1696
for 1914	In this and the following frames, select the correct pronouns. Always choose the same form of the pronoun that you would use if the pronoun were used by itself. **The only two runs were made by Chuck and** (*he, him*). 1915
T, D 2133	**Can you name two ____olidays in ____ebruary?** 2134
store, 2352	**Although he shouted the name could not be heard.** 2353

own
 	
2571
	One of the following sentences requires quotes:
	  a. **The doctor said that I should take a deep breath.**
	  b. **The doctor said now take a deep breath.**
	Which sentence requires quotes because it reports what
	the person said *in his own words?* ___
	2572

announcement 157	The same word can often be used as either a *noun* or a *verb*. Which it is depends on how it is used in the sentence. If the word is used as the subject of the sentence, it is used as a *noun*. If the word makes a statement about the subject, it is a _____. 158
or 377	The three connecting words used to connect the compound parts of sentences are **and, but,** and **or.** Words that connect words or groups of words are called **conjunctions.** Three **conjunctions** are _____, **but,** and **or.** 378
direction 597	A few prepositions show relationships in **time.** TIME: *before, during, after, until, till* The **excitement before the game was tremendous.** The **time** relationship between the **excitement** and the **game** is shown by the preposition _____. 598
True 817	A comma is needed between the adverb clause and the main statement when the adverb clause comes (*first, last*). 818
–ing 1037	Eliminate the **and** in this sentence by changing the italicized part to an *–ing* word group. Write the full sentence. *I tore a page from my notebook* **and left a note at the door.** _____ _____ 1038

spoken
 	
1257
	PRESENT SIMPLE PAST PAST WITH HELPER
	speak **spoke** **have spoken**
	  a. **The customer had spoke to the manager.**
	  b. **The customer had spoken to the manager.**
	Which sentence is wrong because the simple past form, instead of the helper form, is used with the helper **had?** ____
	
	1258

singular 1477	**Dale's parents** (*wasn't, weren't*) **at home.** (*Wasn't, Weren't*) **Dale's parents at home?** Both sentences are alike except that one is a statement and the other is a question. Which verb agrees in number with the plural subject **parents?** _____ 1478
well 1696	In this and the following frames, underline the two correct modifiers in each sentence. (Don't assume that one **good** and one **well** are required in each sentence. Some sentences may call for two of the same word.) **You can't study** (*good, well*) **when the light isn't** (*good, well*). 1697
him 1915	**The gift from** (*her, she*) **and Bert came on Christmas Eve.** 1916
h, F 2134	**This year, _____alloween will fall on a _____aturday.** 2135
shouted, 2353	An introductory word group makes sense by itself—apart from the sentence. (*True, False*) 2354
b 2572	Don't use quotes unless you are quoting someone directly *in his own words*. The word **that** is often a signal that we are reporting someone's remark indirectly *in our words*. a. **Dad said** **you sit in front, Bob.** b. **Dad said** **that I should sit in front.** Which sentence requires quotes? ____ 2573

verb 158	In one of the following two sentences, the italicized word is used as a noun; in the other, as a verb. Write *noun* or *verb* after each sentence. **The *fight* begins at nine o'clock. _____** **Children often *fight* over trifles. _____** 159
and 378	Learn to spell **conjunction.** It has three syllables. **con-junc-tion** The middle syllable of this word is _____. 379
before 598	**We fished <u>until</u> nightfall.** The preposition **until** shows a relationship in (*time, position*). 599
first 818	Earlier in this unit, we learned how to combine two simple sentences into a compound sentence by using the conjunction **and, but,** or **or.** **Hong Kong is an island, *and* Victoria is its main city.** In this compound sentence, the conjunction is _____. 819
Tearing a page from my notebook, I left a note at the door. 1038	An appositive is a noun or pronoun set (*after, before*) another noun or pronoun to explain it. 1039

a
 	
1258
	PRESENT SIMPLE PAST PAST WITH HELPER
	  give **gave** **have given**
	  a. **The cashier had given me the wrong change.**
	  b. **The cashier had gave me the wrong change.**
	Which sentence is wrong because the simple past form, instead of the helper form, is used with the helper **had?** ____
	
	1259

weren't 1478	The pronoun **you** always requires a plural verb in English—even when it refers to only one person. Therefore, we should always say, "You *were*"—never "You *was*." **You** (*was, were*) **driving too fast.** (*Was, Were*) **you driving too fast?** Which verb agrees with the subject **you?** _____ 1479
well, good 1697	Underline the correct modifier in each pair: **If the cloth is** (*good, well*), **a suit will wear** (*good, well*). 1698
her 1916	**The Nortons will meet the Coopers and** (*we, us*) **at the park.** 1917
H, S 2135	Do not capitalize the names of the four seasons. spring summer fall winter **They spent the ____ummer in Wisconsin and the ____inter in Florida.** 2136
False 2354	Unless it is very short, an introductory word group should generally be followed by a comma. (*True, False*) 2355
a 2573	**Dad said, "You sit in front, Bob."** What punctuation mark separates the quotation from the words that introduce it (**Dad said**)? _____ 2574

noun verb 159	Is the italicized word a *noun* or a *verb*? **Sandra's *studies* take most of her time.** _____ **Sandra *studies* Spanish after dinner.** _____ 160
junc 379	**Conjunctions** are a kind or *class* of words. We have now become acquainted with four different classes of words: (1) **nouns,** (2) **pronouns,** (3) **verbs,** (4) **conjunctions.** Nouns, pronouns, verbs, and other words can be connected by _____. 380
time 599	Still other prepositions like *of, for, about, with,* and *except* show many different kinds of relationship between the words they relate. EXAMPLES: **a glass <u>of</u> milk a book <u>about</u> dogs** **a gift <u>for</u> Ruth a boy <u>with</u> freckles** Each of the underlined words is a _____. 600
and 819	When we merely wish to add one idea to another idea, we can connect them with **and.** If the two ideas are *similar* and *of equal importance,* the result is a good _____ sentence. 820
after 1039	Must an appositive word group—like a clause—have a subject and a verb? (*Yes, No*) 1040
b 1259	The form of **grow** that ends with **–en** or **–n** is _____. 1260

were 1479	In this and the following frames, only one of the three subjects in parentheses agrees in number with the verb. Underline this subject. (*You, The sailors, The dog*) **was without water.** 1480
good, well 1698	**A person who reads** (*good, well*) **can't always spell** (*good, well*). 1699
us 1917	**Ellen and** (*him, he*) **spoiled the concert by talking.** (Are you checking each pronoun by trying it by itself in the sentence?) 1918
s, w 2136	**Next ____riday is the first day of ____pring.** 2137
True 2355	It gives variety to your writing to put an introductory word group occasionally ahead of your main statement. (*True, False*) 2356
comma 2574	Use a comma to separate the quotation from the **he said** (or similar expression). **He said, "Stop teasing the dog."** The separating comma comes (*before, after*) the quotes. 2575

noun verb 160	Is the italicized word a *noun* or a *verb*? **This pencil** *breaks* **too easily.** _____ **Some bad** *breaks* **in the pavement slowed down traffic.** _____ 161
conjunctions 380	a. **He and she joined the same club.** b. **Carol and Ken joined the same club.** In which sentence does the conjunction **and** connect two pronouns that are used as subjects? _____ 381
preposition 600	The word **but** is a preposition when it means **except**. **Everybody went except Nancy.** In this sentence, we can replace the preposition **except** with the preposition _____ . 601
compound 820	However, by using an adverb clause, we can often point out a more specific relationship than the word **and** expresses. a. **Phil dropped my radio,** *and* **it wouldn't play.** b. *After Phil dropped my radio,* **it wouldn't play.** Which sentence brings out more clearly the relationship between the two ideas? _____ 821
No 1040	Combine these two sentences by changing the italicized sentence to an appositive word group: **Judy was practicing her piano lesson.** *She is my younger* *sister.* _____ _____ 1041
grown 1260	PRESENT SIMPLE PAST PAST WITH HELPER **grow** **grew** **have** _____ Fill in the helper form of this verb. 1261

The dog	Underline the only subject that agrees in number with the verb:
	(The bank, Schools, Stores) **was closed on Monday.**
1480	1481

well, well	**I can't sleep** *(good, well)* **unless the ventilation is** *(good, well).*
1699	1700

he	**The flat tire made the Todds and** *(us, we)* **late.**
1918	1919

F, s	**Do you know why we celebrate ____hanksgiving ____ay in the ____all rather than in another season?**
2137	2138

True	Lesson **76** **Commas for Setting Off Interrupters**
	[Frames 2358–2395]
2356	

before	**He said, "Stop teasing the dog."**
	The separating comma comes before the quotes.
	The period at the end of the sentence comes *(before, after)* the quotes.
2575	2576

verb noun 161	**plant forget** Which one of the above words could be used as both a *noun* and a *verb*? (Think of actual sentences before writing your answer.) _____ 162
a 381	**Bruce either forgot or broke his date.** In this sentence, the conjunction **or** connects two _____. 382
but 601	**The train goes _____ a tunnel.** Underline the preposition that would make good sense in the above sentence. **among with through of** 602
b 821	A sentence that contains a clause is called a **complex sen- tence.** *After Phil dropped my radio,* **it wouldn't play.** Because the above sentence contains a clause, it is a *compound, complex*) sentence. 822
Judy, my younger sister, was practicing her piano lesson. 1041	UNIT 5: **UNDERSTANDING THE SENTENCE UNIT** Lesson **34** **Avoiding Sentence Fragments** [Frames 1043–1077]
grown 1261	**These tomatoes were . . . in our own backyard.** Which form of the verb **grow** is required? _____ 1262

The bank 1481	Underline the only subject that agrees in number with the verb: (*You, I, We*) **was watching the game.** 1482
well, good 1700	**Our seats were** (*good, well*), **and we heard very** (*good, well*). 1701
us 1919	**Mr. Bailey sat behind Verna and** (*me, I*) **at the play.** 1920

T, D, f
 	
2138
	Capitalize the names of historical events and documents (but not **the** when it precedes these names).
	
	    the Korean War **the Battle of Gettysburg**
	    the Bill of Rights **the Declaration of Independence**
	
	Write the capital letters you would need to use in writing
	
	the war of independence. _____
	
	2139

	We often use expressions that interrupt the smooth flow of the sentence. In speaking them, we drop our voices and pause before and after to set them off from the main idea.
	
	    John, *however,* **is much older.**
	    The breakfast, *for example,* **costs fifty cents.**
	
	The interrupting expressions are set off with _____.
	
	2358

before 2576	Now let's turn the sentence around and put the quotation first instead of last. **"Stop teasing the dog," he said.** Look at the point where the comma and quotes come together. Does the comma still come before the quotes? (*Yes, No*) 2577

plant	Is the italicized word a *noun* or a *verb*?
	The *plant* needs water. _____
	Many farmers *plant* corn. _____
162	163

verbs	The words **and, but,** and **or** are _____.
382	383

through	**The plane _____ New York was late.**
	Underline the preposition that would make good sense in the above sentence.
	against from during except
602	603

complex	a. **Ted insisted on diving,** *and* **the water was too shallow.**
	b. **Ted insisted on diving** *although the water was too shallow.*
	Which sentence is a complex sentence? ____
822	823

	A **fragment** means "a broken piece"—like a fragment of glass or wood.
	A **sentence fragment** is a piece of a sentence that is written as though it were a complete _____.
	1043

grown	PRESENT SIMPLE PAST PAST WITH HELPER
	grow grew have grown
	We (*grew, growed*) these tomatoes in our own back yard.
1262	1263

I 1482	Underline the only subject that agrees in number with the verb: **Was** (*your sister, you, they*) **at Saturday's game?** <div align="right">1483</div>
good, well 1701	**When business is** (*good, well*), **employment is** (*good, well*). <div align="right">1702</div>
me 1920	**The Fields and** (*us, we*) **have been neighbors for years.** <div align="right">1921</div>
W, I 2139	Copy only the words that need to be capitalized, adding the capitals: **Delaware was the first state to ratify the constitution.** _____ <div align="right">2140</div>
commas 2358	The commas that set off interrupting expressions help your reader to keep his mind on the main idea. Underline the interrupter and set it off with commas: **It happened I suppose on an icy pavement.** <div align="right">2359</div>
Yes 2577	<div align="center">**He said, "Stop teasing the dog."** **"Stop teasing the dog," he said.**</div> When a comma and quotes or a period and quotes come together, always put the comma or period first. Punctuate this sentence completely: <div align="center">**The farmer replied These eggs were laid today**</div> <div align="right">2578</div>

Lesson 6 Pronouns Take the Place of Nouns

[Frames 165–192]

---

conjunctions

383

Three common conjunctions used to connect compound subjects, verbs, and other parts of the sentence are **and,**

_____, _____.

384

---

from

603

Our dog jumped _____ **the fence and escaped.**

Underline the preposition that would make good sense in the above sentence.

in   around   near   over

604

---

b

823

a. **Ted insisted on diving,** *and* **the water was too shallow.**
b. **Ted insisted on diving** *although the water was too shallow.*

Which sentence shows more clearly how the two ideas are related? _____

824

---

sentence

1043

To be a sentence, a group of words must pass two tests:

1. Does it have a subject and a predicate?
2. Does it make sense by itself?

A little man in a big hat.

The above word group is a (*fragment, sentence*).

1044

---

grew

1263

The form of **know** that ends with **-en** or **-n** is _____.

1264

your sister 1483	Underline the only subject that agrees in number with the verb: **Was** (*the tickets, the refreshments, the game*) **free?** <div align="right">1484</div>
good, good 1702	**These scissors used to be** (*good, well*)**, but now they don't cut** (*good, well*)**.** <div align="right">1703</div>
we 1921	**We didn't see** (*them, they*) **or the Masons at church today.** <div align="right">1922</div>
Constitution 2140	Copy only the words that need to be capitalized, adding the capitals: **One of the fiercest battles of World war II was the Battle of the bulge.** ——————————————— <div align="right">2141</div>
, I suppose, 2359	Here are other common interrupters that must be fenced off by commas from the sentences in which they occur: **of course by the way on the whole on the other hand** **it seems if possible nevertheless as a matter of fact** Underline the interrupter and set it off with commas: **English on the other hand is easier for me.** <div align="right">2360</div>
replied, "These . . . today." 2578	Punctuate this sentence completely: **These eggs were laid today replied the farmer.** <div align="right">2579</div>

Another kind of word that can serve as the subject of a verb is the **pronoun**. The name *pronoun* comes from a Latin word which means "in place of a noun."

As their name suggests, pronouns are words used in place of _____.

165

---

but, or

384

We can buy or rent a tent.

This sentence has compound _____.

385

---

over

604

(This problem is different. Read the directions carefully.)

We walked _____ the park.

Underline the *one* preposition that would *not* make good sense in the above sentence.

across   around   with   toward

605

---

b

824

a. **Ted insisted on diving,** *and* **the water was too shallow.**
b. **Ted insisted on diving** *although the water was too shallow.*

The relationship between the two ideas is made clearer by using an adverb clause in a (*complex, compound*) sentence.

825

---

fragment

1044

A little man in a big hat . . .

This word group is a fragment because it names something (man) but makes no statement about it.

In other words, this word group is not a sentence because it lacks a (*subject, predicate*).

1045

---

known

1264

The causes of tuberculosis have been . . . for a long time.

Which form of the verb **know** is required? _____

1265

the game 1484	An even more common error is the use of **don't** for **doesn't**. **Don't** is a short cut for **do not; doesn't** is a short cut for **does not.** <div align="center">**My dad** *doesn't* **smoke.**</div> The word **doesn't** takes the place of the two words _____ _____. <div align="right">1485</div>
good, well 1703	**This motor runs** (*good, well*) **if the gasoline is** (*good, well*). <div align="right">1704</div>
them 1922	**The police had trailed his partner and** (*he, him*) **across the state.** <div align="right">1923</div>
War, Bulge 2141	Copy only the words that need to be capitalized, adding the capitals: **The United Nations charter went into effect on october 24,** **1945.** _____ <div align="right">2142</div>
, on the other hand, 2360	When an interrupter begins or ends a sentence, we need, of course, only one comma to set it apart from the main idea. Punctuate this sentence: <div align="center">**As a matter of fact he was telling the truth.**</div> <div align="right">2361</div>
"These . . . today," 2579	The first word of a quotation is always capitalized because it is the beginning of someone's sentence. <div align="center">**The farmer replied, "These eggs were laid today."**</div> The first letter in the above quotation is capital ____. <div align="right">2580</div>

nouns
 	
165
	Notice how a pronoun can take the place of a noun:
	
	      a. **The** *dog* **ran away.**
	      b. *It* **ran away.**
	
	The pronoun *It* in sentence *b* takes the place of the noun
	
	_____ in sentence *a*.
	
	<div align="right">166</div>

verbs 385	**Bob and the new boy soon became friends.** This sentence has a compound _____. <div align="right">386</div>
with 605	**Joan hid the money _____ a book.** Underline the *one* preposition that would *not* make good sense in the above sentence. **in under behind until** <div align="right">606</div>
complex 825	It is easy to change a **compound** sentence to a **complex** sentence. *although* **Tony can play the piano,** ~~and~~ **he has never taken lessons.** We put the clause signal *although* in place of the conjunction *and*. In this way the (*first, second*) part of the compound sentence becomes an adverb clause. <div align="right">826</div>

predicate
 	
1045
	A little man in a big hat . . .
	
	Which of the following items could make a sentence of the
	
	above fragment by providing a predicate? _____
	
	      a. **with a gray band**
	      b. **and a long raincoat**
	      c. **boarded the bus**
	
	<div align="right">1046</div>

known
 	
1265
	PRESENT SIMPLE PAST PAST WITH HELPER
	know **knew** **have known**
	
	    a. **I should have knew better than to depend on Tommy.**
	    b. **I should have known better than to depend on Tommy.**
	
	Which sentence is right? _____
	
	<div align="right">1266</div>

does not 1485	**Eric's parents** *don't* **speak English.** The word **don't** takes the place of the two words _____ _____. 1486
well, good 1704	Lesson **56** Modifiers After "Sense" Verbs [Frames 1706–1742]
him 1923	**Mother had kept the secret from Bert and** (*me, I*). 1924
Charter, October 2142	With two exceptions, which will be explained shortly, the general subjects taught in schools should not be capitalized. **arithmetic algebra history biology** **Ron is excellent in** (*math, Math*). 2143
fact, 2361	a. **I was worried** *by the way* **he acted.** b. **This model** *by the way* **is more expensive.** In one sentence, the italicized phrase is a necessary part of the sentence; in the other, it is an interrupter that might be omitted. In which sentence is it an interrupter—*a* or *b*? _____ 2362
T 2580	a. **Mr. Dole said, "You may use my desk."** b. **Mr. Dole said, "you may use my desk."** Which sentence is correct? _____ 2581

dog 166	a. **Bob drove the car.** b. **He drove the car.** In place of the noun **Bob** in sentence *a*, we have the pronoun _____ in sentence *b*. 167
subject 386	**Fred stayed in his room and studied.** This sentence has compound _____. 387
until 606	**The explosion occurred _____ the fire.** Underline the *one* preposition that would *not* make good sense in the above sentence. **before of after during** 607
second 826	COMPOUND: **Tony can play the piano,** *and* **he has never taken lessons.** COMPLEX: **Tony can play the piano** *although he has never taken lessons.* The contrast between the two ideas is brought out more clearly by the (*compound, complex*) sentence. 827
c 1046	**A little man in a big hat boarded the bus.** This is now a complete sentence because it has both a subject and a _____. 1047
b 1266	If an irregular verb has a form that ends with **–en** or **–n**, use it after any form of the helping verb **be** or _____. 1267

do not 1486	Before using **don't**, see if you can fit **do not** in its place. **He** *don't* **like oysters.** *Don't* **he like oysters?** Can we substitute **do not** for **don't** in these sentences? (*Yes, No*) 1487
	Here are five well-known senses that human beings have: 1. We *hear* with our ears. 2. We *smell* with our noses. 3. We *look* with our eyes. 4. We *taste* with our tongues. 5. We *feel* with our hands. **I looked at my watch.** The verb **looked** means an action of the (*ears, eyes, nose*). 1706
me 1924	**Vincent and** (*me, I*) **played the parts of the two brothers.** 1925
math 2143	a. **Ann likes History better than Algebra.** b. **Ann likes history better than algebra.** Which sentence is correctly capitalized? ____ 2144
b 2362	a. **I was worried by the way he acted.** b. **This model by the way is more expensive.** In which sentence should the phrase **by the way** be set off with commas? ____ 2363
a 2581	a. **The waitress replied, "the pie is all gone."** b. **The waitress replied, "The pie is all gone."** Which sentence is correct? ____ 2582

He 167	a. **The *coat* fits better.** b. *This* **fits better.** Is the italicized word a pronoun in sentence *a* or *b*? _____ 168
verbs 387	**Minneapolis and St. Paul are on opposite sides of the Mississippi River.** This sentence has a compound _____. 388
of 607	Write in the blank a preposition that would make good sense in each sentence: a. **Judy looked** _____ **herself in the mirror.** b. **The address** _____ **the envelope was not clear.** 608
complex 827	Now let's change the **first** part of a compound sentence to an adverb clause: *Because* _____ **The road was under repair, ~~and~~ we had to turn back.** We drop the conjunction *and*. Then we add the clause signal _____ at the beginning of the sentence. 828
predicate 1047	Now we shall add a clause to our sentence: **A little man** *who was wearing a big hat* **boarded the bus.** The clause *who was wearing a big hat* modifies the noun **man**. It is therefore an (*adjective, adverb*) clause. 1048
have 1267	**The cashier gave me the wrong change.** If you added the helper **had** to the verb, you would need to change the verb **gave** to _____. 1268

No

1487

a. He *don't* like oysters.
b. They *don't* like oysters.

In which sentence is **don't** wrong because the words **do not** would be wrong? ____

1488

---

eyes

1706

look   smell   taste   feel   hear

When these "sense" verbs mean the actions we perform with our eyes, nose, hands, etc., we should use *adverbs* to describe these actions.

Melba looked (*sad, sadly*) **at the run in her new nylons.**

1707

I

1925

Between you and (*I, me*)**, it doesn't make any difference.** (**Between** is a preposition.)

1926

---

b

2144

We do, however, capitalize the names of language subjects.

English   Latin   French   Spanish

Underline the names of subjects you would capitalize in the following sentence:

I'm now taking english, algebra, french, and history.

2145

---

b

2363

a. **The watchman** *it seems* **was asleep.**
b. *It seems* **to be warmer today.**

In which sentence should *it seems* be set off with commas because it is an interrupter? ____

2364

---

b

2582

a. **"You can't hunt on this land", warned the farmer.**
b. **"You can't hunt on this land," warned the farmer.**

Which sentence is correct? ____

2583

b 168	a. *Ours* **won the game.** b. **The** *team* **won the game.** Is the italicized word a pronoun in sentence *a* or *b*? ____ 169
subject 388	**My favorite subjects are math and science.** This sentence has compound (*subject complements, subjects*). 389
a. at **b. on** 608	Write in the blank a preposition that would make good sense in each sentence: a. **Vicky is still talking** _____ **her operation.** b. **Everyone in our family** _____ **Ken has had the mumps.** 609
Because 828	_____ **Mother was reading a magazine,** *and* **the rice boiled over.** How would we change the **first** part of this compound sentence to an adverb clause? Drop the conjunction *and.* Then put the clause signal *while* or *as* before the word _____. 829
adjective 1048	Do not mistake a modifier for a predicate. **A little man** *who was wearing a big hat . . .* This is not a sentence. It is just a subject with an adjective clause that modifies it. To make a sentence of this fragment, we would need to add a _____. 1049
given 1268	PRESENT SIMPLE PAST PAST WITH HELPER **throw** **threw** **have thrown** **My test was** (*threw, thrown, throwed*) **out by mistake.** 1269

a	Never use **don't** unless you can put the two words _____ _____ in its place.
1488	1489

sadly	**Mrs. Roe felt the material** (*careful, carefully*). **Felt** is an action performed with one's hands. To describe the action of the verb **felt,** we should choose the adverb _____.
1707	1708

me	**The Devil's Ride made Leora and** (*him, he*) **sick.**
1926	1927

English, French	When the name of a language is combined with the word **history** or **literature,** capitalize only the name of the language. **English literature American history** Underline the words you would capitalize: **Ellen enjoys american literature and english history.**
2145	2146

a	When the word **yes, no,** or **well** begins a sentence, it should be followed by a comma. **Yes, we do own a dog. No, I don't agree.** **Well, this is all the news I have to tell.** Supply *three* necessary commas: **Yes I shall if possible give Iris your message.**
2364	2365

b	One set of quotes ("...") will take care of any number of sentences as long as the same person continues to speak. Punctuate the following quotation: **Walter said I have known Bob for several years. He has a lot of ability. He's a hard worker. You can't elect a better class president.**
2583	2584

a	**The boys washed the car.**
	Underline the *pronoun* that could take the place of the noun **(The) boys** in the above sentence.
	neighbors women they
169	170

subject complements	**The high wind blew down many trees and dead branches.**
	This sentence has compound (*direct objects, subject complements*).
389	390

a. about b. but *or* except	Underline the preposition in each sentence:
	a. **A small sign pointed to the lunchroom.** b. **The paper printed the names of the winner.**
609	610

Mother	_____ **I looked over my paper,** *and* **I noticed several mistakes.**
	After you drop the conjunction *and*, what clause signal would you put at the beginning of the sentence? _____
829	830

predicate	a. **A little man** *who was wearing a big hat.* b. **A little man** *who was wearing a big hat* **boarded the bus.**
	A subject followed by a modifying word group is not a sentence.
	The complete sentence is ____.
1049	1050

thrown	**The catcher should have . . . the ball to second base.**
	Which form of the verb **throw** is required? _____
1269	1270

do not 1489	In this and the following frames, only one of the three subjects in parentheses agrees in number with the verb. Underline this subject. (*The cover, The bolts, The hat*) **don't fit.** 1490
carefully 1708	**Shirley tasted her first cake very** (*hopeful, hopefully*). **Tasted** is an action performed with one's tongue. To describe the action of the verb **tasted,** we should choose the adverb _____. 1709
him 1927	**Here's a snapshot of** (*he, him*) **and his dog.** 1928
American, English 2146	a. **Our coach also teaches American history.** b. **Our coach also teaches American History.** Which sentence is correctly capitalized? ____ 2147
Yes, shall, possible, 2365	a. **No I have never been to Florida.** b. **No small boat could survive in such a gale.** In which sentence should a comma follow the word **No?**____ 2366
said, "I . . . president." 2584	In this and the following frames, supply all the necessary commas and quotes. A few sentences do not require quotes because they do not give the actual words of the speaker. **You meet us in the gym said Bert.** 2585

they 170	Underline the *noun* that the pronoun **she** could take the place of: **girls Peggy sisters** 171
direct objects 390	**My topcoat is light but warm.** This sentence has compound (*direct objects, subject complements*). 391
a. to b. of 610	**I dropped my coin into the slot.** What is the preposition that shows the relationship between **dropped** and **slot**? _____ 611

As (When, While)
 	
830
	A complex sentence is not always better than a compound sentence with **and.** It is better only when there is a more specific relationship than the word **and** can express.
	    a. **Pat's hair is red,** *and* **his eyes are blue.**
	    b. **Don is very bright,** *and* **he gets poor grades.**
	Which compound sentence would you leave as it is? ____
	
	831

b 1050	**The old wooden bridge.** This word group is a (*sentence, fragment*). 1051
thrown 1270	The form of the verb **write** that ends with **–en** or **–n** is _____. 1271

The bolts 1490	Underline the only subject that agrees in number with the verb: *(The tires, It, The car)* **don't look new.** 1491

hopefully
 	
1709
	look smell taste feel hear (sound)
	Besides meaning actions of parts of our bodies, these words have another and more common meaning.
	    a. **Connie smelled the roses.**
	    b. **The roses smelled fragrant.**
	Smelled means an action of the nose in sentence _____.
	1710

him 1928	In this and the following frames, underline the two correct pronouns in each sentence: *(She, Her)* **and** *(I, me)* **first met at Alice's party.** 1929
a 2147	**Next semester we study ∧ literature.** If you inserted the word **American** at the point indicated, would you need to capitalize the noun **literature?** *(Yes, No)* 2148

a
 	
2366
	When the word **why** begins a sentence that does not ask a question, it should be followed by a comma.
	
	    a. **Why did you change your mind?**
	    b. **Why this story is ridiculous!**
	
	In which sentence does **Why** require a comma? _____
	2367

"You . . . gym," 2585	**Bert said You meet us in the gym.** 2586

Peggy 171	The noun **elephant** can mean only one *definite* kind of animal. The pronoun **it,** on the contrary, could mean almost anything—an elephant, a cat, a city, or a cake. A pronoun is generally (*more, less*) definite than a noun. 172
subject complements 391	**His aunt and uncle play both golf and tennis.** Besides having compound subjects, this sentence also has compound (*direct objects, subject complements*). 392
into 611	**Coffee without sugar has a bitter taste.** What is the preposition that shows the relationship between **coffee** and **sugar?** _____ 612
a 831	**Pat's hair is red,** *and* **his eyes are blue.** This is a good compound sentence. We merely wish to state two facts about Pat's appearance, and we connect them with *and.* There is no other relationship between the two facts. Could you improve this sentence by making it complex? (*Yes, No*) 832

fragment
 	
1051
	The old wooden bridge . . .
	Which one of the following word groups could change this fragment to a sentence—*a, b,* or *c?* _____
	
	    a. **which was built 50 years ago**
	    b. **collapsed**
	    c. **across the shallow stream**
	
	1052

written 1271	Supply the right form of the verb **write:** **The new teacher's name was** _____ **on the board.** 1272

The tires
 	
1491
	Underline the only subject that agrees in number with the verb:
	
	    (Archie, We, My dad) **don't like spinach.**
	
	                                            1492

a 1710	Besides meaning an action of the nose, the verb **smelled** has another use. **The roses smelled (= were) fragrant.** In this sentence, **smelled** serves as a linking verb—like **were**— to show that the adjective **fragrant** modifies the subject _____. 1711
She, I 1929	**There isn't room in George's car for both** *(them, they)* **and** *(us, we).* 1930

No
 	
2148
	We also capitalize any school subject that is followed by a *course number*. The course number pins it down as a *particular* course in a general subject.
	
	    algebra—Algebra (1) **literature—Literature II**
	
	Underline the words you would capitalize:
	
	    After completing typewriting (2), I began shorthand. 2149

b 2367	Another type of sentence interrupter is the appositive. An **appositive** is a noun or pronoun—often with modifiers —set after another noun or pronoun to explain it. **Mr. Ebert,** *my English teacher,* **coaches the tennis team.** The appositive explains who _____ is. 2368
said, "You . . . gym." 2586	**Bert said** **that we should meet him in the gym.** 2587

less 172	The noun **teachers** is (*more, less*) definite than the pronoun **they**. 173
direct objects 392	Lesson **14** **Verbs of More Than One Word** [Frames 394–429]
without 612	**The lamp <u>on</u> the table is broken.** **The lamp <u>beside</u> the table is broken.** In these two sentences, the relationship between **lamp** and **table** is different because the _____ are different. 613
No 832	COMPOUND: **Don is very bright,** *and* **he gets poor grades.** COMPLEX: **Don is very bright** *although he gets poor* *grades.* The contrast between the two facts is expressed more clearly in the (*compound, complex*) sentence. 833
b 1052	**The old wooden bridge collapsed.** Now the meaning is complete because the verb _____ makes a statement about the subject **bridge**. 1053

written
 	
1272
	In rapid conversation, the verb **have** and the preposition **of** sound very much alike. Be careful not to write **of** when you mean **have**.
	    a. **You should have started earlier.**
	    b. **You should of started earlier.**
	Which sentence is correct? ____
	1273

We 1492	Underline the only subject that agrees in number with the verb: (*The ladies, My mother, Mr. Henry*) **don't play bridge.** 1493
roses 1711	**The roses were fragrant.** **The roses smelled fragrant.** The verbs **were** and **smelled** both serve the same purpose. They *link* the adjective **fragrant** with the subject **roses,** which it describes. **Were** and **smelled** are, therefore, _____*ing* verbs. 1712
them, us 1930	**Mr. Thomas always gave** (*she, her*) **and** (*I, me*) **the same grades.** 1931
Typewriting (2) 2149	**We are having a test in math ∧ today.** If you inserted the number **(2)** at the point indicated, would you need to capitalize the noun **math?** (*Yes, No*) 2150
Mr. Ebert 2368	**Mr. Ebert,** *my English teacher,* **coaches the tennis team.** Read the above sentence, omitting the italicized appositive. Is it still a complete sentence without the appositive? (*Yes, No*) 2369
None 2587	**The man turned around and said Please don't rattle your program.** 2588

more 173	**Which won the first prize?** We do not know whether *which* refers to a story, a dog, a car, or what. The word *which* is a (*noun, pronoun*). 174
	A verb often needs the help of one or more other verbs to express our exact meaning. **He might study.** **He should study.** These sentences have (*the same, different*) meanings. 394
prepositions 613	A preposition shows the _____*ship* between the noun or pronoun that follows it and some other word in the sentence. 614
complex 833	In this and the following frames, improve each sentence by changing the italicized part to an adverb clause. In other words, change each compound sentence to a complex sentence. Write the full sentence. *I start to eat popcorn,* **and it is hard to stop.** _____ 834
collapsed 1053	a. **The old wooden bridge collapsed.** b. **Because the old wooden bridge collapsed.** Although both word groups have a subject and a verb, which one does *not* make sense by itself? ____ 1054
a 1273	When **have** is a helping verb, it is followed by the main verb. The preposition **of,** on the other hand, is followed by a noun or pronoun. **I could (*of, have*) done this better myself.** **Have** should be used because it is followed by a (*verb, noun*). 1274

The ladies 1493	Underline the only subject that agrees in number with the verb: **Don't** (*Fred, he, the boys*) **want the job?** 1494
link(ing) 1712	**The roses smelled** (*fragrant, fragrantly*). Because the word that follows the linking verb **smelled** describes the subject **roses,** we should choose the adjective _____. 1713
her, me 1931	(*They, Them*) **and** (*we, us*) **are on the same party line.** 1932
Yes 2150	**Jerry does well in Mechanical Drawing (3).** If you dropped the number **(3)** from this sentence, would you still write **Mechanical Drawing** with capital letters? (*Yes, No*) 2151

Yes
 	
2369
	The appositive is an "extra" which may be omitted without damaging the completeness of the sentence.
	    a. **Our target,** *a small tin can,* **was nailed to a post.**
	    b. *A small tin can* **was nailed to a post for our target.**
	
	In which sentence are the italicized words an appositive?
	
	_____ 2370

said, "Please . . . program." 2588	**It's like squeezing blood out of a turnip sighed Rita.** 2589

pronoun 174	a. **Three** *eggs* **broke.** b. *Some* **broke.** Is the italicized word a pronoun in sentence *a* or *b*? ____ 175
different 394	**He** <u>might study</u>. **He** <u>should study</u>. The words that give these sentences different meanings are **might** and _____. 395
relation(ship) 614	Lesson **21** **The Prepositional Phrase as a Modifier** [Frames 616–646]
When (Whenever, After, If) I start to eat popcorn, it is hard to stop. 834	**These coins are valuable,** *and very few of them exist.* _____ _____ 835
b 1054	a. **The old wooden** <u>bridge</u> <u>collapsed.</u> b. **Because the old wooden** <u>bridge</u> <u>collapsed</u> **. . .** By adding the clause signal **because** to sentence *a*, we changed it from a sentence to an adverb _____, which needs a main statement to give it meaning. 1055
verb 1274	**Virginia must** (*of, have*) **waited for over an hour.** Which word is correct in this sentence? _____ 1275

the boys 1494	Underline the only subject that agrees in number with the verb: **Don't** (*the neighbors, your father, she*) **object to the noise?** 1495
fragrant 1713	a. **Mrs. Roe felt the material.** b. **Mrs. Roe felt happy.** In which sentence does **felt** mean an action of the hands— *a* or *b*? _____ 1714
They, we 1932	**Are you going to vote for** (*he, him*) **or** (*she, her*)**?** 1933
No 2151	**There is more to remember in American History II.** If you dropped the number **II,** would you still write **American** with a capital letter? (*Yes, No*) 2152
a 2370	An appositive always comes *after* the noun or pronoun it explains. a. **Harvey Brooks, the editor of our paper, is graduating.** b. **The editor of our paper, Harvey Brooks, is graduating.** In which sentence is **Harvey Brooks** an appositive? _____ 2371
"It's . . . turnip," 2589	**I told the driver that one of his headlights was out.** 2590

b 175	a. *People* **wanted their money back.** b. *Customers* **wanted their money back.** c. *Many* **wanted their money back.** In which sentence is the subject a pronoun, not a noun? ____ 176
should 395	a. **He might study.** b. **He should study.** In sentence *a*, the verb consists of two words—**might study.** In sentence *b*, the verb consists of two words— _____ _____. 396
	The noun or pronoun that follows a preposition is called its **object.** **Fred works for his uncle.** The object of the preposition **for** is the noun _____. 616
These coins are valuable because (since, as) very few of them exist. 835	*The winners were being announced,* **and everyone held his breath.** _____ _____ 836
clause 1055	*Because the old wooden bridge collapsed,* **we took the longer road.** The adverb clause answers the question (*How? Why?*) about the action of the verb in the main statement. 1056
have 1275	Fill in the right word: **Nobody could** _____ **tried harder.** 1276

the neighbors 1495	Lesson **48** The Useful "Rule of *S*" [Frames 1497–1520]
a 1714	**Mrs. Roe felt the material** (*careful, carefully*). In this sentence, **felt** means an action of the hands. To describe this action, we should choose the adverb _____. 1715
him, her 1933	Lesson **63** The Problem of Omitted Words [Frames 1935–1968]
Yes 2152	In this and the following frames, cross out each capital letter that is not correct: **We study the Bill Of Rights in American History.** 2153
b 2371	Because an appositive interrupts the sentence, it is set off with commas (or with a comma if it ends the sentence). Punctuate this sentence: **Colgate Clock the largest clock in the world is in New York.** 2372
None 2590	**Miss Gaines said You look out the window. You play with your pen. You talk to your neighbors. You do everything except pay attention.** 2591

c 176	a. *Everybody* **liked this program.** b. *Roger* **liked this program.** In which sentence is the subject a pronoun, not a noun? _____ 177
should study 396	Verbs that help the main verb to express our meaning more exactly are called **helping verbs** or **helpers**. **He <u>must</u> study.** The main verb is **study;** the helping verb is _____. 397
uncle 616	**The sound of heavy footsteps awoke me.** The object of the preposition **of** is the noun _____. 617
As (While, When) the winners were being announced, everyone held his breath. 836	*We fed our cat salmon,* **and it would eat no other food.** _____ _____ 837
Why? 1056	*Because the old wooden bridge collapsed,* **we took the longer road.** The adverb clause modifies the verb _____ in the main statement. 1057
have 1276	**One <u>of</u> the pupils must <u>of</u> lost some <u>of</u> the tickets.** There are three **of**'s in this sentence. Write the word which follows the **of** which should have been **have.** _____ 1277

The <u>dog</u> <u>barked</u>.

If we made the subject **dog** plural, would we need to change the simple past verb **barked?** (*Yes, No*)

1497

---

carefully

a. **Mrs. Roe felt the material.**
b. **Mrs. Roe felt happy.**

In which sentence is **felt** a linking verb which links an adjective with the subject **Mrs. Roe?** ____

1715

1716

A comparison expressed by the word **than** or **as** is usually an abbreviated sentence. By supplying the omitted words, you will see instantly which pronoun to choose.

Gerald stayed later than I (stayed).

The omitted verb in this sentence is _____.

1935

Øf, History

Cross out each capital letter that is not correct:

We shall have tests in English and Algebra when we return from our Spring vacation.

2153

2154

Clock, world,

Punctuate this sentence:

A heavy snowstorm held up our train the Lexington Express.

2372

2373

---

said, "You . . . attention."

This wasn't my lucky day   groaned Mike.

2591

2592

a 177	a. **Wayne and Gary were absent.** b. **Both were absent.** How many names in sentence *a* does the word **Both** in sentence *b* take the place of? _____ 178
must 397	Learn to recognize these important helping verbs. Each has its own special meaning. HELPING VERBS: **shall, will** **may, can** **could, would, should** **must, might** Two helping verbs that rhyme with **could** are _____ and _____. 398
footsteps 617	**The band marched across the muddy field.** The object of the preposition **across** is the noun _____. 618
After (Since, Because, If, When) we fed our cat salmon, it would eat no other food. 837	**Bob is always broke,** *and he gets a good salary.* _____ _____ 838
took 1057	a. *Because the old wooden bridge collapsed,* **we took the longer road.** b. *Because the old wooden bridge collapsed.* **We took the longer road.** Which is correct because the adverb clause is in the same sentence with the verb it modifies? _____ 1058
lost 1277	Lesson **41** **Straightening Out** *Lie* **and** *Lay* [Frames 1279–1317]

No 1497	SINGULAR: **The <u>dog</u> <u>barked</u>.** PLURAL: **The <u>dogs</u> <u>barked</u>.** We use the same simple past verb whether its subject is singular or _____. 1498
b 1716	**Mrs. Roe felt (= was) happy.** In this sentence, **felt** is a linking verb which links the adjective **happy** with the subject _____, which it describes. 1717
stayed 1935	**Gerald stayed later than <u>I</u> (stayed).** The subject form **I** is correct because it is the (*subject, object*) of the omitted verb **stayed.** 1936
A̶lgebra, S̶pring 2154	Cross out each capital letter that is not correct: **Myra's Shorthand teacher got her a job with the Company that manufactures Princess Shoes.** 2155
train, 2373	Punctuate this sentence: **With the help of Bob Morely the boy across the street I built a model jet plane.** 2374
"This . . . day," 2592	**Tommy announced firmly that he didn't want any supper.** 2593

Two 178	**Both were absent.** The word **Both** is a _____. 179
would, should 398	HELPING VERBS: **shall, will** **may, can** **could, would, should** **must, might** Two helping verbs that begin with **m** and end with **t** are _____ and _____. 399
field 618	A group of words that begins with a preposition and ends with its object is called a **prepositional phrase.** **The sound of heavy footsteps awoke me.** In this sentence, the **prepositional phrase** begins with the preposition **of** and ends with its object _____. 619
Bob is always broke although he gets a good salary. 838	**We'll mark our route on the map,** *and we won't lose our way.* _____ _____ 839
a 1058	**The kettle whistles. When the water boils.** The second word group is not a sentence. It is an adverb clause that modifies the verb _____ in the main statement to which it should be attached. 1059
	The verbs **lie** and **lay** are often confused. First, let's see how these slippery little verbs differ in meaning. **To lie** means "to rest in a flat position" or "to be in place." **Don't _____ in the hot sun.** 1279

plural 1498	Except for the verb **be,** all verbs have one simple past form that is used with both singular and plural subjects. SINGULAR: **The <u>dog was</u> hungry.** PLURAL: **The <u>dogs were</u> hungry.** The verb **be,** however, has two simple past forms: the singular form **was** and the plural form _____. <div align="right">1499</div>
Mrs. Roe 1717	**Mrs. Roe felt** (*happy, happily*). Because the word that follows the linking verb **felt** describes the subject **Mrs. Roe,** we should choose the word _____. <div align="right">1718</div>
subject 1936	**We live closer to the school than <u>they</u> (_____).** The omitted verb in this sentence is _____. <div align="right">1937</div>
$horthand, ¢ompany, $hoes 2155	**George plans to take Chemistry and Geometry (2) at Summer School.** <div align="right">2156</div>
Bob Morley, street, 2374	Here is another type of interrupter that requires commas. When we address (talk to) a person directly, we often interrupt a sentence to insert his name or other words that identify him. This is called **direct address.** *Donna* **wants you to write her,** *Nancy,* **about your plans.** The name used in direct address is (*Donna, Nancy*). <div align="right">2375</div>
None 2593	**A sign on the lawn says Your feet are killing me.** <div align="right">2594</div>

pronoun
 	
179
	To show ownership, nouns and pronouns have a **possessive** form. Possessive pronouns take the place of possessive nouns.
	
	      a. **Sharon's hair is red.**
	      b. **Her hair is red.**
	
	What pronoun in sentence *b* takes the place of **Sharon's** in sentence *a*? _____
	
	180

must, might 399	HELPING VERBS: **shall, will** **may, can** **could, would, should** **must, might** Two helping verbs that end with **–ll** are _____ and _____. 400
footsteps 619	**My cousin lives on a very large ranch.** In this sentence, the **prepositional phrase** begins with the preposition **on** and ends with its object _____. 620
We'll mark our route on the map so that we won't lose our way. 839	Lesson **28** **Understanding the Adjective Clause** [Frames 841–875]
whistles 1059	a. **The kettle whistles. When the water boils.** b. **The kettle whistles when the water boils.** Because an adverb clause should be in the same sentence as the verb it modifies, (*a, b*) is correct. 1060
lie 1279	A rug **lies** on the floor, a letter **lies** on the desk, and a person _____ in bed. 1280

were
 	
1499
	Now we shall change to present time.
	
	       SINGULAR: **The dog** *barks.*
	       PLURAL: **The dogs** *bark.*
	
	The verbs in both sentences show present time.
	
	Is the same form of the verb used with both a singular and a plural subject? (*Yes, No*)
	
	                                     1500

happy 1718	When the "sense" verbs **look, smell, taste, feel,** and **hear** mean actions of the body, we use (*adjectives, adverbs*) to describe the action. 1719
live (*or* do) 1937	We live closer to the school than <u>they</u> (live). The subject form **they** is correct because **they** is the (*subject, object*) of the omitted verb **live.** 1938

¢hemistry,
$ummer
$chool
 	
2156
	In this and the following frames, underline the words that lack required capitals:
	
	   My birthday is on the first sunday in april.
	
	                                     2157

Nancy
 	
2375
	Because words of direct address interrupt the sentence, they are set off with commas.
	
	Punctuate this sentence:
	
	   I am happy ladies and gentlemen to be here tonight.
	
	                                     2376

says, "Your . . .
me."
 	
2594
	Now let's see what happens when the quotation is a question rather than a statement of fact.
	
	   "Have you heard the news?" he asked.
	
	The question mark is at the end of the (*quotation, sentence*).
	
	                                     2595

Her 180	a. **Linda won't drink her milk.** b. **Linda won't drink hers.** The pronoun **hers** in sentence *b* takes the place of two words in sentence *a*. What are these two words? _____ _____ 181
shall, will 400	HELPING VERBS: **shall, will** **may, can** **could, would, should** **must, might** One helping verb besides **may** that has only three letters is _____. 401
ranch 620	a. **Mary was raised by an aunt.** b. **Mary was raised by a very strict aunt.** How many words does the **prepositional phrase** in sentence *a* contain? ____ In sentence *b*? ____ 621
  	He consulted *important* **people.** The adjective *important* modifies the noun _____. 841
b 1060	**We have bought new equipment. Which saves us much time.** The second word group is not a sentence. It is an adjective clause that modifies the noun _____ in the main statement. 1061
lies 1280	**To lay** means "to put or to place something." Never use this word unless you name the "something" that is put or placed somewhere (or use a pronoun in its place). **You can lay (put) the box on the shelf.** What is the "something" that you can **lay (put)** on the shelf? It is the _____. 1281

No 1500	**The <u>dog</u> <u>barks</u>.** The subject **dog** is singular, and the verb **barks** is singular. Which word ends in *s*—the *subject* or the *verb*? _____ 1501
adverbs 1719	If we can substitute for the "sense" verb some form of **be (am, is, are—was, were, been)**, it is used as a linking verb and should be followed by an (*adjective, adverb*) which describes the subject. 1720
subject 1938	Here, to fill in the sentence, we must add two words, not just a verb: **The dress fits you better than (it fits) her.** The two omitted words in this sentence are _____ and _____ . 1939
Sunday, April 2157	Underline the words that need to be capitalized: **After the Merrills bought their new plymouth convertible, Dick's grades in latin and history went down.** 2158
happy, gentlemen, 2376	Punctuate this sentence: **I have decided my friend to take your advice.** 2377
quotation 2595	**"Have you heard the news?" he asked.** Because the quotation itself is a question, the question mark is placed (*inside, outside*) the quotes. 2596

her milk 181	**Hers is newer than yours.** How many pronouns are there in this sentence? _____ 182
can 401	a. **write, sell, swim, bring** b. **shall, would, may, might** Which group of words consists of helping verbs? _____ 402
a. 3 b. 5 621	**The smoke from this great fire darkened the sky.** The **prepositional phrase** begins with the preposition _____ and ends with its object _____. 622
people 841	A **prepositional phrase** can be used exactly like an adjective. **He consulted people** *of importance.* The prepositional phrase *of importance* is an adjective phrase because it modifies the _____ **people.** 842
equipment 1061	a. **We have bought new equipment which saves us much time.** b. **We have bought new equipment. Which saves us much time.** An adjective clause should not be cut off from the word it modifies. Therefore, (*a, b*) is correct. 1062

box
 	
1281
	Once again, **to lie** means "to rest in a flat position" or "to
	be in place."
	
	In which of the following sentences does this definition
	fit? ____
	
	    a. **You will get sunburnt if you . . . on the beach.**
	    b. **Don't . . . the hot pan on the table.**
	
	1282

verb 1501	**The <u>dogs</u> <u>bark</u>.** Now the subject **dogs** is plural, and the verb **bark** is plural. Which word ends in *s*—the *subject* or the *verb*? _____ 1502
adjective 1720	a. **Jennifer's make-up looked very** (*curious, curiously*). b. **Everyone looked at Jennifer very** (*curious, curiously*). In which sentence does **looked** mean an action of the eyes—*a* or *b*? ____ 1721
it, fits 1939	**The dress fits you better than (it fits) <u>her</u>.** The object form **her** is correct because it is the object of the omitted verb _____. 1940
Plymouth, Latin 2158	Underline the words that need to be capitalized: **The speaker expressed the idea that the constitution was inspired by god.** 2159
decided, friend, 2377	Punctuate this sentence: **Why did you spend your money on this you foolish girl?** 2378
inside 2596	**"Have you heard the news?" he asked.** Is the separating comma used between the quotation and **he asked?** (*Yes, No*) 2597

Two	Is the italicized word in each sentence a *noun* or a *pronoun*?
	a. *Corn* grows fast in hot weather. _____
	b. *It* grows fast in hot weather. _____
182	183
b	The three helping verbs below have several forms.
	HELPING VERBS: **be (is, am, are—was, were, been)**
	have (has, had)
	do (does, did)
	Has and **had** are forms of the verb _____.
	Does and **did** are forms of the verb _____.
402	403
from, fire	a. **healthy people**
	b. **people in good health**
	In *a*, the adjective **healthy** modifies the noun **people**.
	In *b*, the prepositional phrase **in good health** also modifies
	the noun _____.
622	623
noun	A **clause**, too, can do the work of an adjective by modifying a noun or pronoun.
	He consulted people *who are important.*
	Because the clause *who are important* modifies the noun **people**, it is an (*adjective, adverb*) clause.
842	843
a	**Don read until midnight. And finished the book.**
	The (*first, second*) word group is a sentence fragment.
1062	1063
a	**You will get sunburnt if you . . . on the beach.**
	The meaning we want is "to rest in a flat position."
	Therefore, the correct word is _____.
1282	1283

subject 1502	**The <u>boy</u> <u>swims</u>.** The subject **boy** is singular, and the verb **swims** is singular. Which word ends in *s*—the *subject* or the *verb*? _____ 1503
b 1721	**Everyone looked at Jennifer very** (*curious, curiously*). In this sentence, **looked** means an action of the eyes. To describe this action of the eyes, we should choose the word _____. 1722
fits 1940	Write in the omitted words: **The collision hurt the car more than (**_____ _____**)** **us.** 1941
Constitution, God 2159	**The Vogue shop on Washington boulevard is showing the** **newest fall fashions.** 2160
this, 2378	Because names are often used as appositives and direct address, some pupils thoughtlessly put commas around every name they write. Don't use commas unless the words interrupt the sentence and could be omitted. **The next time you come Dave you must bring Earl along.** 2379
No 2597	**"Have you heard the news?" he asked.** The comma that usually separates the quotation from the rest of the sentence is no longer needed. The question mark alone is enough to separate the quotation from **he asked.** Punctuate the following sentence: **Where did you buy that hat asked Sally.** 2598

noun
pronoun
 	
183
	Is the italicized word a *noun* or a *pronoun*?
	
	    a. *Who* **reported the fire?**_____
	
	    b. *Jane* **reported the fire.**_____
	
	184

have **do** 403	a. <u>Tom</u> <u>is</u> my brother. b. <u>Tom</u> <u>is washing</u> the car. Is the verb **is** used by itself as the *main verb* in sentence *a* or *b*? ____ 404
people 623	a. <u>healthy</u> **people** b. **people** <u>in good health</u> Because the prepositional phrase **in good health** serves the same purpose as the adjective _____, we call it an **adjective phrase.** 624
adjective 843	a. **He consulted** *important* **people.** b. **He consulted people** *who are important.* The adjective clause *who are important* does the same job in sentence *b* that the adjective _____ does in sentence *a.* 844
second 1063	<u>Don</u> <u>read</u> **until midnight. And** <u>finished</u> **the book.** The second word group is a sentence fragment because the verb **finished** lacks a _____. 1064
lie 1283	PRESENT SIMPLE PAST PAST WITH HELPER **lie** **lay** **have lain** **Last night I** _____ **down on the sofa and fell asleep.** Supply the right form of the verb **lie.** 1284

verb 1503	**The <u>boys</u> <u>swim</u>.** Now the subject **boys** is plural, and the verb **swim** is plural. Which word ends in *s*—the *subject* or the *verb*? _____ 1504
curiously 1722	a. **Jennifer's make-up looked very** (*curious, curiously*). b. **Everyone looked at Jennifer very** (*curious, curiously*). In which sentence can we substitute **was** for **looked**? _____ 1723
it hurt 1941	Underline the correct pronoun: **The collision hurt the car more than** (*we, us*). 1942
Shop, Boulevard 2160	**The battle of San Jacinto won for texans their independence from mexico.** (Remember that historical events are capitalized.) 2161
come, Dave, 2379	In this sentence, only one of the two names is used as an appositive and, therefore, requires commas. Insert the necessary commas: **The hero of this story Dick Crothers saves Allan Merrick from drowning.** 2380
"Where . . . hat?" 2598	a. **"Does coffee ever keep you awake,"** asked Mr. Horn? b. **"Does coffee ever keep you awake?"** asked Mr. Horn. Which sentence is correct? _____ 2599

pronoun
noun
 	
184
	Is the italicized word a *noun* or a *pronoun*?
	
	    a. *These* **won prizes.** _____
	
	    b. **The** *stories* **won prizes.** _____
	
	185

a 404	a. **I have the measles.** b. **I have caught the measles.** Is the verb **have** used as a *helping verb* in sentence *a* or *b*? _____ 405
healthy 624	**people in good health** We call **in good health** an **adjective phrase** because it does exactly the same work as an _____. 625
important 844	Think of an adjective clause as a "stretched-out" adjective of several words that modifies a noun or pronoun, like any ordinary _____. 845
subject 1064	a. **Don read until midnight. And finished the book.** b. **Don read until midnight and finished the book.** A verb should be in the same sentence as its subject. Therefore, (*a, b*) is correct. 1065

lay
 	
1284
	This little rhyme will help you to remember that the simple
	past form of **lie** is **lay**:
	
	            Yes-ter-**day**
	            In bed I **lay.**
	
	Write the correct past form of the verb **lie**:
	
	    I don't know how long I _____ **there.**
	
	1285

subject 1504	Add an *s* where it will make the sentence plural: **The tree_____ grow_____.** 1505
a 1723	**Jennifer's make-up looked (= was)** (*curious, curiously*). Because **looked** is a linking verb here, it must be followed by a word that modifies the subject. Therefore, we should choose the word _____. 1724

us
 	
1942
	Sometimes the meaning of a sentence depends on whether we use the subject or object form of a pronoun.
	
	  a. **I like her sister more than <u>she</u> (likes her sister).**
	  b. **I like her sister more than (I like) <u>her</u>.**
	
	In which sentence does the pronoun come before the omitted verb as its subject? _____
	
	194

Battle, Texans, Mexico 2161	**The American legion presented a flag to our high school on Veterans day.** 2162
story, Dick Crothers, 2380	Punctuate the appositive in this sentence: **The winners of the game Kent High had never defeated Marston High before.** 2381

b
 	
2599
	We follow the same procedure with a quotation that requires an exclamation point (**!**).
	
	  "What a beautiful sunset!" exclaimed Virginia.
	
	Punctuate the following sentence:
	
	  Look out for the car shouted Ken
	
	2600

pronoun
noun
 	
185
	Is the italicized word a *noun* or a *pronoun*?
	
	    a. **The** *car* **broke down.** _____
	
	    b. *Ours* **broke down.** _____
	
	    186

b
 	
405
	a. **Judy does her lessons.**
	    b. **Yes, Judy does study her lessons.**
	
	Is the verb **does** used by itself as the *main verb* in sentence *a* or *b*?
	
	    406

adjective
 	
625
	a. **The natives live in <u>straw</u> houses.**
	    b. **The natives live in houses <u>of straw</u>.**
	
	In *a*, **straw** is an adjective.
	
	In *b*, the phrase **of straw** is an *adjective* _____.
	
	    626

adjective
 	
845
	a. **A** *friendly* **squirrel comes to our door.**
	    b. **A squirrel** *that is friendly* **comes to our door.**
	
	The adjective clause *that is friendly* does the same job in sentence *b* that the _____ *friendly* does in sentence *a*.
	
	    846

b
 	
1065
	a. **Vern had many opportunities but threw them all away.**
	    b. **Vern had many opportunities. But threw them all away.**
	
	Which is correct—*a* or *b*? ____
	
	    1066

lay
 	
1285
	(An object can *lie* on a chair, table, or floor just as a person can *lie* on a bed.)
	
	    My missing wallet (*lay, laid*) **in the snow all winter.**
	
	    1286

(tree)s 1505	Add an *s* where it will make the sentence singular: **The tree_____ grow_____.** 1506
curious 1724	**The doctor felt my ankle very gently.** The adverb **gently** is correct because it modifies the verb _____. 1725
a 1943	a. **Cliff likes dogs more than <u>she</u> (. . .).** b. **Cliff likes dogs more than (. . .) <u>her</u>.** Each of the above sentences has a different meaning. To see this difference, think of the missing words in each sentence. Which sentence means that Cliff likes dogs more than the girl likes them? ____ 1944
Legion, Day 2162	**A boy in my english class found a presto camera on the Woodlawn avenue bus.** 2163
game, Kent High, 2381	Don't put commas around the titles of books, stories, poems, etc., unless they are used as appositives. a. **I am reading** *The Call of the Wild* **for my book report.** b. **I am reading an interesting book** *The Call of the Wild* **for my book report.** In which sentence does the title require commas? ____ 2382
"Look . . . car!" shouted Ken. 2600	a. **"We've won again!" screamed Betty.** b. **"We've won again," screamed Betty!** Which sentence is correct? ____ 2601

noun
pronoun
 	
186
	Is the italicized word a *noun* or a *pronoun*?
	
	    a. **Do you want** *mustard*? _____
	
	    b. **Do you want** *any*? _____
	
	187

a 406	**The bus will be leaving soon.** The main verb **leaving** has two helpers—_____ and _____. 407

phrase
 	
626
	Think of an **adjective phrase** as being a stretched-out **adjective** consisting of two or more words.
	
	    a. **The team with the greater strength will win.**
	    b. **The stronger team will win.**
	
	Is the **adjective phrase** in sentence *a* or *b*? ____
	
	627

adjective 846	a. **A** *friendly* **squirrel comes to our door.** b. **A squirrel** *that is friendly* **comes to our door.** In sentence *a*, the adjective *friendly* comes *before* the noun it modifies. In sentence *b*, the adjective clause *that is friendly* comes (*before, after*) the noun it modifies. 847
a 1066	In this and the following frames, write an **S** for each word group that is a **sentence,** and an **F** for each word group that is a **fragment.** Write your answers in the same order as the two word groups. **I feel sorry for Judy. Because her birthday comes on Christmas.** ___ ___ 1067
lay 1286	PRESENT SIMPLE PAST PAST WITH HELPER **lie** (be in place) **lay** **have lain** **The boat lies on the beach all summer.** If we changed this sentence from present to past time, we would need to change **lies** to _____. 1287

(grow)s 1506	SINGULAR: **The boy swims.** SINGULAR: **The tree grows.** PLURAL: **The boys swim.** PLURAL: **The trees grow.** When we add an *s* to the subject, we do not add an *s* to the verb. When we add an *s* to the verb, we do not add an *s* to the _____. 1507
felt 1725	**This wood feels too rough to use.** The adjective **rough** is correct because it modifies the noun _____. 1726
a 1944	**Cliff likes dogs more than <u>she</u> (likes them).** The subject form **she** is the subject of the omitted verb _____. 1945
English, Presto, Avenue 2163	**Lesson 70 Learning to Capitalize Titles** [Frames 2165–2201]
b 2382	In this and the following frames, supply the necessary commas. Some of the sentences do not require commas. **A surplus of corn for example always produces a surplus of hogs.** 2383
a 2601	When the question or exclamation comes at the end of the sentence, the usual comma is needed as a separator. **Terry asked, "Did you finish the test?"** Punctuate this exclamation the same way: **Judy exclaimed What a beautiful sunset** 2602

noun pronoun 187	Pronouns help us to avoid the tiresome repetition of nouns. *Connie* **denied that the writing was** *Connie's.* Avoid this repetition by substituting a pronoun: **Connie denied that the writing was** _____. 188
will, be 407	<p align="center">a. **Frank is working.** b. **Frank has been working.** c. **Frank should have been working.**</p>In which sentence does the main verb **working** have three helpers? ____ 408
a 627	<p align="center">a. **spoke <u>angrily</u>** b. **spoke <u>with anger</u>**</p>In *a*, the adverb **angrily** modifies the verb **spoke.** In *b*, the prepositional phrase **with anger** also modifies the verb _____. 628
after 847	<p align="center">**A squirrel** *that is friendly* **comes to our door.**</p>Now let's remove the adjective clause from this sentence and look at it more closely: <p align="center">*that <u>is</u> friendly*</p>Although this clause has both a subject and a verb, does it form a complete sentence by itself? (*Yes, No*) 848
S F 1067	Put down an **S** (for **sentence**) or an **F** (for **fragment**) for each of the two word groups: **I feel sorry for Judy. Her birthday comes on Christmas.** <p align="center">____ ____</p>1068
lay 1287	PRESENT SIMPLE PAST PAST WITH HELPER **lie** (in bed) **lay** **have lain** <p align="center">**Dad had** _____ **down after dinner.**</p>1288

subject 1507	**The tree grows.** **The trees grow.** When the subject is singular, there is no *s* on the subject, but there is an *s* on the verb. When the subject is plural, there is an *s* on the subject but none on the _____. 1508
wood 1726	In this and the following frames, underline the adverb **(–ly)** if the subject is smelling with his nose, looking with his eyes, feeling with his hands, etc., and if the word describes this action. **The cashier looked at the check** (*suspicious, suspiciously*). 1727
likes 1945	a. **Cliff likes dogs more than she.** b. **Cliff likes dogs more than her.** Which sentence means that Cliff likes dogs more than he likes the girl? ____ 1946
	Capitalize the first word and all important words in titles of books, stories, poems, etc. *The Sea Wolf* **"Our Schools Today"** **"The Split Cherry Tree"** **"Paul Revere's Ride"** Write the capital letters you would need to use in writing *the red pony*. _____ 2165
corn, example, 2383	Insert any necessary commas: **His two brothers George and Martin are in the Navy.** 2384
exclaimed, "What . . . sunset!" 2602	In this and the following frames, supply the necessary punctuation. Each sentence requires either a question mark or an exclamation point. **When do we eat asked Charlie.** 2603

Stanley **is training** *Stanley's* **dog to obey** *Stanley's* **commands.**

Avoid this repetition by substituting pronouns:

Stanley is training _____ **dog to obey** _____ **commands.**

189

The two or more words that make up the verb may come together, or they may be interrupted by other words that are not verbs.

     a. **The <u>bus</u> <u>will be leaving</u>** *soon.*

     b. **The <u>bus</u> <u>will</u>** *soon* **<u>be leaving</u>.**

The verb is interrupted by another word in sentence (*a, b*).

409

---

     a. **spoke <u>angrily</u>**
     b. **spoke <u>with anger</u>**

Because the prepositional phrase **with anger** in sentence *b*

does exactly the same work as the adverb **angrily** in sen-

tence *a*, we call it an _____ *phrase.*

629

ADJECTIVE CLAUSE SIGNALS

The following pronouns are often used to start adjective clauses: **who (whom, whose), which, that.**

     Bill owns a collie *which has won many prizes.*

The adjective clause in this sentence begins with the pronoun _____.

849

Unless you are willing to care for a dog properly. You should not get one.

     ____   ____

1069

Another little rhyme will help you to remember that the helper form of **lie** is **have lain:**

     In **pain**
     I **have lain.**

     The cow had . . . down on the railroad track.

Write the correct helper form: _____

1289

verb 1508	The store clos**e**s. The store**s** close. Which verb is singular—**closes** or **close**? _____ 1509
suspiciously 1727	Underline the adjective (without **–ly**) if the verb is used as a linking verb and the word that follows it describes the subject. **Your dress looks** (*beautiful, beautifully*) **on you.** 1728
b 1946	**Cliff likes dogs more than (he likes) <u>her</u>.** The object form **her** is the object of the omitted verb _____. 1947
T R P 2165	a. *The Covered Wagon* b. *the Covered Wagon* Which title is correctly capitalized? ____ 2166
brothers, Martin, 2384	Insert any necessary commas: **Yes that was the last time that I saw Tom Chapman.** 2385
"When . . . eat?" 2603	Supply the necessary punctuation, including either a question mark or an exclamation point: **Just look at your shoes exclaimed Mother.** 2604

his, his 189	*The boys* **washed** *the boys* **in the lake.** Avoid repeating *the boys* by substituting a pronoun: **The boys washed** _____ **in the lake.** 190
b 409	**Dad has always collected stamps.** The main verb is separated from its helper by the word _____ . 410
adverb 629	a. **Tom ate <u>hurriedly</u>.** b. **Tom ate <u>in a hurry</u>.** In sentence *a*, **hurriedly** is an adverb. In sentence *b*, **in a hurry** is an *adverb* _____ . 630
which 849	**Bill owns a collie** *which has won many prizes.* The adjective clause *which has won many prizes* modifies the noun _____ . 850
F S 1069	**Gunpowder was invented by the Chinese. Who used it only for fireworks.** ____ ____ 1070
lain 1289	**I lay down and couldn't get up.** If we added the helper **had** to the verb, what word would we need to put in place of **lay?** _____ 1290

closes 1509	**The store closes.** **The stores close.** Adding an *s* to the noun makes it plural. Adding an *s* to the verb makes it _____. 1510
beautiful 1728	**This perfume smells** (*different, differently*) **from the last.** (*Hint:* Perfume has no nose for smelling.) 1729
likes 1947	We use the word **as,** as well as **than,** in making comparisons. **I have as many friends as <u>she</u> (has).** The subject form **she** is correct because it is the subject of the omitted verb _____. 1948

a
 	
2166
	Unless they are the first word in a title, do not capitalize:
	
	    ARTICLES: **a, an, the** CONJUNCTIONS: **and, but, or**
	    SHORT PREPOSITIONS: **of, in, to, for, with,** etc.
	
	Underline the words you would capitalize in the following
	title: *the call of the wild.*
	
	2167

Yes, 2385	**It won't be easy to win old boy with Larry Schultz pitching** **for the Wildcats.** 2386
"Just . . . shoes!" 2604	Supply the necessary punctuation, including either a ques- tion mark or an exclamation point: **Mr. Mitchell inquired** **Is parking allowed here** 2605

themselves	A noun is the name of a person, place, thing, or an idea. A word used in place of a noun is a _____.
190	191
always	**I could hardly read the address.** The main verb is separated from its helper by the word _____.
410	411
phrase	**We drove <u>over a very shaky bridge</u>.** The prepositional phrase **over a very shaky bridge** modifies the verb **drove**—just like an ordinary *adverb*. We therefore call it an _____ _____.
630	631
collie	*which has won many prizes* The verb of this clause is *has won;* the subject is the pronoun _____.
850	851
S F	**Ellen put the key in the lock. And tried to turn it.** ____ ____
1070	1071
lain	**To lay** means "to put or to place something." You can't just put—you have to put *something*. Unless the sentence names this "something," this is not the word you want. **Don't lay the hot pan on the table.** The "something" in this sentence is _____.
1290	1291

singular 1510	People frequently make mistakes in the agreement of subject and verb because they think that a verb that ends in *s* is plural. **My friend lives in Florida.** A present-tense verb that ends in *s* is always (*singular, plural*). 1511
different 1729	**We now smelled smoke very** (*distinct, distinctly*). 1730
has 1948	Underline the correct pronoun: **We made as many hits as** (*they, them*). 1949
the <u>call</u> of the wild 2167	Copy the following title, adding the needed capitals: *a tale of two cities* _____ 2168
win, boy, 2386	**Well this is all the news I have Steve.** (More than one comma is needed.) 2387
inquired, "Is . . . here?" 2605	**Alex bawled angrily I told you to shut off the water** (Use an !) 2606

pronoun 191	A pronoun is usually (*more, less*) definite than a noun. 192
hardly 411	**Shirley will surely stay with the baby.** The verb **will stay** is interrupted by the word _____. 412

adverb phrase
 	
631
	Think of an adverb phrase as being a stretched-out adverb consisting of two or more words.
	
	   a. **I glued the broken pieces together carefully.**
	   b. **I glued the broken pieces together with great care.**
	
	Is the **adverb phrase** in sentence *a* or *b*? ____
	
	632

which 851	**Bill owns a collie** *which has won* **many prizes.** An adjective clause signal is always a pronoun. This pronoun stands for the word which the clause modifies. In the above sentence, the pronoun *which* stands for the noun _____, as the arrow shows. 852
S F 1071	**After Ellen put the key in the lock. She tried to turn it.** ___ ___ 1072
pan 1291	PRESENT SIMPLE PAST PAST WITH HELPER **lay** (put) **laid** **have laid** This verb is the simpler of our two verbs. The two past forms of **lay** are (*alike, different*). 1292

singular 1511	This is the **"Rule of S"** that we have been building up: When the subject ends in *s*, the verb does not; when the verb ends in *s*, the _____ does not. 1512
distinctly 1730	**Chad's scheme sounded rather** (*dishonest, dishonestly*) **to me.** 1731
they 1949	**We made as many hits as <u>they</u> (made).** The subject form **they** is correct because it is the subject of the omitted verb _____. 1950
A Tale of Two Cities 2168	Copy and capitalize this title: *the prince and the pauper* _____ 2169
Well, have, 2387	**General Lafayette named his son after George Washington.** 2388
angrily, "I . . . water!" 2606	**Can't you read that sign shouted the policeman.** 2607

Lesson **7** Unit Review

[Frames 194–215]

---

surely

412

The words **not** and **never** make a statement negative. They are never a part of the verb.

> **Shirley will not stay with the baby.**
> **Shirley will never stay with the baby.**

In both sentences, the verb consists of only two words—

_____ _____ .

413

---

b

632

An **adjective phrase** is used like a single adjective.

An **adverb phrase** is used like a single _____ .

633

---

collie

852

which has won many prizes

really means:

collie *has won* many prizes

In this clause, the pronoun _____ stands for the noun **collie.**

853

F S

1072

Ellen tried to turn the key. Which she had put in the lock.

_____ _____

1073

---

alike

1292

Mother . . . a cold cloth on my forehead.

This sentence names the "something" that Mother put on my forehead. It was a cloth.

Therefore, our verb should be a form of (*lay, lie*).

1293

subject 1512	Our rule does *not* state that there must always be an *s* on either the subject or the verb. **Men work.** **I dive.** **Children play.** **We swim.** In these sentences, do either the subjects or the verbs end in *s*? (*Yes, No*) 1513
dishonest 1731	**I tasted the hot soup** (*cautious, cautiously*). 1732
made 1950	a. **We must invite the Kirks as well as <u>they</u>.** b. **We must invite the Kirks as well as <u>them</u>.** Which sentence means that we must invite both the Kirks and the other family? _____ 1951
The Prince and the Pauper 2169	Capitalize, too, the titles of movies, works of art, musical compositions, etc. *Wings of the Eagle* "Tea for Two" "After the Rain" "March of the Toy Soldiers" Write the capital letters you would need to use in writing the movie title *the shadow of a doubt.* _____ 2170
None 2388	**Don't forget you lucky guy that I voted for you.** 2389
"Can't . . . sign?" (*or*) !" 2607	**What a ridiculous idea exclaimed George** 2608

A sentence normally consists of two parts.

The *predicate* makes a statement about the _____.

194

---

will stay

413

Supply a suitable helping verb:

Someone _____ taken your seat.

414

---

adverb

633

An adverb phrase—just like an adverb—can tell **when, where, how,** or **how much** about the _____.

634

---

which

853

The fish *that we caught* **were too small to keep.**

The adjective clause *that we caught* modifies the noun

_____.

854

S F

1073

Mr. Nolan grabbed his bag. And ran for the train.

_____ _____

1074

---

lay

1293

PRESENT	SIMPLE PAST	PAST WITH HELPER
lay (put)	**laid**	**have laid**

Write in the correct verbs:

a. **Mother _____ a cold cloth on my forehead.**

b. **Mother had _____ a cold cloth on my forehead.**

1294

No 1513	In this and the following frames, underline the verb that agrees in number with the subject. Avoid having an *s* on both the subject and the verb. **school** (*open, opens*) 1514
cautiously 1732	**The customer felt the cloth very** (*rough, roughly*). 1733
b 1951	**We must invite the Kirks as well as (invite) them.** The pronoun **them** is the (*object, subject*) of the omitted verb **invite.** 1952
T S D 2170	a. **"On The Road To Mandalay"** b. **"On the Road to Mandalay"** c. **"On the road to Mandalay"** Which song title is correctly capitalized? ____ 2171
forget, guy, 2389	**The band then played my favorite march "The Stars and Stripes Forever."** 2390
"What . . . idea!" exclaimed George. 2608	**I called to Mother Is this piece of pie for me** 2609

subject 194	a. **disappeared into the clouds** b. **the man on third base** c. **escaped from its cage** Which group of words could be the subject of a sentence? _____ 195
has *or* had 414	Supply a suitable helping verb: **Every driver _____ have a license.** 415
verb 634	**We reached Niagara Falls in the late afternoon.** The adverb phrase tells (*how, when*) about the verb **reached.** 635
fish 854	**The fish *that we caught* were too small to keep.** The clause signal *that* is a pronoun. The pronoun *that* stands for the noun _____, the word that the clause modifies. 855
S F 1074	**If there were no such thing as gravity. A person would weigh nothing at all.** ____ ____ 1075
a. laid b. laid 1294	Here are the two verbs to compare: | PRESENT	SIMPLE PAST	PAST WITH HELPER
---	---	---
lie (in bed)	**lay**	**have lain**
lay (put)	**laid**	**have laid**	 The simple past form of **lie** is _____. The simple past form of **lay** is _____. *page 389* 1295

opens 1514	Underline the verb that agrees in number with the subject: **schools** (*open, opens*) 1515
roughly 1733	**Mayor Kearney felt** (*unhappy, unhappily*) **about his defeat.** (This does not mean an action of the hands.) 1734
object 1952	a. **We must invite the Kirks as well as <u>they</u>.** b. **We must invite the Kirks as well as <u>them</u>.** Which sentence means that we, as well as the other family, must invite the Kirks? ____ 1953
b 2171	Now we turn to another kind of title—the titles of **people,** like **Doctor Klein, Captain Craig,** or **Aunt Ruth.** **a doctor** **Doctor Klein** Which words mean a *particular* doctor? _____ 2172
march, 2390	**The band then played "The Stars and Stripes Forever."** 2391
Mother, "Is . . . me?" 2609	**Mrs. Kerney cried out** **My feet are killing me** (Use an !) 2610

b 195	a. **most of the new cars** b. **the decision of the referee** c. **started on time** Which group of words could be the predicate of a sentence? ____ 196
must *or* should 415	Supply a suitable helping verb: **If I were George, I _____ <u>find</u> a job.** 416
when 635	**Jack opened the screen door <u>with a wire.</u>** The adverb phrase tells (*how, when*) about the verb **opened.** 636
fish 855	*that <u>we caught</u>* really means: **fish** <u>*we caught*</u> (<u>*we caught*</u> **fish**) In this clause, the pronoun _____ stands for the noun **fish.** 856
F S 1075	**Mr. Bosley would get his own breakfast. Or eat at a drugstore near his office.** ——— ——— 1076
lay laid 1295	PRESENT SIMPLE PAST PAST WITH HELPER **lie** (in bed) **lay** **have lain** **lay** (put) **laid** **have laid** The verb whose two past forms are the same—just like any regular verb—is _____. 1296

open 1515	**stores** (*sell, sells*) 1516
unhappy 1734	**Her playing must have sounded** (*frightful, frightfully*). 1735
a 1953	**We must invite the Kirks as well as <u>they</u> (must invite) them.** The pronoun **they** is the (*object, subject*) of the omitted verb **must invite.** 1954
Doctor Klein 2172	**I called a doctor. I called Doctor Klein.** We capitalize the noun **doctor** only when it is used (*with, without*) a person's name. 2173
None 2391	**No our neighbors the Sullivans don't have their collie any more.** 2392
out, "My . . . me!" 2610	Lesson **83** Unit Review [Frames 2612–2633]

c 196	a. **the hungry dog waited at the door** b. **the only boy on the committee** c. **walked briskly across the stage** Which group of words is a sentence because it has both a subject and a predicate? _____ (The capital letter and the period are omitted to avoid revealing the answer.) 197
would 416	Supply a suitable helping verb: **Some animals** _____ **see in the dark.** 417
how 636	**Ross buys most of his clothes <u>at one store</u>.** The adverb phrase tells *(when, where)* about the verb **buys.** 637

that
 	
856
	When we remove an adjective clause from a sentence, we should have a complete sentence remaining.
	
	    a. **The fish** *that we caught* **were too small to keep.**
	    b. **The fish** **were too small to keep.**
	
	Is sentence *b*, without the clause, a complete sentence? *(Yes, No)*
	857

S F 1076	In this frame there are three word groups to be judged. **Although the novel is long. The reader never loses interest. Because the plot is loaded with suspense.** _____ _____ _____ 1077
lay 1296	PRESENT SIMPLE PAST PAST WITH HELPER **lie** (in bed) **lay** **have lain** Write in the missing words: **Ken** _____ **on the beach longer than I had** _____ **there.** 1297

sell 1516	**show** (*start, starts*) 1517
frightful 1735	**This snapshot looks more** (*natural, naturally*) **than the other.** 1736
subject 1954	In this and the following frames, underline the correct pronoun. Make sure that you select the correct pronoun by thinking of the omitted word or words in each comparison. **You live closer to the school than** (*they, them*). 1955
with 2173	Capitalize titles that show a person's profession, rank, or position when they are used as part of a person's name. a. **The order was given by major Stokes.** b. **The order was given by Major Stokes.** Which sentence is correctly capitalized? ____ 2174
No, neighbors, Sullivans, 2392	**The courage of one officer Lieutenant Bates saved the ship.** 2393
	Apostrophes are used with nouns to show ownership. Place the apostrophe so that the letters that come before it indicate the owner. a. **one boy's test** b. **one boys' test** Because the test belongs to one **boy,** the apostrophe is correctly placed in (*a, b*). 2612

a 197	The most important word in the predicate is called the _____. <div align="right">198</div>
can *or* do 417	Fill each blank with a suitable helping verb. **You** _____ _____ **started earlier to get a good seat.** <div align="right">418</div>
where 637	An adverb phrase does not need to be next to the verb it modifies. <div align="center">**Ross buys most of his clothes at one store.**</div> How many words stand between the adverb phrase and the verb which it modifies? ____ <div align="right">638</div>
Yes 857	Let's look at the adjective clause signals once again: <div align="center">**who (whom, whose) which that**</div> These words are used to start adjective clauses, which modify _____ and pronouns. <div align="right">858</div>
F S F 1077	**Lesson 35 More Types of Sentence Fragments** [Frames 1079–1106]
lay, lain 1297	PRESENT SIMPLE PAST PAST WITH HELPER **lay** (put) **laid** **have laid** Write in the missing words: **Paul _____ his books where he always had _____ them.** <div align="right">1298</div>

starts 1517	**doctors** (*agree, agrees*) 1518
natural 1736	When the "sense" verb means action, use the adverb *well* to describe this action. When the "sense" verb links a word that follows it to the subject, use the adjective *good* to describe the subject. **You can't smell** (*good, well*) **when you have a cold.** 1737
they 1955	**Mosquitoes always bit Dad more than** (*I, me*). 1956
b 2174	a. **Ken saluted captain Marsh.** b. **Ken saluted the captain.** In which sentence should **captain** be capitalized? ____ 2175
officer, Lieutenant Bates, 2393	**It was the courage of Lieutenant Bates that saved the ship.** 2394
a 2612	a. **several student's tests**　　b. **several students' tests** Because the tests belong to several **students,** the apostrophe is correctly placed in (*a, b*). 2613

verb 198	When we change a sentence from present to past time, or from past to present time, the only word that usually changes its form is the _____. 199
should (could, might) have 418	In the following frames, write the *initials* (first letters) only of the words that make up the *complete* verb. EXAMPLE: **I should have followed your advice.** Initials of verb: *s h f* The initials of the verb **may be waiting** are _____. 419
4 638	**With no hesitation, the owner of the store refunded my money.** How many words stand between the adverb phrase and the verb which it modifies? _____ 639
nouns 858	**The lady** *whose baby was crying* **left the theater.** The adjective clause starts with the word _____ and ends with the word _____. 859

	Here, again, are the two tests for a complete sentence:
	     1. Does it have a subject and a predicate?
	     2. Does it make sense by itself?
	 Adverb and adjective clauses fail to pass the (*first, second*) of these tests.
	
	 1079

laid, laid 1298	**to lie** **to lay** Which of these verbs means "to rest in a flat position" or "to be in place"? _____ 1299

agree	**glue** (*stick, sticks*)
1518	1519
well	**A hot drink tastes** (*good, well*) **after ice-skating.**
1737	1738
me	**Are you as old as** (*he, him*)**?**
1956	1957
a	**Our dentist is doctor Ridley.** In this sentence, capitalize (*dentist, doctor*).
2175	2176
None	**If you want to read a good book about horses Pete read** *My Friend Flicka.*
2394	2395
b	**a. The men's department is having a sale.** **b. The mens' department is having a sale.** Look at the letters that come before the apostrophe. Since the department belongs to **men**—not **mens**, the apostrophe is correctly placed in sentence (*a, b*).
2613	2614

verb	PRESENT: **My dad takes many pictures.** To change this sentence to past time, we would need to change the verb **takes** to _____ .
199	200

m b w	**Sonny did not wipe his feet on the mat.** Initials of verb: _____ (Be careful not to include a word that is not part of the verb.)
419	420

5	An adverb phrase—just like an adverb—can often be moved to another part of the sentence.
	
	    We reached Niagara Falls <u>in the late afternoon</u>.
	    <u>In the late afternoon</u>, we reached Niagara Falls.
	
	The fact that the prepositional phrase can be moved shows that it is an (*adjective, adverb*) phrase.

639	640

whose, crying	**The lady** *whose baby was crying* **left the theater.** **The lady left the theater.** When we omit the adjective clause from this sentence, do we have a complete sentence remaining? (*Yes, No*)
859	860

second	Now we will look at other types of sentence fragments. **The young man apologized. Realizing his mistake.** The sentence fragment is the (*first, second*) word group.
1079	1080

to lie	Remember these rhymes. They will help to straighten you out when using the two past forms of **lie**.
	
	    Yes-ter-**day** In **pain**
	    In bed I **lay.** I have **lain.**
	
	The two past forms of **lie** are (*alike, different*).

1299	1300

sticks	**dogs** *(have, has)*
1519	1520
good	**Feel the paint** *(good, well)* **to make sure that it's dry.**
1738	1739
he	**Mother bakes her beans much longer than** *(she, her).*
1957	1958
Doctor	**Sam introduced lieutenant Dobbs to the major.** In this sentence, capitalize *(lieutenant, major).*
2176	2177
horses, Pete,	Lesson **77** **Commas in Addresses and Dates** [Frames 2397–2421]
2395	
a	Be sure that the letters coming before the apostrophe spell the owner or owners correctly. Underline the correct word: **These** *(ladys', ladies')* **handkerchiefs are very expensive.**
2614	2615

took 200	PAST: **The old map showed the location of the treasure.** To change this sentence to present time, we would need to change the verb from _____ to _____. 201
d w 420	**The meeting will surely end by ten o'clock.** Initials of verb: _____ 421
adverb 640	**Jack opened the screen door <u>with a wire</u>.** **<u>With a wire</u>, Jack opened the screen door.** The prepositional phrase **with a wire** is an (*adverb, adjective*) *phrase*. 641
Yes 860	**The lady** *whose baby was crying* **left the theater.** Because the clause *whose baby was crying* modifies the noun **lady,** it is an (*adjective, adverb*) clause. 861
second 1080	**The young man apologized.** *Realizing his mistake.* *Realizing his mistake* is an **–ing** word group. It is not a complete sentence because it has neither a subject nor a _____. 1081
different 1300	In this and the following frames, underline the correct verb in each pair: **Keith must** (*lie, lay*) **in bed for several days.** 1301

have 1520	Lesson **49** Keeping Track of the Subject [Frames 1522–1543]
well 1739	Home certainly looked (*good, well*) to me after living in a tent. 1740
she 1958	The referee penalized them more often than (*we, us*). 1959
Lieutenant 2177	Our superintendent appealed to mayor Kirby. In this sentence, capitalize (*superintendent, mayor*). 2178
	The following sentence gives only one part of Bob's address —the street address: Bob has lived at *464 Oak Street* for ten years. Is this one-part address set off with commas? (*Yes, No*) 2397
ladies' 2615	Place the apostrophe accurately in each italicized word: My *mothers* calendar shows all her *friends* birthdays. 2616

showed, shows 201	It is better to find the verb before looking for the sub-ject. Underline just the verb with two lines: **A tall, husky guard in uniform stood at the entrance to the camp.** 202
w e 421	**The use of safety glass has saved many lives.** Initials of verb: _____ 422
adverb 641	a. **A herd of cows blocked the road.** b. **Jerry delivers papers after school.** Can the prepositional phrase be moved to another position in sentence *a* or *b*? _____ 642
adjective 861	**The pupil** _____ *name the teacher called* **was absent.** Underline the pronoun that would serve as an adjective clause signal in this sentence. **who which whose that** 862
predicate (*or* verb) 1081	**The young man apologized.** *Realizing his mistake.* The **–ing** word group *Realizing his mistake* modifies the noun _____ in the main statement. 1082
lie 1301	**Where did Peggy (***lie, lay***) her coat?** 1302

Now we shall study a type of sentence that often leads people to choose the wrong verb.

One (*is, are*) **broken.**

Which verb agrees with the singular subject **One?** _____

1522

---

good

1740

I looked at his face (*good, well*) **so that I would recognize him the next time we met.**

1741

---

us

1959

My brother gets home much earlier than (*me, I*)**.**

1960

Mayor

2178

The judge is a friend of superintendent Welch.

In this sentence, capitalize (*judge, superintendent*).

2179

No

2397

Now to make Bob's address more complete, we add a second part—the city.

Bob has lived at 464 Oak Street, *Columbus,* **for ten years.**

Is the second part of the address set off with commas? (*Yes, No*)

2398

---

mother's, friends'

2616

Place the apostrophe accurately in each italicized word:

Two other *fellows* **scores were higher than my** *dads.*

2617

<u>stood</u> 202	A tall, husky guard in uniform <u>stood</u> at the entrance to the camp. Now that you have found the verb **stood,** ask yourself, "Who **stood?**" The answer to this question tells you the subject, which is _____. 203
h s 422	**The other car must have been speeding.** Initials of complete verb: _____ 423
b 642	**Jerry delivers papers <u>after school</u>.** The prepositional phrase **after school** is an _____ *phrase*. 643
whose 862	**The pupil whose name the teacher called was absent.** Write the sentence that remains when we omit the adjective clause. _____ 863
man 1082	a. **The young man apologized,** *realizing his mistake.* b. **The young man apologized.** *Realizing his mistake.* An **–ing** word group should be in the same sentence as the word it modifies. Therefore, (*a, b*) is correct. 1083
lay 1302	**The doctor told me to (*lie, lay*) down.** 1303

is 1522	a. **One is broken.** b. **One (of the eggs) is broken.** In sentence *a*, we don't know whether **One** means an egg, a window, a chair, or a cup. We therefore add a prepositional phrase **(of the eggs)** to make our meaning clear. The subject in both *a* and *b* is the pronoun _____. 1523
well 1741	**A cold shower feels** (*good, well*) **on a hot day.** 1742
I 1960	**The sudden storm caught us as well as** (*them, they*). 1961

Superintendent
 	
2179
	Also capitalize a word that shows family relationship, like **uncle, cousin,** or **grandmother,** when used with a person's name.
	
	    a. **This gift was from my uncle John.**
	    b. **This gift was from my Uncle John.**
	
	Which sentence is correctly capitalized? ____
	
	2180

Yes 2398	To make the address still more complete, we now add a third part—the state. **Bob has lived at 464 Oak Street, Columbus,** *Ohio,* **for ten years.** Is the third part of the address set off with commas? (*Yes, No*) 2399
fellows', dad's 2617	When apostrophes are used with nouns to measure time (*a week's work*) or money (*ten cents' worth*), apply the same rule that you follow to show ownership. Place the apostrophe accurately in each italicized word: **In less than an** *hours* **time, my customer selected over two hundred** *dollars* **worth of dresses.** 2618

guard 203	First, underline the verb with two lines. Then underline the subject with one line: **The owner of this car drove it only on weekends.** 204
m h b s 423	**This could never have happened to anyone else.** Initials of complete verb: _____ 424
adverb 643	**A blind man <u>with a cane</u> was waiting <u>at the curb</u>.** This sentence contains both an adjective phrase and an adverb phrase. The **adverb phrase** is the (*first, second*) phrase. 644
The pupil was absent. 863	**There are many interesting hobbies which are not expensive.** The adjective clause starts with the word _____ and ends with the word _____. 864
a 1083	*Standing on a box.* **Ronnie watched the parade.** The sentence fragment is the (*first, second*) word group. 1084
lie 1303	**Don't (*lie, lay*) near the open window.** 1304

One 1523	A verb agrees with its subject, not with another noun that may come between the subject and the verb. **One (of the eggs) is broken.** **Eggs** is not the subject of the verb. It is the object of the preposition _____. 1524
good 1742	Lesson **57** **Making Comparisons Correctly** [Frames 1744–1779]
them 1961	**Eleanor doesn't spend as much as (*me, I*) on movies.** 1962
b 2180	a. **My uncle owns an airplane.** b. **My uncle Pete owns an airplane.** In which sentence should **uncle** be capitalized? ____ 2181
Yes 2399	**Bob has lived at 464 Oak Street, Columbus, Ohio, for ten years.** After the first part of the address, is there a comma both *before* and *after* each additional part? (*Yes, No*) 2400
hour's, dollars' 2618	Apostrophes have very exact uses. Do not insert an apostrophe before the final *s* on a verb or on an ordinary plural noun that does not show ownership. Place an apostrophe in the *one* word that requires it: **One of our neighbors sometimes prunes and sprays my fathers apple trees.** 2619

owner drove 204	A word used to name a person, place, thing, or an idea is a _____. 205
c h h 424	**A crowd of people were watching the steam shovel.** Initials of complete verb: _____ 425
second 644	**The smell of fresh bread came from the kitchen.** This sentence contains both an adjective phrase and an adverb phrase. The **adjective phrase** is the (*first, second*) phrase. 645
which, expensive 864	**People who live in glass houses should not throw stones.** The adjective clause starts with the word _____ and ends with the word _____. 865
first 1084	*Standing on a box*. **Ronnie watched the parade.** *Standing on a box* is an **–ing** word group. It modifies the noun (*Ronnie, parade*) in the second word group. 1085
lie 1304	(*Lie, Lay*) **your packages on the back seat.** 1305

of 1524	**One (of the eggs) is broken.** The subject of this sentence is not the plural noun **eggs** but the singular pronoun _____. 1525
	John is tall. Here we are talking about only one boy. If we were to compare the tallness of John with the tallness of another boy, how would we need to change the word **tall?** **John is _____ than Fred.** 1744
I 1962	**We have lived in Nashville as long as** (*they, them*). 1963
b 2181	**My aunt lives with grandma Olson.** In this sentence, capitalize (*aunt, grandma*). 2182
Yes 2400	After writing the first part of an address, put a comma both *before* and *after* each additional part. Of course, if an added part ends the sentence, a period—not a comma—is used. Punctuate the following sentence: **The package was sent to 94 Park Avenue Portland Oregon.** 2401
father's 2619	SINGULAR: **Mr. Jones Mrs. Sims Miss Barnes** PLURAL: **the Joneses the Simses the Barneses** In forming the possessive of names ending in *s*, be sure that the letters before the apostrophe spell the name of the owner or owners correctly. (*Jame's, James's*) **uncle fixed the** (*Joneses', Jone's*) **car.** 2620

noun 205	A good test for a noun is to see if it can be used as the subject of a sentence. If a word cannot be used as a subject, it (*is, is not*) a noun. 206
w w 425	**Someone must have carelessly dropped this pen.** Initials of complete verb: _____ 426
first 645	**During the summer, I read a book about rockets.** The **adverb** phrase is the (*first, second*) phrase. 646
who, houses 865	In a previous lesson, we saw that an **adverb clause** can often be moved from one position to another in a sentence. **A squirrel** *that is friendly* **comes to our door.** Can the adjective clause *that is friendly* be moved to another position in this sentence? (*Yes, No*) 866
Ronnie 1085	a. *Standing on a box*. **Ronnie watched the parade.** b. *Standing on a box,* **Ronnie watched the parade.** An **–ing** word group should be in the same sentence as the word it modifies. Therefore, (*a, b*) is correct. 1086
Lay 1305	lay laid Which one of these past forms means that someone or something "rested in a flat position" or "was in place"? _____ 1306

One 1525	**One of the tires . . . flat.** We are not making a statement about all four tires but about only one of them. Is the subject of this sentence the singular pronoun **One** or the plural noun **tires?** _____ <div align="right">1526</div>
taller 1744	**John is taller than Fred.** To show that John has more tallness than Fred, we add the letters _____ to the word **tall.** <div align="right">1745</div>
they 1963	**Although they both did the same work, Mr. Smith paid Linda more than** (*she, her*). (Think of the omitted words before making your choice.) <div align="right">1964</div>
Grandma 2182	**My uncle Burt inherited the farm from his grandmother.** In this sentence, capitalize (*uncle, grandmother*). <div align="right">2183</div>

Avenue,
Portland,
 	
2401
	If an address is put right after a name with no preposition like **at, in, on,** or **of** to tie it in with the name, even a one-part address is set off with commas.
	
	    a. **Mr. A. C. Roe** *of* **461 Avery Road is the owner.**
	    b. **Mr. A. C. Roe 461 Avery Road is the owner.**
	
	The street address requires commas in sentence _____.
	<div align="right">2402</div>

James's,
Joneses'
 	
2620
	Unlike nouns, possessive pronouns show ownership without the addition of apostrophes.
	POSSESSIVE PRONOUNS: **his, hers, yours**
	                                its (belonging to **it**), **ours, theirs**
	Add the *one* necessary apostrophe:
	    Neither yours nor hers will open Carols locker.
	<div align="right">2621</div>

is not 206	His _____ surprised me. Underline the word that is a noun and could therefore be used as the subject of the above sentence: **generous generosity generously** 207
m h d 426	**never shall will soon** The two helping verbs in the above group are _____ and _____. 427
first 646	Lesson **22** Unit Review [Frames 648–669]

No
 	
866
	An adjective clause, generally, is fixed in position.
	
	    a. **Gwen arrived** *as I was leaving.*
	    b. **We took the road** *which was shorter.*
	
	In which sentence can the clause be moved to another position? ____
	
	867

b 1086	Don't mistake an *–ing* word group for a predicate. **My mother,** *wanting to please me* . . . *Wanting to please me* is not a predicate. It merely describes the subject _____, as any ordinary adjective might do. 1087
lay 1306	He (*lay, laid*) **awake and counted sheep most of the night.** 1307

One 1526	**One of the tires** (*was, were*) **flat.** The subject **One** is singular. Therefore, we choose the singular verb _____. 1527
–er 1745	**John is tall.** **John is taller than Fred.** When we speak about the tallness of one boy, we use the word **tall.** When we compare the tallness of two boys, we use the word _____. 1746
her 1964	**The other team made twice as many touchdowns as** (*us, we*). 1965
Uncle 2183	**My grandfather Shaw put my cousin through college.** In this sentence, capitalize (*grandfather, cousin*). 2184
b 2402	a. **The Speedy Cleaners, 666 Belmont Avenue, give 4-hour service.** b. **The Speedy Cleaners, at 666 Belmont Avenue, give 4-hour service.** From which sentence should the commas be omitted? ____ 2403

Carol's
 	
2621
	In writing contractions, always put the apostrophe in place of the missing letter or letters.
	
	     a. **doesn't, couldn't, hasn't, wasn't**
	     b. **does'nt, could'nt, has'nt, was'nt**
	
	Which group of words is correct—*a* or *b*? ____
	2622

generosity 207	Underline the one word which is a noun: **eager eagerly eagerness** 208
shall, will 427	**should surely make would** The two helping verbs in the above group are_____ and _____. 428
  	Adjectives can modify two classes of words: _____ and _____. 648
a 867	a. **Gwen arrived** *as I was leaving.* b. **We took the road** *which was shorter.* In sentence *a,* the clause modifies the verb **arrived.** In sentence *b,* the clause modifies the _____ **road.** 868
mother 1087	**My mother,** *wanting to please me . . .* Which one of the following word groups could make a sentence of the above fragment by providing a predicate? ____ a. **on my birthday** b. **and my dad** c. **made my favorite dessert** 1088
lay 1307	 **I can't remember where I** (*lay, laid*) **the car keys.** 1308

was 1527	**One of the tires** (*was, were*) **flat.** In sentences like this, don't let a noun that follows the subject run off with the verb. The plural noun **tires** is not the subject of the sentence. It is the object of the preposition _____. 1528
taller 1746	When we compare the tallness of three (or more) boys, how would we need to change the word **tall?** **John is tall.** (one) **John is taller than Fred.** (two) **John is the** _____ **boy in the class.** (three or more) 1747
we 1965	**Although I was just as guilty, the teacher scolded Fred more often than** (*me, I*). 1966

Grandfather
 	
2184
	When **Mother, Father, Dad,** etc., are used as names, you may capitalize them or not, as you please.
	
	       Hello, Mother (mother). How is Father (father)?
	In the following sentence, which word is used as a name—
	Dad or **mother?** _____
	       Dad, I'd like you to meet Jim's mother.
	
	2185

b 2403	**Mrs. John Porter** *of* **2211 Pinecrest Road is in charge of ticket sales.** If you omitted the preposition *of* from this sentence, should commas be added? (*Yes, No*) 2404
a 2622	Do not confuse contractions with possessive pronouns that sound exactly like them. CONTRACTIONS: **you're they're it's who's** POSSESSIVE PRONOUNS: **your their its whose** (*You're, Your*) **always thinking about** (*you're, your*) **mistakes.** 2623

eagerness
 	
208
	Some words can be used as either nouns or verbs.
	
	    a. **The Smiths** *travel* **every summer.**
	    b. *Travel* **provides interesting experiences.**
	
	In which sentence is the italicized word used as a noun?
	
	_____
	
	                                              209

should, would 428	**always may not can** The two helping verbs in the above group are _____ and _____ . 429

nouns,
pronouns
 	
648
	The most common position of adjectives is right before the nouns they modify.
	
	Underline *three* adjectives:
	
	    Several students received perfect scores on this test.
	
	                                            649

noun
 	
868
	a. **Gwen arrived** *as I was leaving.*
	    b. **We took the road** *which was shorter.*
	
	Which sentence contains an adjective clause? _____
	
	                                            869

c
 	
1088
	A subject followed by only an *–ing word group* is not a sentence. An *–ing word group* has no power to make a statement about a subject.
	
	    a. **My mother,** *wanting to please me.*
	    b. **My mother,** wanting to please me, **made a chocolate pie.**
	
	The complete sentence is _____ .
	
	                                            1089

laid 1308	**A hundred miles of bad roads still** (*lay, laid*) **ahead of us.** 1309

of 1528	The tricky phrases that make people choose the wrong verb often begin with the following prepositions: **of** (of the car) (of the books) (of the voters) **on** (on the floor) (on his clothes) (on the field) **The spots (on the floor) were ink.** Is the subject of this sentence **spots** or **floor?** _____ 1529
tallest 1747	**John is the tallest boy in the class.** To show that John has the most tallness of all the boys in the class, we add the letters _____ to the word **tall.** 1748
me 1966	**I am taking just as many subjects as** (*her, she*). 1967
Dad 2185	When **mother, father, dad,** etc., are used merely to show family relationship, do not capitalize them. **My mother knew his dad at college.** In the following sentence, which word is used to show family relationship—**mother** or **dad?** _____ **Dad, I'd like you to meet Jim's mother.** 2186
Yes 2404	**Joe Wilson, Union City, is the newly elected chairman.** If you inserted the preposition **of** after the name **Joe Wilson,** would you keep the commas? (*Yes, No*) 2405
You're, your 2623	a. *Their* **trying to sell** *they're* **farm.** b. *They're* **trying to sell** *their* **farm.** In which sentence are the italicized words correct? ____ 2624

b 209	a. **The new** *shop* **opened yesterday.** b. **Many people** *shop* **in the new store.** In which sentence is the italicized word used as a noun— *a* or *b*? _____ 210
may, can 429	Lesson **15** Unit Review [Frames 431–455]
Several, perfect, **this** 649	When an adjective is used as a subject complement, it comes (*before*, *after*) the noun or pronoun it modifies. 650
b 869	One sentence contains an adverb clause, and one sentence contains an adjective clause: a. **People** *who are selfish* **make poor friends.** b. **Hilda had few friends** *because she was selfish.* Which sentence contains an adjective clause? _____ 870
b 1089	**We talked about photography. My favorite hobby.** Which word group does not have both a subject and a predicate—the *first* or *second*? _____ 1090
lay 1309	**The strikers** (*lay, laid*) **down their tools and went home.** 1310

spots 1529	Other tricky phrases begin with these prepositions: **in** (in the box) (in the cities) (in the room) **for** (for his success) (for his absences) **with** (with the case) (with the records) **The reason (for his absences) was illness.** The subject of this sentence is _____. <div style="text-align:right">1530</div>
–est 1748	Most adjectives and adverbs have three degrees (or steps) of power. The *first degree* merely states the quality—**new, quiet, fast.** **strong stronger strongest** Underline the adjective in the first degree. <div style="text-align:right">1749</div>
she 1967	**Jimmy is jealous because he thinks that his parents like the new baby better than** (*him, he*). <div style="text-align:right">1968</div>
mother 2186	**Mother, father, dad,** etc., show family relationship and should not be capitalized whenever they are used after **a, the,** or any possessive word **(my, his, their, Bob's).** a. **Is dinner ready, Mother?** b. **Their mother was not at home.** Does **mother** show relationship in sentence *a* or *b*? ____ <div style="text-align:right">2187</div>
No 2405	The name of a state following the name of a city is usually set off with commas. Supply the necessary commas: **The Tournament of Roses is held in Pasadena California every New Year's Day.** <div style="text-align:right">2406</div>
b 2624	The word **who's** is a contraction that means *who is.* The word **whose** is a possessive pronoun that means *belonging to whom.* a. *Who's* **the batter** *whose* **home run won the game?** b. *Whose* **the batter** *who's* **home run won the game?** In which sentence are the italicized words correct? ____ <div style="text-align:right">2625</div>

a

A word that can take the place of a noun is called a

_____.

210 | 211

---

a. **The <u>outfielder</u> <u>has dropped</u> the ball.**
b. **The <u>price</u> of eggs <u>has dropped</u> again.**

In one sentence, the action verb makes a complete statement about its subject. It needs no word to show *what* received the action. This sentence is (*a, b*). ____

431

---

after

a. **This store is** *generous* **to its employees.**
b. **This store gives** *generous* **treatment to its employees.**

In which sentence does the italicized adjective come after

the noun it modifies? ____

650 | 651

---

a

a. **The telephone rang while I was taking a bath.**
b. **The car which Jerry bought needs new tires.**

Which sentence contains an adjective clause? ____

870 | 871

---

second

We talked about photography. My favorite hobby.

Which word group does not make sense by itself—the *first*

or *second*? _____

1090 | 1091

---

laid

has lain   **has laid**

Which of these helper forms is a form of the verb **lie**, which means "to rest in a flat position" or "to be in place"?

_____

1310 | 1311

reason 1530	Remember the **"Rule of S"**: When we add an *s* to the subject, we do not add an *s* to the verb. When we add an *s* to the verb, we do not add an *s* to the _____ . 1531
strong 1749	The *second degree* shows that one thing has *more* of this quality than another thing—**newer, quieter, faster.** **cold colder coldest** Underline the adjective in the second degree. 1750
him 1968	Lesson **64** **Pronouns That Show Ownership** [Frames 1970–1992]
b 2187	a. **Why don't you ask your father?** b. **Why don't you ask Father?** Is **father** used to show family relationship, and not as a name, in sentence *a* or *b*? ____ 2188
Pasadena, California, 2406	**We drove from Atlanta to Detroit in only one day.** If we inserted **Georgia** after **Atlanta,** and **Michigan** after **Detroit,** how many commas would we need to add? ____ 2407

a
 	
2625
	Be especially careful to use the contraction **it's** only when you can substitute the two words **it is.** To show ownership, use the possessive pronoun **its** without an apostrophe.
	    a. *It's* **owner is sure that** *its* **genuine.**
	    b. *Its* **owner is sure that** *it's* **genuine.**
	In which sentence are the italicized words correct? ____
	
	2626

pronoun 211	a. **The** *lock* **broke.** c. *One* **broke.** b. *It* **broke.** d. **The** *window* **broke.** In which two sentences is the italicized word used as a pronoun? ____ and ____ 212
b 431	An action verb often needs to be completed with another word. This word shows *who* or *what* receives its action or shows the result of this action. Such a word is called a _____ _____. 432
a 651	Some words can be used as either adjectives or nouns. a. **The** *road* **was very winding.** b. **The** *road* **map showed a detour.** In which sentence is the italicized word used as an adjec- tive? ____ 652
b 871	a. **because, when, if, unless, although, after** b. **who (whom, whose), which, that** Which words can be used as adjective clause signals— those in group *a* or *b*? ____ 872
Second 1091	**We talked about photography. My favorite** *hobby*. The noun *hobby* in the second word group means the same thing as the noun _____ in the first word group. 1092
has lain 1311	**Gail caught cold because she had** (*lain, laid*) **in a draft.** 1312

subject 1531	**The cost of the repairs** (*seem, seems*) **too high.** Since **cost,** the subject of the sentence, does not end in *s,* which verb would you choose? _____ 1532
colder 1750	The *third degree* shows that one thing has this quality to the *highest* degree—**newest, quietest, fastest.** Write the third degree of the adjective **cheap.** _____ 1751
	Apostrophes are needed to make nouns show ownership or possession. **My <u>sister's</u> coat is dark.** The noun that shows the ownership of the coat is _____. 1970
a 2188	a. **A father has many responsibilities.** b. **I invited father to our meeting.** In which sentence would it be wrong to capitalize **father** because it is used to show family relationship? ____ 2189
4 2407	We punctuate **dates** in the same way as addresses. If only one part of a date is given, no commas are used. **It was decided that** *October 4* **would be the date of our first meeting.** Is a one-part date set off with commas? (*Yes, No*) 2408
b 2626	Use quotation marks only when you report what a person said directly in his own words. a. **Bob said** **I'll be home by ten.** b. **Bob said** **that he would be home by ten.** Which sentence requires quotation marks? ____ 2627

b, c

212

The *wind* **damaged** *some* **of the** *trees.*

Which one of the italicized words is a pronoun? _____

213

---

direct object

432

a. **They** <u>started</u> after a short *delay.*
b. **They** <u>started</u> the *game* on time.

In which sentence is the italicized word a direct object?

___

433

---

b

652

Although adverbs can modify three classes of words, they usually modify _____.

653

---

b

872

who (whom, whose)   which   that

Because these adjective clause signals stand for a noun in the main statement of the sentence, they are (*adverbs, pronouns*).

873

---

photography

1092

We talked about photography. *My favorite hobby.*

Because the noun *hobby* comes after the noun **photography** and explains it, it is (*a clause, an appositive*).

1093

---

lain

1312

Where could I have (*lain, laid*) **my keys?**

1313

seems 1532	**The windows in the kitchen** (*need, needs*) **washing.** Since **windows,** the subject of this sentence, ends in *s,* which verb would you choose? _____ 1533

cheapest
 	
1751
	FIRST DEGREE SECOND DEGREE THIRD DEGREE
	   high **higher** **highest**
	   happy **happier** **happiest**
	With short words of one and sometimes two syllables, the
	second degree is formed by adding **–er;** the third degree is
	formed by adding _____.
	
	1752

sister's 1970	a. **My <u>sister's</u> coat is dark.** b. **<u>Yours</u> is light.** In sentence *a*, the word that shows ownership is the noun **sister's.** In sentence *b*, the word that shows ownership is the pro- noun _____. 1971
a 2189	**I should have phoned Mother or Dad.** Since **Mother** and **Dad** are used as names in the above sentence, you may capitalize them or not, as you wish. If you inserted the pronoun **my** before **Mother** and **Dad,** would you still capitalize these words? (*Yes, No*) 2190
No 2408	If the date consists of more than one part, put a comma both *before* and *after* each additional part. **October 4,** *1966,* **was the date of our first meeting.** Punctuate the following sentence: **On August 15 1914 the first ship passed through the Panama Canal.** 2409
a 2627	a. **Mother said to Henry "Don't read while you eat."** b. **Mother said to Henry, "Don't read while you eat."** Which sentence is correct? _____ 2628

some 213	*They* **bought a new** *house* **on our** *street.* Which one of the italicized words is a pronoun? _____ 214
b 433	A word that shows by its position alone *to whom* or *for whom*, or *to what* or *for what*, something is done is called a(n) _____ *object.* 434
verbs 653	We form many adverbs by adding the suffix (*–ly, –ous*) to adjectives. 654
pronouns 873	If a clause can be moved from one position to another, it is likely to be an (*adverb, adjective*) clause. 874
appositive 1093	a. **We talked about photography.** *My favorite hobby.* b. **We talked about photography,** *my favorite hobby.* Which is correct because the appositive is in the same sentence with the noun it explains? ____ 1094
laid 1313	**Gordy must have** (*lain, laid*) **the paint on too thick.** 1314

need 1533	In this and the following frames, underline the verb that agrees with its subject. Don't be fooled by an object of a preposition that might come between the subject and the verb. **The weight of the big trucks** (*injure, injures*) **the pavement.** 1534
–est 1752	Let's see what happens when we make comparisons with longer words: **John is more intelligent than Fred.** To avoid such a clumsy word as **intelligenter,** we do not add **–er.** Instead, we form the second degree of longer words by using the adverb _____. 1753
Yours 1971	**My sister's coat is dark.** **Yours is light.** The word that shows ownership without the use of an apostrophe is the (*noun, pronoun*). 1972
No 2190	**I enjoy talking to ˄ Dad.** If you inserted **Tom's** at the point indicated, would you capitalize the word **Dad?** (*Yes, No*) 2191
August 15, 1914, 2409	A period used after an abbreviation in an address or a date does not take the place of a required comma. Use commas just as you would with the complete words. Punctuate the following sentence: **We moved to 1700 Lakeshore Ave. Oakland Calif. on Sept. 5 1965.** 2410
b 2628	a. **"Where did you get your facts?,"** asked Mr. Reagan. b. **"Where did you get your facts?"** asked Mr. Reagan. Which sentence is correct? ____ 2629

They 214	**The** *soldier* **camouflaged** *himself* **with** *branches*. Which one of the italicized words is a pronoun? _____ 215
indirect 434	**Mrs. Dow made a dress** *for Bertha*. If you changed the phrase *for Bertha* to an indirect object, you would insert the indirect object right after the word _____. 435
–ly 654	**When? Where? How? How much? How often?** Words that answer these questions about the actions of verbs are called _____. 655
adverb 874	Only *one* of the following statements is correct: a. An adjective clause is one that does the work of a single adjective. b. An adjective clause is one that begins with an adjective. Which definition of an adjective clause is correct? ____ 875
b 1094	In this and the following frames, write an **S** for each word group that is a **sentence,** and an **F** for each word group that is a **fragment.** Write your answers in the same order as the two word groups. **Grabbing his bag. Mr. Nolan ran after the train.** ____ ____ 1095
laid 1314	**You shouldn't have** (*lain, laid*) **down in your best suit.** 1315

injures 1534	**One of the car's headlights** (*is, are*) **out.** 1535
more 1753	**John is the most intelligent boy in the class.** To avoid such a clumsy word as **intelligentest,** we form the third degree of longer words not by adding **–est,** but by using the adverb _____. 1754
pronoun 1972	Although nouns need apostrophes to show ownership, pronouns show ownership *without apostrophes*. The ownership idea is built right into the pronouns themselves. **My <u>sister's</u> coat is darker than <u>yours</u>.** Do both of the underlined words in this sentence show ownership? (*Yes, No*) 1973
No 2191	a. **Tommy was raised by his Grandma.** b. **Tommy was raised by his Grandma Schultz.** Which sentence is correctly capitalized—*a* or *b*? _____ 2192
Ave., Oakland, Calif., Sept. 5, 2410	In this and the following frames, supply the necessary commas. Several sentences do not require commas. **The Dionne quintuplets were born on May 28 1934 in Callender Ontario.** 2411
b 2629	a. **Mr. Dobbs said that we had only five minutes left.** b. **Mr. Dobbs said, "That we had only five minutes left."** Which sentence is correct? _____ 2630

Lesson 8 — The Subject–Verb and Direct Object Patterns

[Frames 217–248]

himself

215

---

made

Only one of the following statements is true:

a. An *action verb* must always be completed by a direct object.
b. A *linking verb* must always be completed by a subject complement.

The true statement is (*a, b*). ____

435 436

---

adverbs

Underline *two* adverbs:

My polite friend graciously stepped aside for the lady.

655 656

Lesson 29 — How to Make Adjective Clauses

[Frames 877–911]

a

875

F S

I saw the Illinois game. The biggest game of the season.

____ ____

1095 1096

---

lain

Lay and **have lain** are past forms of the verb (*lie, lay*).

1315 1316

is 1535	The reasons for his dismissal (*has, have*) not been stated. 1536
most 1754	a. Our backyard is more beautiful than our front yard. b. Our backyard is beautifuller than our front yard. In which sentence is the comparison made correctly— *a* or *b*? ____ 1755
Yes 1973	My <u>sister's</u> coat is darker than <u>yours</u>. Which underlined word shows ownership without the use of an apostrophe—the *noun* or the *pronoun*? _____ 1974
b 2192	In this and the following frames, cross out each capital letter that is not correct: Many famous actors had small parts in the movie *Around The World In Eighty Days.* 2193
May 28, 1934, Callender, 2411	Insert any necessary commas: We drove from El Paso Texas to Phoenix Arizona in a single day. 2412
a 2630	a. "How did the movie end?" asked Rita. b. "How did the movie end," asked Rita? Which sentence is correct? ____ 2631

Many action verbs are able to make *complete statements* about their subjects without the help of other words.

EXAMPLES: <u>Birds</u> <u>fly</u>. The <u>motor</u> <u>stalled</u>.
<u>Ice</u> <u>melts</u>. The <u>game</u> <u>began</u>.

The verbs in these sentences make (*complete, incomplete*) statements about their subjects.

217

---

b

436

The most common linking verbs are the various forms of the verb (*have, be, do*). _____

437

---

graciously,
aside

656

Underline *two* adverbs:

Some fans usually come early to get good seats.

657

Adjective clauses are useful for combining sentences.

We had a large *map*. *It* showed all the small towns.

First, find a word in the second sentence (*It*) that means the same as a word in the first sentence (_____).

877

S F

1096

I saw the Illinois game. It was the biggest game of the season.

1097

---

lie

1316

Laid and **have laid** are past forms of the verb (*lie, lay*).

1317

have 1536	The footprints in the snow (*was, were*) the only clue. 1537
a 1755	a. **This is the wonderfullest trick I have ever seen.** b. **This is the most wonderful trick I have ever seen.** In which sentence is the comparison made correctly? ____ 1756
pronoun 1974	<u>His</u> is next to <u>hers</u>. The two pronouns in this sentence that show ownership are **His** and _____. 1975
The, In 2193	Cross out each capital letter that is not correct: **Our High School band is rehearsing Leroy Anderson's "Jazz Pizzicato" for our Spring concert.** 2194
El Paso, Texas, Phoenix, Arizona, 2412	Insert any necessary commas: **Your complaint should be sent to the Longwear Tire Company in Akron.** 2413
a 2631	a. **"That's what friends are for", smiled Paul.** b. **"That's what friends are for," smiled Paul.** Which sentence is correct? ____ 2632

complete 217	PATTERN 1: *Subject—Action Verb* A sentence built around a subject and an action verb is our first and simplest sentence pattern. **The exciting <u>game</u> with Knox <u>began</u> on time at two o'clock.** This entire sentence of 11 words is built around a two-part framework—the subject _____ and the action verb _____. 218

be
 	
437
	a. **is, am, are** c. **has, may, will**
	      b. **does, can, make** d. **was, were, been**
	The various forms of the verb **be** are found in lines ____ and ____.
	     438

usually, early 657	Besides modifying verbs, adverbs can also modify other modifiers: _____ and other _____. 658

map
 	
877
	↙*which*
	    We had a large *map.* ~~It~~ **showed all the small towns.**
	Next, put the adjective clause signal *which* in place of the word *It,* thus changing the second sentence into an _____ *clause.*
	     878

S   S
 	
1097
	Homer was in the basement. Trying to iron his shirt.
	
	    ____ ____
	     1098

lay 1317	Lesson **42** **Learning the Difference Between** *Sit* **and** *Set* [Frames 1319–1347]

were 1537	**One of the wheels** (*squeak, squeaks*). 1538
b 1756	FIRST DEGREE SECOND DEGREE THIRD DEGREE expensive **more expensive** **most expensive** skillfully **more skillfully** **most skillfully** The second degree of **successful** would be _____ **successful.** 1757
hers 1975	<u>His</u> is next to <u>hers</u>. Pronouns show ownership without apostrophes. To write **hers** with an apostrophe **(her's)** is just as incorrect as to write **his** with an apostrophe **(hi's)**. Should either **his** or **hers** be written with an apostrophe? (*Yes, No*) 1976
~~H~~igh ~~S~~chool, ~~S~~pring 2194	Cross out each capital letter that is not correct: **For my Birthday, my Aunt gave me a copy of** *Lightning On Ice.* 2195
None 2413	**F. W. Woolworth opened his first five-and-ten store in Utica N.Y. on Feb. 22 1879.** 2414
b 2632	a. **"What a perfect day for a picnic," exclaimed Alison!** b. **"What a perfect day for a picnic!" exclaimed Alison.** Which sentence is correct? ____ 2633

game (subject)
began (verb)
 	
218
	Some action verbs, however, are *not* able to make complete statements about their subjects.
	    a. **The <u>rain</u> <u>stopped</u>.**
	    b. **The <u>dog</u> <u>needs</u> . . .**
	Does the verb in sentence *a* or *b* fail to make a complete statement about its subject? ____
	    219

a, d 438	We can often substitute another verb for a form of the linking verb **be.** This word would also be used as a linking verb. **The trip** *was* **tiresome.** Underline *two* of the following verbs that could be used as linking verbs in the above sentence. **became drove seemed planned** 439
adjectives, adverbs 658	Special adverbs such as **very, quite, rather, extremely,** and **too** can modify either adjectives or adverbs. (*True, False*) 659

adjective
 	
878
	a. **It showed all the small towns.**
	    b. *which showed all the small towns*
	We have now changed *a*, which is a sentence, to *b*, which is a _____.
	    879

S F 1098	**Homer was in the basement. He was trying to iron his shirt.** ____ ____ 1099
	To sit means "to take a sitting position" or "to be in place." **Dick sits next to Fred.** **The clock sits on his desk.** **The children like to _____ in the front row.** 1319

squeaks 1538	The effects of sunburn (*is, are*) often quite serious. 1539
more 1757	FIRST DEGREE SECOND DEGREE THIRD DEGREE **expensive** **more expensive** **most expensive** The third degree of **courteous** would be _____ **courteous.** 1758
No 1976	<u>Hers</u> writes better than <u>Karens</u>. Both the underlined words in this sentence show owner-ship. Which of these words requires an apostrophe? _____ 1977
~~B~~irthday, ~~A~~unt, ~~O~~n 2195	Cross out each capital letter that is not correct: **My Uncle Steve was promoted from Captain to Major.** 2196
Utica, N.Y., Feb. 22, 2414	**The Pickwick Restaurant at 851 Concord Avenue was sold to Gus Evans in March 1959.** (Only one comma is needed.) 2415
b 2633	

b 219	After an incomplete action verb, we keep wondering "What?" or "Whom?" until another word is added. The <u>dog needs</u> ... (What?) The <u>dog needs</u> a bath. The word that completes the meaning of the verb **needs** is _____. CONTINUED WITH FRAME 221 ON PAGE 1 220
became, seemed 439	The coat *is* too tight. Underline *two* of the following verbs that could be used as linking verbs in the above sentence. **sells feels looks makes** CONTINUED WITH FRAME 441 ON PAGE 1 440
True 659	a. **The train made *very* frequent stops.** b. **The train stopped *very* frequently.** In which sentence does the italicized adverb modify another adverb? _____ CONTINUED WITH FRAME 661 ON PAGE 1 660
clause 879	**We had a large map** *which showed all the small towns.* The clause *which showed all the small towns* is an adjective clause because it modifies the noun _____. CONTINUED WITH FRAME 881 ON PAGE 1 880
S S 1099	**The camp is on Lake Superior. The largest of the Great Lakes.** _____ _____ CONTINUED WITH FRAME 1101 ON PAGE 1 1100
sit 1319	A person **sits** on a chair, a kettle **sits** on the stove, and a radio _____ on the table. CONTINUED WITH FRAME 1321 ON PAGE 2 1320

INDEX

Each entry is indexed by frame number, followed by the page, in parentheses, on which the frame appears. The references included in each entry direct the reader to Key frames. Additional information and related exercises may be found in the frames preceding and following those listed. Complete review exercises for major topics are listed in the table of contents.

C D E F G H I J
4 5 6 7 8 9 0 1 2